Through the Year with
The Pilgrim Fathers

To each and every fellow-pilgrim endeavouring to steer a course through life's voyage: making mistakes along the way, but refusing to abandon their calling, with respect and affection.

Through the Year with

The Pilgrim Fathers

365 Daily Readings Inspired by the Journey of the *Mayflower*

Stephen J. Poxon

MONARCH
BOOKS

Published by
Lion Hudson Limited
Wilkinson House, Jordan Hill Business Park
Banbury Road, Oxford OX2 8DR, England
www.lionhudson.com

Hardback ISBN: 9780 8572 1972 5
Paperback ISBN: 978 0 8572 1970 1
e-ISBN: 978 0 8572 1971 8

First edition 2020

Acknowledgments

Scripture quotations are primarily taken from the Holy Bible, New International Verison NIV® Copyright © 1973, 1978, 1984, 2011 by Biblica, Inc.® formerly International Bible Society. Used by permission of Hodder & Stoughton Ltd, an Hachette UK company. All rights reserved. "NIV" is a registered trademark of Biblica. UK trademark number 1448790.

Scripture quotations marked KJV are from The Authorized (King James) Version. Rights in the Authorized Version are vested in the Crown. Reproduced by permission of the Crown's patentee, Cambridge University Press.

Scripture quotations marked ESV are from The Holy Bible, English Standard Version® (ESV®) copyright © 2001 by Crossway, a publishing ministry of Good News Publishers. All rights reserved.

Scripture quotations marked NLT are taken from the Holy Bible, New Living Translation, copyright © 1996, 2004, 2007 by Tyndale House Foundation. Used by permission of Tyndale House Publishers, Inc., Carol Stream, Illinois 60188. All rights reserved.

Scripture taken from The Message. Copyright © by Eugene H. Peterson 1993, 1994, 1995, 1996, 2000, 2001, 2002. Used by permission of NavPress Publishing Group.

A catalogue record for this book is available from the British Library

Printed and bound in the UK, April, LH29

Atlantic Charter

What were you carrying, Pilgrims, Pilgrims?
What did you carry beyond the sea?
We carried the Book, we carried the Sword,
A steadfast heart in the fear of the Lord,
And a living faith in his plight and word
That all men should be free.

What were your memories, Pilgrims, Pilgrims?
What of the dreams you bore away?
We carried the songs our fathers sung
By the hearths of home when they were young,
And the comely words of the mother-tongue
In which they learned to pray.

What did you find there, Pilgrims, Pilgrims?
What did you find beyond the waves?
A stubborn land and a barren shore,
Hunger and want and sickness sore;
All these we found and gladly bore
Rather than be slaves.

How did you fare there, Pilgrims, Pilgrims?
What did you build in that stubborn land?
We felled the forest and tilled the sod
Of a continent no man had trod
And we established there, in the grace of God,
The rights whereby we stand.

What are you bringing us, Pilgrims, Pilgrims?
Bringing us back in this bitter day?
The selfsame thing we carried away;
The Book, the Sword,
The fear of the Lord,
And the boons our fathers dearly bought:
Freedom of worship, speech and thought,
Freedom from want, freedom from fear,
The liberties we hold most dear,
And who shall say us nay?

From *The Island* by Francis Brett Young

THE PILGRIM FATHERS quite rightly hold a particularly special and secure place in the history of Protestant Christianity. Regarded with enormous and equal quantities of respect and affection on both sides of the Atlantic, their legendary exploits have secured them a unique reputation as pioneers, courageous (albeit somewhat naïve) missionaries, and a group of people who almost single-handedly changed the course of the Anglo-American historical narrative.

To refer to the motley crew who bravely voyaged from the shores of England to the largely unknown shores of Massachusetts as the Pilgrim Fathers, though, is of course grossly unfair to the women among their party who demonstrated just as much courage, foresight, and initiative as their more illustrious male counterparts. That they are only mentioned with relative infrequency throughout published records is indeed unfortunate, but merely a symptom of their times, their day and age, rather than anything deliberately misogynistic as we would understand gender bias in a significantly more enlightened culture. That should be borne in mind when reading this book.

What should also be taken into consideration when these pages are studied is that this is, first and foremost, a *devotional* publication intended to aid prayers and personal Bible reading. It is certainly not any kind of adequate historical account, but merely a brief glimpse into the lives and circumstances of a group of people who followed Christ to the best of their knowledge and ability. The reader who picks up this book in the hope of discovering a documented, detailed version of their story will, I'm afraid, be disappointed. *Through the Year with the Pilgrim Fathers* is written to inspire and encourage. It does not pretend to include every detail of swashbuckling adventures – far from it – but seeks to provide a flavour of what became of this remarkable company of (very!) amateur sailors.

The Pilgrim Fathers are fully entitled to our admiration. When we analyse and discuss their deeds from a comfortable distance of some four centuries, it is all-too-easy to gasp in shock and even disbelief at some of their miscalculations and questionable judgments. We have the benefit of 400 years' worth of hindsight, whereas they had to work within the confines of their understanding and enlightenment. They were by no means perfect – nor, for that matter, did they ever claim to be – but they withstood intense religious persecution and held impressively tightly to a faith that was severely tested. In context, then, their achievements were nothing less than outstanding, and it is therefore fitting that their legacy lives on.

This commemorative volume celebrates one of the greatest landmarks in Christian folklore. It is my hope and prayer that these pages will help each reader to realize afresh something of the great mercy and faithfulness of the God they served and that inspiration will be found within these selected and edited accounts.

I am more than grateful to everyone who has helped me in the compilation of this modest effort. My family members have been as patient, supportive, and encouraging as ever, and they have my gratitude, as do my friends and colleagues at Lion Hudson/Monarch whose expertise and cooperation are never taken for granted, but are deeply appreciated. I must immediately state that any mistakes are mine, not theirs. To those who have pointed me in the direction of research materials, and have chipped in with kind words of encouragement and interest every now and then, I also offer my thanks.

S.J.P.

> THEN ANSWERED PETER AND SAID UNTO HIM, BEHOLD,
> WE HAVE FORSAKEN ALL, AND FOLLOWED THEE;
> WHAT SHALL WE HAVE THEREFORE?
> (Matthew 19:27 *KJV*)

THE LINES ARE FALLEN UNTO ME IN PLEASANT PLACES; YEA, I HAVE
A GOODLY HERITAGE.

(Psalm 16:6 KJV)

Under the auspices of the Cape Cod[1] Pilgrim Memorial Association[2]... was laid the corner-stone of the monument at Provincetown commemorating the landing there of the *Mayflower* passengers [in] 1620. In his address delivered upon that occasion, President Roosevelt said:

The coming hither of the Puritan three centuries ago shaped the destinies of this continent, and therefore profoundly affected the destiny of the whole world... We cannot as a nation be too profoundly grateful for the fact that the Puritan has stamped his influence so deeply on our national life... The splendid qualities which he left to his children, we other Americans who are not of Puritan blood also claim as our heritage. You, sons of the Puritans, and us, who are descended from races whom the Puritans would have deemed alien – we are all Americans to-day. We all feel the same pride in the genesis, in the history of our people; and therefore this shrine of Puritanism is one at which we all gather to pay homage, no matter from what country our ancestors sprang.[3] [4]

Heavenly Father, as this New Year opens up before me, I thank you for all those people whose influence upon my life has been godly and edifying. Thank you for those who have played their part in "shaping" my spiritual beliefs and convictions, thereby granting me "a goodly heritage". My prayer as this year begins is that I would, with your help, live up to their investment of prayer and example.

---

1   A peninsula of the state of Massachusetts, USA.
2   See https://www.guidestar.org/profile/04-2157040
3   The Pilgrims had intended to settle near the Hudson River, but prevailing weather conditions forced them to shelter at Cape Cod. The passengers decided not to sail further, but to remain there.
4   From Albert Matthews, *The Term Pilgrim Fathers*, Cambridge (MA): John Wilson and Son, 1915.

**AND THIS DAY SHALL BE UNTO YOU FOR A MEMORIAL; AND YE
SHALL KEEP IT A FEAST...**
(Exodus 12:14 *KJV*)

The Old Colony Club,[1] agreeable in a vote... met in commemoration of the landing of their worthy ancestors in this place [Massachusetts] ... After discharging a cannon, was hoisted upon the Hall an elegant silk flag with the following inscription, "Old Colony 1620." At eleven o'clock A.M. the members of the Club appeared at the Hall, and from thence proceeded to the house of Mr. Howland,[2] innholder (which is erected upon the spot where the first licensed House in the Old Colony formerly stood). At half after two a decent repast was served up, which consisted of the following dishes; namely, –

1. A large baked Indian whortleberry[3] pudding.
2. A dish of sauquetash.[4]
3. A dish of clams.
4. A dish of oysters and a dish of codfish.
5. A haunch of venison roasted by the first jack brought to the Colony.
6. A dish of sea-fowl.
7. A ditto of frost-fish and eels.
8. An apple pie.
9. A course of cranberry tarts, and cheese made in the Old Colony; dressed in the plainest manner (all appearances of luxury and extravagance being avoided, in imitation of our worthy ancestors whose memory we shall ever respect).[5]

> **Thank you, Lord, for significant occasions in my life; times of celebration and feasting. Thank you too, for those "flag raising" days, as it were, when spiritual milestones are commemorated – church anniversaries and so on. May they always bring you glory and pleasure; your people eating and drinking together as they mark your faithfulness and steadfast love.**
> **May this year be full of such events!**

---

1   The Old Colony Club, one of the oldest Gentlemen's Clubs in the USA, having been founded in 1769 in Plymouth, Massachusetts. The club is famous for its annual celebration of Forefathers' Day.
2   Mr Thomas Southworth Howland (1734–79).
3   Bilberry.
4   Or succotash. A dish consisting of sweetcorn, lima beans or other shell beans, tomatoes, and peppers.
5   From *The Term Pilgrim Fathers*.

WHETHER YOU TURN TO THE RIGHT OR TO THE LEFT, YOUR EARS
WILL HEAR A VOICE BEHIND YOU, SAYING,
"THIS IS THE WAY; WALK IN IT."
(Isaiah 30:21)

The Brownist emigration,[1] known to Americans as the "Sailing of the Pilgrim Fathers," was a little part of a great movement towards independence of judgment in spiritual affairs. The great movement began in the latter half of the sixteenth century in many parts of England. The little part of it which concerns us began in the early years of the seventeenth century in the country about the borders of the three counties of Nottingham, Lincoln and York. The Separatists were members of the lower and middle classes, who accepted the ruling of the Church of England in articles of faith, but refused her judgment in points of discipline. They held (in opposition to the Church) that the priesthood is not a distinct order, but an office temporarily conferred by the vote of the congregation.

Their attitude and action have been thus described by one of their number: "They entered into covenant with God and one with another, in the enjoyment of the Ordinances of God. But finding by experience they could not peaceably enjoy their own liberty in their Native Country, without offence to others that were differently minded, they took up thoughts of removing."[2]

> Guiding God, my prayers today are with those who are on the brink of life-changing decisions. Bless them with your guidance, perhaps especially if those decisions are of a spiritual nature. I pray too, for church leaders who are sometimes confronted with matters of division and even discord.

---

1   The Brownists were a group of English Dissenters (or Separatists) from the Church of England, named after their leader, Robert Browne. The majority aboard the *Mayflower* were Brownists. Robert Browne (c. 1550–1633) became an Anglican priest late in life. As a student at Cambridge University, he was influenced by Puritan theologians.

2   From Alexander Young, *Chronicles of the Pilgrim Fathers*, Boston: C.C. Little and J. Brown, 1841.

... HOLDING FAITH AND A GOOD CONSCIENCE.
(1 Timothy 1:19 *ESV*)

One party of [the Separatists]... "removed" from Gainsborough, in Lincolnshire, to Amsterdam, in the year 1606. Another party organized in that year in the district of Scrooby, in Nottinghamshire... began to make itself obnoxious to the country authorities. This second party contained two prominent men, William Brewster,[1] the chief layman, and John Robinson,[2] one of the two ministers.

The members of the party were accustomed to meet together "to worship God in their own manner." Church discipline, which forbade their meetings, imposed a persecution upon them. Religious persecution that endeavours to drive a flock along a path is successful, as a rule, only with the sheep. It makes the goats unruly. The persecution failed to bend the brethren, but it gave them enough annoyance to make them wish to leave the country. The leaders among them planned an exodus to Holland. In the autumn of 1607 a large party tried to escape to Holland from the port of Boston, in Lincolnshire. At that time it was not lawful for a person to leave the country without license. A large party could not hope to get away without the connivance of a ship's captain. The ship's captain to whom this escaping party appealed, accepted the bribe, then, fearing the consequences of his action, or hoping to obtain a reward, betrayed his passengers to the authorities. The members of the party were sentenced to a month in gaol; their goods were confiscated.[3]

> **Lord, there are those times when we have to obey our conscience, even though doing so might set us at odds with church authorities. It cannot reasonably be expected that we always see eye-to-eye with everyone, even those we love and respect! At such moments, Lord, I pray that grace may prevail, and that disagreements may be handled with Christ-like maturity.**

---

1   William Brewster (1566–1644), a *Mayflower* passenger in 1620. Within what eventually became the established Plymouth Colony, Brewster became a senior elder and the leader of the community.
2   John Robinson (1576–1625), pastor to the Pilgrim Fathers before they set sail on the *Mayflower*. A leader of the English Separatists, Robinson is regarded as one of the founders of what became known as the Congregational Church.
3   From *Chronicles of the Pilgrim Fathers*.

FOR WHO HATH DESPISED THE DAY OF SMALL THINGS?
(Zechariah 4:10 *KJV*)

In 1620, a little band of English people – men, women, and children – to the number of about one hundred, sailed from Plymouth in a ship called the *Mayflower* to settle on the bleak and then almost unknown coast of North America.

There they landed at a spot where a huge stone, one of those ice-borne boulders that strew the low shores of Massachusetts Bay, is said to mark the place at which they stepped ashore, now become a place of pilgrimage to which many come from all over the United States, visiting it with reverence. There this storm-tossed and sea-weary company built their huts and a wooden block-house for defence against the native Indians, and prepared to cultivate the soil.

Not long before an English settlement had been planted in Virginia, and other English colonists came a few years later to another part of the New England coast, where is now the town of Salem. But this Plymouth Settlement (for that was the name they gave it) was the most remarkable of the three, just because it was the smallest and weakest, carried out with the least official favour, least noticed by the world in its own day.[1]

> Lord, your ways are sometimes found in the mundane and unspectacular. You often choose to reveal your will through the most ordinary means. Help me, I pray, to see you at work in "the day of small things" – the everyday, the routine – lest I fail to discern your presence and activity.

---

1   From the Foreword to Basil Matthews, *The Argonauts of Faith*, New York: George H. Doran Co., 1920.

... THE PEOPLE THAT DO KNOW THEIR GOD SHALL BE STRONG, AND
DO EXPLOITS.
(Daniel 11:32 *KJV*)

The Pilgrims were humble men, none of them persons of any consequence or influence. But the historical significance and moral dignity of an event are not to be measured by the power or honour, or rank, or wealth of those who bear a part in it.

This was one of the great events in the annals of the English race. It was the second migration of that race. The first was made in war-ships coming from the mouth of the Elbe, manned by fierce heathen warriors, who came as plunderers and conquerors, and took nearly three centuries of fighting to complete their conquest of South Britain (except Wales).[1] This second migration from the Old England of Angles and Saxons, across a far wider sea, to the New England in America marked the beginning of a nation which was to increase and multiply till it overspread a vast continent. It was a peaceful migration. But the Plymouth Pilgrims had the qualities which belong to the English race. They had courage, constancy, loyalty to their convictions. They stamped these qualities upon the infant colony. They gave that distinctive quality to the men of those north-eastern American colonies which has told upon and determined the character of the whole American people.[2]

> Lord, how reassuring it is to learn from this story that you prize availability over ability. You take the ordinary and produce the extraordinary – humble people who have given you their all, and through whom you work great deeds. Take my life, and use it as you will. Take this day.

---

1   The Roman invasion of the British Isles.
2   From *The Argonauts of Faith*.

I EXHORT THEREFORE, THAT, FIRST OF ALL, SUPPLICATIONS, PRAYERS, INTERCESSIONS, AND GIVING OF THANKS, BE MADE FOR ALL MEN; FOR KINGS, AND FOR ALL THAT ARE IN AUTHORITY; THAT WE MAY LEAD A QUIET AND PEACEABLE LIFE IN ALL GODLINESS AND HONESTY. FOR THIS IS GOOD AND ACCEPTABLE IN THE SIGHT OF GOD OUR SAVIOUR ...

(1 Timothy 2:1–3 *KJV*)

[Queen Elizabeth I][1] was angry concerning some of her subjects, who were counted among the Puritans, or, as many termed them, Precisians.[2]

"Have they been especially unreasonable, Madame?" [Bernard Vincent][3] ventured ...

She stared at him, and did not answer the question. She went on to speak slightingly of some whom Bernard knew to be godly men and women, and he thought it grossly unfair that they should be so maligned, and classed among Papists[4] and criminals. He ventured to say so, and the Queen, who was moving up and down the room in the worst of tempers, halted, and swung round to face him.

"What was that you said?" she asked sharply; and there was a flash in her eyes not pleasant to witness.

"I was saying, Madame, that they are blamed for much when their faults are so few."

He stopped abruptly, but she insisted that he should say what was in his mind, and he obeyed willingly, knowing that he had ventured too far.

"It has always seemed to me, Madame, that the Puritans are troubled on trifling points, and I have heard it said that many of them complain that the faithful ministers of the Word are marshalled with the worst malefactors, arraigned and condemned for what some count matters of slender moment."[5]

My prayers today, Almighty God, are for those in authority – and those who work beneath them, handling matters of diplomacy and importance. I lift them all to you in prayer.

---

1   "Elizabeth had her own private chapel in most of her palaces, and reputedly prayed there every day. She saw herself as God's vessel on earth, and would pray to determine God's will so that he would reveal it to her, and she could implement it. Although Elizabeth's actual beliefs elude us, we are able to get an indication of them from her attitudes and gestures. Her chapels were conservative – the crucifix was displayed, and she also liked candles and music. She disliked long Protestant sermons, but also expressed displeasure at some Catholic rituals such as the elevation of the host, which implied that she rejected the Catholic belief of transubstantiation. She also did not really approve of the clergy marrying as she expressed on several occasions, but as this was an integral aspect of Protestantism, she had to accept it." (From https://www.elizabethi.org/contents/elizabethanchurch/queenandchurch.html)

2   A nickname for Puritans who were fastidious in their ways. It was meant as an insult, and a form of ridicule.

3   Private Secretary to Queen Elizabeth I.

4   A derogatory name for Roman Catholics.

5   From Albert Lee, *The Maid of the Mayflower*, London: Morgan & Scott Ltd. Date unknown.

THE LORD SAID TO MOSES, "GO TO PHARAOH AND SAY TO HIM,
'THIS IS WHAT THE LORD, THE GOD OF THE HEBREWS, SAYS:
"LET MY PEOPLE GO, SO THAT THEY MAY WORSHIP ME."
(Exodus 9:1)

The Queen interrupted [Bernard Vincent].

"What things do some count matters of slender moment?" she asked…

"Some, Your Majesty, are punished for leaving the Holy Days unobserved; some for singing the Nunc Dimittis in the morning; some for turning the questions in baptism concerning faith from the infants to the godfathers; some for leaving out the cross in baptism; some for omitting the ring in marriage."

He paused.

"Bernard Vincent, go on!" cried the Queen sharply, and her eyes flashed like steel.

"I would rather say no more, Madame."

"I should think not, indeed," came the angry retort, "It is my pleasure that these creatures be treated as rogues, and felons, and Papists, or anything else that is bad within my realm! They shall think as I think, or I will make the land too hot to hold them!"

Bernard had ventured to differ from his royal mistress at other times on some points, and had been forgiven, and he presumed on past indulgences now. In his blindness he went on to what might well be his destruction.

"But, Madame, may not these godly men and women have consciences of their own?"

"Certainly not, while I am Queen!"

"Surely, Madame, you would not expect them to give up everything to the Crown, and yield to it the absolute direction of their consciences?" he exclaimed incredulously.

"Why not? I will permit no latitude in these matters," the Queen retorted. "There shall be an exact uniformity in doctrine and ceremonies within my realm!"[1]

Lord God, I pray for those who have what is sometimes the unenviable responsibility of speaking truth to power, be that in the political realm or within the church. I pray for them especially when truth is unwanted, and met with hostility. Grant them your authority, your courage, and your wisdom.

---

1   From *The Maid of the Mayflower*.

… THE FATHER OF THE HEAVENLY LIGHTS, WHO DOES NOT CHANGE.

(James 1:17)

At Cambridge [University] young Brewster[1] found himself at the very centre of the conflict. In spite of his youth he followed it with some attention, it appears, early embracing the rebel cause, for it was here, in Bradford's phrase, that he was "first seasoned with ye seeds of grace and vertue [sic]".[2]

On one side… stood the master of his college, Dr. Andrew Perne,[3] possessed of an elasticity of conscience seldom found outside academic circles. First a Catholic, he had become a Protestant under Edward VI,[4] reverted to Catholicism under Mary,[5] and frantically embraced Protestantism again under Elizabeth,[6] thus managing to hold his mastership of Peterhouse,[7] which he ruled with a firm high hand. It was he who in Mary's reign had officiated at the trial and burning of the corpses of two long-buried Protestants,[8] both men of mild views. Many of his students scorned Perne as the "old Turner", and certainly Brewster was among them. But the master of Peterhouse lived and died a power in the church, the intimate friend and adviser of John Whitgift,[9] once a fellow of the college, now well on his way to becoming Archbishop of Canterbury.

But there were many at Cambridge, both among the fellows and the students of the colleges, who were disturbed by the state of the church. True radicals in seeking the root of things, they dug into Scripture to discover just where the "disorder" had first crept in. The more they dug and explored, the less warrant they could find for a great deal of current belief and observance. The originally simple Christian faith had been corrupted, they declared, by time and "human invention".[10]

Lord, human beings are fickle! We change our minds and sometimes sail with ships of convenience. You do not alter. Your ways are fixed, stable, and utterly reliable. You are my God. In a world of shifting values, your standards remain.

---

1   See Footnote 1, January 4ᵗʰ.

2   William Bradford (1590–1657), English Puritan who emigrated on the *Mayflower*. Bradford became Governor of the Plymouth Colony, and recorded the story in his journal *Of Plymouth Plantation*.

3   Andrew Perne (c. 1519–89), Vice-Chancellor of Cambridge University and Dean of Ely.

4   The first English monarch to be raised as a Protestant.

5   Mary took the throne in 1553, as the first queen regnant of England and Ireland. She sought to return England to the Catholic Church, persecuting hundreds of Protestants.

6   See Footnote 1, January 7ᵗʰ.

7   Peterhouse College, University of Cambridge.

8   Not an entirely unusual course of action at the time. See accounts of the "Cadaver Synod".

9   John Whitgift (c. 1530–1604), Archbishop of Canterbury from 1583 to his death.

10   From George F. Willison, *Saints and Strangers*, Time-Life Books, 1981.

THESE THINGS SAITH THE AMEN, THE FAITHFUL AND TRUE
WITNESS, THE BEGINNING OF THE CREATION OF GOD; I KNOW THY
WORKS, THAT THOU ART NEITHER COLD NOR HOT: I WOULD THOU
WERT COLD OR HOT…
(**Revelation 3:14–15 KJV**)

The… need of the hour was to restore [the Church] to its "ancient purity" – or, as the Pilgrims later phrased it, "to its primitive order, libertie, & bewtie". Such views upset the orthodox, and in 1565 Archbishop Parker[1] denounced those who advanced them as "these precise men". The phrase was graphic and seemed to fit, and the reformers were soon known as the Precisians, somewhat later as the Puritans – so named, it should be observed, not for their moral code but for their theological doctrine.

The discontented had many telling points to make against the church. They particularly objected to the great host of "dumb" ministers who seldom or never preached.[2] A sermon once a quarter or even once a month was not enough. Ministers should preach every Sunday, and "not to please the ears but move the heart".[3]

**Lord, it is not difficult to see trouble brewing here! An apathetic church and a
group of dissenters longing for something more. In your mercy, restore your
Church where it is flagging, and where many are discouraged. Send the fire today!**

---

1   Matthew Parker (1504–75), Archbishop of Canterbury from 1559 until his death.
2   Lazy clergy were the scourge of Christendom for a season. Some ordained priests spent their time playing cards, eating fine meals, and hunting on horseback, but doing very little otherwise. This problem also features in my book *Through the Year with John Newton*.
3   From *Saints and Strangers*.

January 11th

… Saul was still breathing out murderous threats against
the Lord's disciples.

(Acts 9:1)

There were so many people going from the villages round Scrooby[1] to Gainsborough[2] on Sundays that they felt it was unnecessary to walk every week so far across the country to [the parish church in] Gainsborough. They could form a little church themselves. They believed that if two or three were gathered together in Christ's name to worship Him there was the Church. So William Brewster,[3] about the year 1600, asked the friends to come and meet under the roof at the Manor House at Scrooby.

This was very brave of Brewster; for Archbishop Whitgift[4] was driving to prison men who dared to worship in this way. At any hour he might find himself robbed of his home and his living, and carried away to a dungeon and even a scaffold. But that did not stop him…

As a young clergyman in Norwich,[5] [John] Robinson[6] had already been thrown into prison for gathering people in worship and for declaring their freedom to meet as they desired.

So on a Sunday morning the men and women came with their boys and girls from the farmsteads and the villages round about the Manor House…

Sometimes they had warning that the Queen's officers would arrest them if they worshipped there. That week they would arrange secretly to meet in some other place close by in another village. But in one place or another they did meet, in spite of everything.[7]

> Almighty God, today I pray for "the persecuted church" – those believers who live in countries where oppressive regimes persecute Christians to the point of imprisonment and execution. Strengthen your people as they meet in secret. Meet their fears with courage. Touch the hearts of dictators who instigate such persecution. Show me if there is anything I can do to help and support my brothers and sisters in such situations.

1   Nottinghamshire, England.
2   Lincolnshire, England. (Nottinghamshire and Lincolnshire share a border.)
3   See Footnote 1, January 4th.
4   See Footnote 9, January 9th.
5   Norfolk, England.
6   See Footnote 2, January 4th.
7   From The Argonauts of Faith.

"Leave your country and your people..."
(Acts 7:3)

Prisoners in country gaols were then supported out of the rates. The keeping of large numbers of people in prison, in idleness, proved to be a great burden upon the rates of the towns where they were gaoled. The authorities who felt the burden soon became anxious to get rid of their prisoners. They released them and connived at their leaving the country. By August 1608, the whole party [of religious persecuted] was safely in Amsterdam.

During the next few months, after some contention with the party from Gainsborough, a hundred of the Scrooby party obtained leave to go to Leyden[1], where they settled down to the manufacture of woollen goods. They were joined from time to time by other Separitists [*sic*] from England. In a few years their communion numbered some three hundred souls, among whom were Edward Winslow,[2] John Carver,[3] and Miles Standish.[4][5]

Heavenly Father, human history is littered with accounts of people leaving their homes in order to seek a better life elsewhere: political exiles, refugees, and those seeking religious freedom. Bless those who migrate, Lord, especially those who travel in fear and poverty, and whose circumstances are desperate.

---

1   Leyden (or Leiden), a city in the Dutch province of South Holland.
2   Edward Winslow (1595–1655), a Separatist who was a passenger on the *Mayflower*. He became a senior leader within the Plymouth Colony.
3   John Carver (c. 1584–1621), a *Mayflower* passenger who became the first governor of Plymouth Colony.
4   Myles (or Miles) Standish (c. 1584–1656), English military officer hired by the Pilgrims as military adviser for Plymouth Colony. He sailed on the *Mayflower* and was influential in the administration and defence of Plymouth Colony.
5   From *Chronicles of the Pilgrim Fathers*.

ALL YOUR CHILDREN WILL BE TAUGHT BY THE LORD, AND GREAT
WILL BE THEIR PEACE.
(Isaiah 54:13)

In the year 1617, these exiles began to realize that Holland, though a seasonable refuge, could not be their abiding place. The children were growing up. The parents did not wish to send them to Dutch schools, because the Dutch children were of bad behaviour. The parents feared that the children, if sent to school in Holland, would receive evil communications and lose something of their nationality. No one is so proud of his nationality as the exile. The fear that the colony might become a part of the Dutch population caused the leaders to think of travelling elsewhere. Guiana, the first place suggested, was rejected as unsuitable, because it was supposed to contain gold. Gold, or the prospect of finding gold, would be a temptation, if not a curse, to weak members of the community. There was also the danger from the Spaniards. Virginia, the next place suggested, was considered unsafe. The English were there. It was doubtful whether the English would allow in their midst a large community the members of which held unauthorized religious opinions. No other place offered such advantages as Virginia. The settlers there were Englishmen and Protestants. It was decided that members of the community should go to London to ask leave of the Virginia Company.[1] [2]

Heavenly Father, I pray for children who are moving schools on account of their parents' occupations or decisions. Bless them, and help them to settle quickly. Bless their mums and dads too in such times of transition!

---

1   The London Company (also called the Virginia Company of London) was an English joint-stock company established in 1606 by royal charter by King James I with the purpose of establishing colonial settlements in North America (from https://en.wikipedia.org/wiki/London_Company).

2   From *Chronicles of the Pilgrim Fathers*.

JESUS REPLIED, "FOXES HAVE DENS AND BIRDS HAVE NESTS, BUT THE
SON OF MAN HAS NO PLACE TO LAY HIS HEAD."
(Luke 9:58)

In September 1617, two of the Separatists (John Carver[1] and Robert Cushman)[2] laid before the Virginia Company in London a declaration in seven articles. This declaration was designed to show that the Separatists would not be rebellious nor dangerous colonists. It stated that they assented to the Doctrines of the Church of England and acknowledged the King's authority.[3] The Virginia Company, accepting the declaration, was inclined to welcome the party as colonists; but a fear, suggested by the bishops, that they intended for Virginia, "to make a free popular state there," caused delay.[4]

> Lord, my prayers today reach out to those who are seeking to make their new home in a foreign country, and whose applications are delayed or obstructed by bureaucracy. Lord, for those whose lives are held in the balance by people who might not be sympathetic, or in any particular hurry to help, I ask your blessing. Soften the hearts of bureaucrats, I pray, as they deal with applications for citizenship or sanctuary.

1   See Footnote 2, January 12th.
2   Robert Cushman (1577–1625), leader and organizer of the *Mayflower* voyage, who served as negotiator in London for the Leiden Separatist contingent.
3   King James I.
4   From *Chronicles of the Pilgrim Fathers*.

"NAZARETH! CAN ANYTHING GOOD COME FROM THERE?"
(John 1:46)

[There] follows the ode written by Judge John Davis…
I am aware it will be a political apostasy… to trace up a descent from the wicked island of Great-Britain. But from no country…, had I rather be descended…

AN ODE,
For… the anniversary of our ancestors' landing at Plymouth,[1] 1620:
By JOHN DAVIS, ESQUIRE:[2]
Sung by CAPTAIN J. THOMAS.[3]
Sons of renowned sires,
Join in harmonious choirs,
Swell your loud songs:
Daughters of peerless dames,
Let their revered names
Dwell on your tongues!
Columbia, child of heaven –[4]
The best of blessings, given,
Rest on thy head:
Beneath thy peaceful skies,
While prosperous tides arise,
Here turn thy grateful eyes,
Revere the DEAD![5]

How wonderful, Lord, that the very people who were despised and ostracized in England should eventually be celebrated in song in America! And even more wonderful, Lord Jesus, is the fact that that even though your ethnicity as a Nazarene was once treated with derision, we now acknowledge you as King of Kings! You came as an outcast and endured rejection, just because of love.

1   Plymouth, Massachusetts, USA.
2   John Davis (1761–1847) lawyer, member of both the House of Representatives and the Senate of the Commonwealth of Massachusetts, comptroller, and federal judge. He was born in Plymouth, Massachusetts.
3   Uncertain.
4   Here, "Columbia" is a poetic term used for the United States, originating from the name of Christopher Columbus … Columbia … is the personification of the United States. It was also a historical name used by some Europeans and Americans to describe the Americas, the New World (from *Wikipedia*).
5   From *The Term Pilgrim Fathers.*

"... I will build my church..."
(Matthew 16:18)

Pluralism[1] had nominally been abolished by Henry VIII, but many clerics still held scores of pulpits and church livings, appearing only to collect their stipends. Country parishes frequently went for years without religious services of any kind. Those who enjoyed multiple livings defended themselves by arguing that there were insufficient educated men to go around, sneeringly asking critics if they would place cobblers and tailors in the pulpit.

"Yea!" came the sharp reply, "a great deale better were it so to do than place popishe Priestes, the devourers of Christe's Lambes. For their priest crafte is the wickedest occupation that ever was in the world, and the most craftie" [sic].

Under the circumstances it was no wonder that the English church was "a pache of popery, and a pudle of corruption" [sic]. Was not the sign of the cross, hated as part of the Roman church, still made over infants at baptism? Were not dispensations sold to those who could afford them? To dispense with publication of banns before marriage cost 10s.[2] Eating flesh on fast days came higher at 40s. And did not the church still operate to its immense profit that elaborate fee and fine system known as the Indulgences, a primary cause of Luther's revolt and still a noisome scandal in the Roman church?[3]

Almighty God, look upon your Church with mercy. Today, I pray for the church to which I belong. Bless my minister and help him/her to successfully manage any difficulties and problems. Send the fire of your Holy Spirit afresh.

---

1   The practice of holding more than one ecclesiastical office at a time.
2   Shillings.
3   From *Saints and Strangers*.

Who dared deny that the higher clergy were brazenly "making merchandise of the Church of God"? They not only bestowed scores of benefices upon themselves and resided in none, but many were alienating their lands, wasting their woods, and disposing of ecclesiastical rights and revenues quite as if these were their personal property, with the result, as even the biographer of Archbishop Parker[1] had to confess, that "the churchs ran greatly to decays, were kept filthy and nasty, and undecent for God's worship" [sic].

Even more devout churchmen were engaged in this nefarious traffic.[2]

Little wonder, Lord, that the Pilgrim Fathers felt the need to break away, if this was the state of affairs! Lord of the Church, look upon your people and forgive us where we have things wrong. Pardon our failings and, where necessary, restore us. Gracious Spirit, visit us with the blessing of conviction and lead us to repentance.

---

1 See Footnote 1, January 10th.
2 From *Saints and Strangers*.

THOSE WHO REPAY MY GOOD WITH EVIL LODGE
ACCUSATIONS AGAINST ME, THOUGH I SEEK ONLY TO DO WHAT IS
GOOD.
(Psalm 38:20)

The Queen had died… Then King James sat on her throne… His Majesty made it known that he "would have no canting Puritans" about his Court…

[The King]… was making unhappiness throughout the kingdom by his resolution to assert his kingly right to interfere in men's religious opinions and sacrifices. It was not alone the King's intrusion.[1]

Heavenly Father, once again I pray for those whose religious freedom is obstructed or curtailed. I pray for those who face opposition at the highest level. Help them, Lord. Grant them strength and holy belligerence.

---

1   From *The Maid of the Mayflower.*

THEY THAT GO DOWN TO THE SEA IN SHIPS ...

(Psalm 107:23 *KJV*)

OUTWARD BOUND

Dear Earth, near Earth, the clay that made us men,
  The land we sowed,
The hearth was glowed –
O mother, must we bid farewell to thee?
Fast dawns the last dawn,
And what shall comfort then
The lonely hearts that roam the outer sea?
Gray wakes the daybreak,
The shivering sails are set,
To misty deeps
The channel sweeps –
O mother, think on us who think on thee!
Earth-home, birth-home, with love remember yet
The sons in exile on the eternal sea.[1]

(Sir Henry Newbolt)[2]

**Lord of the seas, draw close to those who sail the oceans, for whichever reason
they do so: fishermen, sailors, military personnel, migrants, and passengers.
Protect them from the perils of the deep, I pray.**

---

1   I have included this poem as it reflects some of the feelings and emotions surrounding the voyage of
    the *Mayflower*, even though it was not written with any direct reference to that sailing. It is included in
    the hope of granting readers some insight into the emotional turmoil the Pilgrim Fathers must have
    experienced.
2   Sir Henry John Newbolt (1862–1938), poet, novelist, and historian. He was also a government adviser.

… THEY SEIZED PAUL AND SILAS AND DRAGGED THEM INTO THE
MARKETPLACE TO FACE THE AUTHORITIES. THEY BROUGHT THEM
BEFORE THE MAGISTRATES… THE CROWD JOINED IN THE ATTACK
AGAINST PAUL AND SILAS, AND THE MAGISTRATES ORDERED THEM
TO BE STRIPPED AND BEATEN WITH RODS. AFTER THEY HAD BEEN
SEVERELY FLOGGED, THEY WERE THROWN INTO PRISON, AND THE
JAILER WAS COMMANDED TO GUARD THEM CAREFULLY.

(Acts 16:19–23)

William Brewster and John Robinson and their friends in Scrooby and the country round about were at last forced to see very clearly that they could not stay in England any longer. If they did remain, they knew that they would be hunted from pillar to post, and, at the worst, die of fever in some dark dungeon in those foul gaols, like the Fleet[1] or Brideswell[2] or in the foetid cells of Boston prison… [3]

William Bradford,[4] who was now seventeen years old… told how they were "hunted and persecuted on every side; so as their former afflictions were but as flea-bitings in comparison of those which now came upon them. For some were taken and clapt up in prison, others had their houses beset and watcht night and day, and hardly escaped their hands, and ye most were faine to flie and leave their houses and habitations and the means of their livelihood" [sic].[5]

> Stand up, stand up for Jesus,
> The strife will not be long;
> This day the noise of battle,
> The next the victor's song.
> To those who vanquish evil
> A crown of life shall be;
> They with the King of Glory
> Shall reign eternally.[6]

---

1   A notorious prison that stood by the River Fleet in London. Built in 1197, but rebuilt several times, it was finally demolished in 1846.

2   Brideswell Prison & Hospital, London (or Bridewell), established for the disorderly poor. Demolished in 1864. The term "Brideswell" became synonymous with large prisons everywhere, even in the USA.

3   "The Scrooby Separatists" were held in squalid cells beneath Boston Guildhall, Lincolnshire, England. (An interesting aside is that when the settlement in Massachusetts was eventually founded, it was named Boston in honour of the Separatists' home town.)

4   See Footnote 2, January 9th.

5   From The Argonauts of Faith.

6   From George Duffield's hymn "Stand Up, Stand Up for Jesus".

WHEN ALL THE NATION HAD FINISHED PASSING OVER THE JORDAN, THE LORD SAID TO JOSHUA, "TAKE TWELVE MEN FROM THE PEOPLE, FROM EACH TRIBE A MAN, AND COMMAND THEM, SAYING, 'TAKE TWELVE STONES FROM HERE OUT OF THE MIDST OF THE JORDAN, FROM THE VERY PLACE WHERE THE PRIESTS' FEET STOOD FIRMLY, AND BRING THEM OVER WITH YOU AND LAY THEM DOWN IN THE PLACE WHERE YOU LODGE TONIGHT.'" THEN JOSHUA CALLED THE TWELVE MEN FROM THE PEOPLE OF ISRAEL, WHOM HE HAD APPOINTED, A MAN FROM EACH TRIBE. AND JOSHUA SAID TO THEM, "PASS ON BEFORE THE ARK OF THE LORD YOUR GOD INTO THE MIDST OF THE JORDAN, AND TAKE UP EACH OF YOU A STONE UPON HIS SHOULDER, ACCORDING TO THE NUMBER OF THE TRIBES OF THE PEOPLE OF ISRAEL, THAT THIS MAY BE A SIGN AMONG YOU. WHEN YOUR CHILDREN ASK IN TIME TO COME, 'WHAT DO THOSE STONES MEAN TO YOU?' THEN YOU SHALL TELL THEM THAT THE WATERS OF THE JORDAN WERE CUT OFF BEFORE THE ARK OF THE COVENANT OF THE LORD. WHEN IT PASSED OVER THE JORDAN, THE WATERS OF THE JORDAN WERE CUT OFF. SO THESE STONES SHALL BE TO THE PEOPLE OF ISRAEL A MEMORIAL FOREVER."
(Joshua 4:1–7 *ESV*)

The important achievements and pious examples of illustrious characters of former times, are both interesting and instructive to rising generations. Among the glorious events recorded in our history, none claim our grateful recollection more, than the pilgrimage of our venerable fore-fathers. As a testimony of high respect for their characters and memory, the anniversary of their landing and establishment on our shores, should be commemorated as "the glory of children are their fathers." What scene can be more interesting to the best feelings of the human heart, than a social union, celebrating the virtues and recounting the sufferings of our pious ancestors. While in the full enjoyment of their inestimable inheritance, let it not be imagined that prosperity has contracted our hearts, or debased our character; but, let us pay our annual tribute to their shrine, and perpetuate the theme to future generations.[1]

> Eternal God, thank you for helpful and encouraging memorials – those in the heart, of blessings in times past, those recorded in the Bible, of your great deeds throughout history, and those commemorated in the life of my church. Lord, help us never to rest on our laurels and succumb to complacency, but neither to forget that marvellous record of your historic actions.

---

1   From *The Term Pilgrim Fathers*.

How can we sing the songs of the Lord while in a foreign land?

(Psalm 137:4)

[William Brewster, William Bradford, John Robinson & Co.] were driven at last in 1607 to leave the homesteads where they had been born; the old meadow by the river Idle, where they had played and fished; the smithy where their fathers' and grandfathers' and great-grandfathers' horses had been shod. They must sail into a strange land; and they would never see the wild-duck fly over their native meadows again.

As William Bradford said:

"To goe into a countrie they knew not (but by hearsay), wher they must learne a new language, and get their livings they knew not how, it being a dear place and subjecte to ye misseries of war, it was by many thought an adventure almost desperate, a case intolerable, and a misserie worse than death" [*sic*].[1]

> God of compassion, my prayers today reach out towards those who are away from home and homesick. I pray for family members who are separated from each other, for whatever reason. I pray for those whose contact with loved ones and friends is limited by circumstance. I pray for those who live apart from their nearest and dearest. Grant them your consolation, Lord.

---

1   From *The Argonauts of Faith*.

BEWARE OF THE SCRIBES, WHICH LOVE TO GO IN LONG CLOTHING,
AND LOVE SALUTATIONS IN THE MARKETPLACES...
(Mark 12:38 *KJV*)

Elizabeth's bishops were, by and large, a worldly and avaricious lot. Several were just plain rascals and had to be unseated for brazenly looting the parishes in their charge. The grossly sensual lives of others created scandal at a time when a gargantuan love of the fleshpots, even among the clergy, scarcely caused comment. All lived in the greatest magnificence and luxury. On their travels the Archbishops of Canterbury were accompanied with a great troop of white horse and hundreds of flunkeys in scarlet livery set off with gold chain and gold braid.

And such were the prelates who, to clothe their worldly pride and arrogance, clung so passionately to "the rags of Rome"!, exclaimed the reformers with disgust. Churchmen, they said, should be distinguished, "by their doctrines, not their garments; their conversation, not their dress; their purity of mind, not their adornment of person".[1]

Oh Lord! This is an extreme example but, for all that, I ask your forgiveness
for those times when we, your people, may have placed appearance above
application, and have emphasized style over substance. Have mercy, Lord, and
teach your Church more about rolling its sleeves up and getting its hands dirty in
the service of suffering humanity.

---

1   From *Saints and Strangers*.

AND WHEN [JESUS] ENTERED JERUSALEM, THE WHOLE CITY WAS
STIRRED UP…
(Matthew 21:10 *ESV*)

The Puritan animus against "gay apparel" originated here in this dispute about clerical vestments. Anyone bedecked in silks and flounces must be as "antichristian" as a bishop. There were many at the time who belittled this controversy as trivial and illiberal on the Puritans' part. Many have since joined them in charging the latter with a "peevish forwardness and a zeal for discord". This is, at best, a very superficial view. At worst, it is the kind of special pleading employed at all times and all places by defenders of the *status quo*. The latter are always for peace and harmony and unity – but strictly on their own terms, of course. They have no use for "agitators" given to asking embarrassing questions, and are savage in their attack upon any and all not content to let well enough alone.

If clerical vestments were of no importance, as traditionalists pretended in this instance, why did they fight so fiercely to retain them? It was because they quite realistically appreciated their inestimable value as symbols, and the Puritans can hardly be blamed for likewise appraising them as just that – the flaunting banners of the old order. As the Pilgrims later declared, all this "popish & antichristian stuffe" merely encouraged the Papists "to hope againe for a day" [*sic*].[1] [2]

Oh Lord! The importance of being awkward and stirring things up! Bless those who agitate and disturb the status quo, if they are doing so under your guidance and inspiration. Grant me the courage to take a stand if and when the need arises.

---

1   Hoping for the restoration of Roman Catholicism in England.
2   From *Saints and Strangers*.

So Pharaoh said to Joseph,
"I hereby put you in charge of the whole land of Egypt."
(Genesis 41:41)

The reformers found increasing support throughout the realm, even in the most exalted circles. The Queen's ruling favourite, the highly decorative Earl of Leicester, was an avowed Puritan,[1] as were the poets Spenser[2] and Sir Philip Sidney,[3] both with influence at Court. The great Lord Burghley,[4] treasurer and virtually the prime minister of the land, more than once publicly urged a "reduction of the church to its former puritie [sic]" in spite of the Queen's jibes at him and "his brothers in Christ". Nothing ever said by the Puritans, even the most extreme, quite matched the vehement denunciation of the "abuses" uttered… at Cambridge in 1578 in a remarkable sermon[5] by a distinguished and devout churchman, Dr. Laurence Chaderton,[6] one of the inspired scholar-poets who later gave us the magnificent King James Version of the Bible.[7]

Thank you, Lord, for friends in high places! My prayers today are for Christians who occupy places of influence within parliament or even royal circles. Bless their witness, I pray. Grant them courage, courtesy, and wisdom.

1   Robert Dudley, 1ˢᵗ Earl of Leicester (1532–88).
2   Edmund Spenser (1552 or 1553–99), a poet whose famous work *The Faerie Queene* [sic] celebrated the Tudor dynasty and Elizabeth I.
3   Sir Philip Sidney (1554–86), poet, courtier, scholar, and soldier.
4   William Cecil, 1ˢᵗ Baron Burghley (1520–98), chief advisor of Queen Elizabeth I.
5   See https://en.wikipedia.org/wiki/Laurence_Chaderton
6   Laurence Chaderton (c. 1536–1640), Puritan divine and one of the translators of the King James Version of the Bible.
7   From *Saints and Strangers*.

REST IN THE LORD, AND WAIT PATIENTLY FOR HIM …
(Psalm 37:7 *KJV*)

When the patent [from the Virginia Company] had been obtained more delay was caused by the difficulty of obtaining money for the equipment of the expedition. The London merchants saw little prospect of rich returns. They were slow to invest in an undertaking so hazardous. It was one thing to subscribe money "for the glory of Christ and the advancement of the beaver trade," another to equip a large party of religious enthusiasts for an experimental setting in a savage country. John Robinson, wearying of the delays, tried to persuade the Dutch to encourage his party to settle in the new Netherlands. His request led to nothing. Early in 1620, Thomas Weston,[1] a London merchant, suggested that the settlement should be made in Northern Virginia. About seventy other merchants offered to subscribe. The business began to go forward. A Common Stock was formed. Ten pound shares in this Stock could be taken up either by money or by goods.[2]

> **Heavenly Father, we aren't always very good at waiting! Help those, I pray, who need extra patience today – grant them your peace, even if what they are hoping for hasn't yet come to pass. Help them to resist the temptation to rush ahead without you, so to speak. Bless them with the grace of trusting!**

---

1 Thomas Weston (c. 1584–c. 1646), ironmonger, colonist, merchant, and adventurer.
2 From *Chronicles of the Pilgrim Fathers*.

"IT IS WRITTEN," [JESUS] SAID TO THEM, "'MY HOUSE WILL BE
CALLED A HOUSE OF PRAYER,' BUT YOU ARE MAKING IT 'A DEN OF
ROBBERS.'"

(Matthew 21:13)

The church was, [Dr. Laurence Chaderton][1] declared, mincing no words, "a huge masse of old and stinking works, of conjuring, witchcraft, sorcery, charming, blaspheming the holy name of God, swearing and forswearing, profaning of the Lord's Sabbothe, disobedience to superiours, contempt of inferiours; murther, manslaughter, robberies, adultereye, fornication, covenant-breaking, false witness-bearing, lieing…" It was filled with arrogant hypocrites and renegades. There was everywhere a crying need for honest and zealous pastors "to admonish, correct, suspende, and excommunicate such noysome, hurtfull, & monstrous beastes out of the house of God, without respect of persons" [sic].[2]

What a dreadful state of affairs, Lord! This highlights, though, your great
faithfulness towards your Church over the centuries, even when we, your people,
have made mistakes, sinned and erred. Thank you, Lord, that you are a redeemer,
and that however hopeless things may seem, your grace prevails. Help me to
remember that, and take heart from it.

---

1   See Footnote 6, January 25th.
2   From *Saints and Strangers*.

THEN CALEB SILENCED THE PEOPLE BEFORE MOSES AND SAID,
"WE SHOULD GO UP AND TAKE POSSESSION OF THE LAND, FOR WE
CAN CERTAINLY DO IT."

(Numbers 13:30)

In their franker moments even some of the bishops agreed, but they always had some excuse to postpone action. Now was not the time for reform – and "now never came. Besides, it would be necessary to retain certain "harmless" beliefs and ceremonies if "ye weake & ignorant [*sic*]" were not to be lost to the Lord. And there could be no question, of course, of touching the revenues of the higher clergy.

"When they that serve God's altar shall be exposed to poverty," growled Archbishop Whitgift[1] in an aspersion on the early church and Christ himself, "then religion shall be exposed to scorn and become contemptible."

All in all, critics made little impression upon the "antichristian prelates" who more and more insistently demanded that all strictly conform and hold their tongues. Under increasing pressure many of the Puritans, especially those who were more comfortably situated in life, began to give way and resign themselves to at least a nominal conformity, fearing to jeopardize their personal safety, their bread and butter, even their creature comforts. But those of greater faith and courage were determined to go on.[2]

> Heavenly Father, I pray to be a Caleb today! I pray to be someone who will see
> opportunities, and not only obstacles. Easier said than done, I know, but make
> me one of "those of greater faith and courage".
> Equip me for the challenges of this day.

---

1   See Footnote 9, January 9ᵗʰ.
2   From *Saints and Strangers*.

WITH YOUR HELP I CAN ADVANCE AGAINST A TROOP; WITH MY GOD
I CAN SCALE A WALL.

(Psalm 18:29)

[The Separatists] hated to go; for they loved England, though they felt that her government treated them harshly. Indeed the boys who lived then loved England as people had never done in all her history. For at last she had become really one land and one people. She had passed through terrible perils. A boy – like William Bradford – would listen at night by the fire in the Manor House at Scrooby, with his chin in his hands, while he was told the story of how, only two years before he was born, the Great Armada of Spain had sailed to destroy England, and how Drake had "drummed them down the Channel."

Fancy hearing the story of the great victory over the Armada from the very lips of a sailor who had fought in the greatest naval battle! The boy might even possibly have read Sir Walter Raleigh's book *The Fight About the Azores* and his *Discoveries*, and perhaps Hakluyt's[1] wonderful *Voyages and Discoveries*, of which the last volume had only been published seven years earlier in 1600. And only a few years before that there had come into print for the first time those words of the love of England written by a man William Shakespeare, who in those very days walked the streets of London town – words that have set the blood of three centuries of boyhood in a tingle.

> ... *This little world,*
> *This precious stone set in the silver sea,*
> *Which serves it in the office of a wall,*
> *Or as a moat defensive to a house,*
> *Against the envy of less happier lands;*
> *This blessed spot, this earth, this realm, this England.*[2][3]

Thank you, Lord, for people who inspire and encourage! Thank you for stories and testimonies that stir the blood! Thank you for books that fire the imagination! Help me, I pray, to inspire those who come within the remit of my influence. Grant me the gift of encouragement, so that those who meet me may be strengthened in their resolve and emboldened in their hopes and dreams.

---

1   Richard Hakluyt (1553–1616), writer. Some of his works promoted the English colonization of North America. He also promoted a petition to King James I for letters patent to colonize Virginia, which were granted to the Virginia Company in 1606.
2   From Shakespeare's *King Richard II*, Act II, Scene I, published in 1597, nine years after the defeat of the Spanish Armada.
3   From *The Argonauts of Faith*.

"... HE WILL BIND UP OUR WOUNDS."

(Hosea 6:1)

These men did love their own land which had so narrowly escaped with its life from the Armada of Spain. Yet England tried their love sorely and wore out their patience. They were men who knew that "patriotism is not enough"; – they had gone to prison for disobeying the law of their country in obedience to what was – they were sure in their own mind – a still higher law. They could say to England what the soldier-poet said to his lady-love:

"I could not love thee, Dear, so much,
Loved I not Honour more."[1] [2]

That awful moment, Lord, when love goes wrong! I pray for those today whose devotion has been sorely tried, and whose patience is wearing thin: with a friend, an organization, a church, or a loved one. In your mercy, Lord, bring resolution and healing. Mend broken relationships and fractured situations.

1   Richard Lovelace (1617–57). From his poem "To Lucasta, on going to the Wars".
2   From *The Argonauts of Faith*.

... GOD'S ELECT, EXILES SCATTERED THROUGHOUT THE PROVINCES
OF PONTUS, GALATIA, CAPPADOCIA, ASIA AND BITHYNIA ...
(1 Peter 1:1)

A great stir had been raised... by Robert Browne[1]... The most creative religious thinker of his day, he was to exert a profound influence upon Brewster and all the Pilgrim leaders. He soon abandoned his advanced principles and rejoined the Church, creeping "back into Egypt to live off the spoils of it", as a Pilgrim leader declared in rather lightly dismissing him as "a man of insinuating manners, but very unsteady in his views of men and things". Certainly, his was an always restless mind and its volatility in later years more than suggested mental derangement. But his leadership, however brief, laid the foundation upon which others were to build. So pervasive was his influence that all of the religious radicals, regardless of creed, were known as Brownists ...

Browne created such a storm with his... sermons that... he was forced to retire to Norwich, one of the most active Puritan centres. There he was soon jailed, on the complaint of the local bishop, for holding private meetings "of the vulgar sort of people... to the number of one hundred at a time." Appealing to Lord Burghley[2]... Browne obtained his release, only to be jailed again by the bishop. Once more Burghley released him, again the bishop jailed him, whereupon "Troublechurch" Browne and his company seized the first opportunity to flee to Holland, blazing a trail that many were to follow. The exiles settled down at Middelburg, where... Browne published two works of the greatest consequence. *A Treatise of Reformation without Tarying for Anie* and *A Booke which sheweth the Life and Manner of all True Christians* [sic].[3]

Lord, whatever the idiosyncrasies of Robert Browne's leadership, there can be no doubt that you used him to lay the foundations of intelligent spiritual revolution. Thank you, then, for his influence. I offer this day to you, in the hope that I too can be of some use and service to your Kingdom in these hours. I pray that you would work through me according to your will.

1   See Footnote 1, January 3rd.
2   See Footnote 4, January 25th.
3   From *Saints and Strangers*.

THEN THE APOSTLES AND ELDERS, WITH THE WHOLE CHURCH, DECIDED TO CHOOSE SOME OF THEIR OWN MEN…
(Acts 15:22)

Formulating the basic principles upon which the revolutionary Independent movement took shape, giving clear and ringing expression for the first time to ideas that had been vaguely circulating for some time, Browne rejected Calvin's thesis that reform of the Church[1] had to wait until the state took action, a most unrealistic view at a time when Church and State were one. No, said Browne, the kingdom of God was "not to be begun by whole parishes, but rather by the worthiest, were they ever so few". In every parish these should withdraw from the Church – secede, separate, as they had warranted to do by Scripture* – and organize themselves under a mutual covenant to "forsake & denie all ungodliness and wicked fellowship, and to refuse all ungodlie communion with Wicked Persons" [sic]. This concept of a free covenant was borrowed from the execrated German Anabaptists[2] and their descendants, the Dutch Mennonites,[3] whom Browne had known at Norwich,[4] for many of them had come to live there as workers in the woollen trade.[5]

*2 Corinthians vi.17: "Come out from them, and be ye separate, saith the Lord, and touch not the unclean thing."

> Heavenly Father, how it must grieve you when your Church is divided and torn apart. I thank you, Lord, for those who agitate in order to move the church forward in ways of good and healthy progress, but at the same time, I pray for those whose lives are affected and for any who might be hurt, albeit inadvertently. Lord, at such times, draw close to your people.

---

1   A useful explanation of this can be found at https://www.ligonier.org/blog/john-calvin-necessity-reforming-church/
2   The belief in the validity and worth of a second baptism.
3   A Protestant sect originating in Friesland, Netherlands, in the sixteenth century.
4   Norwich, England, enjoyed prosperity on the back of the wool trade in the Middle Ages.
5   From *Saints and Strangers*.

All the believers were together and had everything in
common. They sold property and possessions to give to
anyone who had need.

(Acts 2:44–45)

John Carver[1] went to Southampton to engage a ship. Robert Cushman,[2] acting for the brethren, drew up an agreement with the merchant adventurers, or, as we should call them, the speculators. He agreed that all the labour of the colonists should be for the common benefit, and that, after seven years, the results of the labours (houses, tilled lands and goods) should be divided equally between the planters and adventurers.[3]

What an example, Lord!

---

1   See Footnote 2, January 12th.
2   See Footnote 2, January 14th.
3   From *Chronicles of the Pilgrim Fathers.*

THEREFORE ENCOURAGE ONE ANOTHER AND BUILD
EACH OTHER UP...
(1 Thessalonians 5:11)

They thought of only one land where they might find freedom, the land that we call Holland, which was then usually named the Netherlands, or the Low Country. Many of the Dutchmen from Holland in those days came across the seas to England on business. Some of them actually lived not far off in Norwich, where you could hear the "click-clumph, clickety-clump" of the looms at which they worked at the worsted-making.[1]

Other of the Dutch countrymen would come from time to time to the Post-house at the Manor of Scrooby... They told of the freedom of their native land of Holland, where – they said – in spite of the threats of the Spanish king,[2] they held freely opinions like those for which their friends in England were thrown into prison and persecuted in other ways. William Brewster... had lived in Holland himself for years, would nod his head in agreement with what they said.[3]

Thank you, Lord, for those who tell of freedom! Thank you for those who encourage – those who, literally, impart courage. Thank you for those who inspire and build up. May I be one such person today!

---

1 See Footnote 4, February 1st.
2 See https://en.wikipedia.org/wiki/Eighty_Years%27_War for background information to this point.
3 From. *The Argonauts of Faith*.

... THEY WERE STRANGERS AND PILGRIMS ON THE EARTH.
(Hebrews 11:13 *KJV*)

In such talks as these the Pilgrims began to think of sailing over the seas to the freedom of Holland to escape from the tyranny of the rule of England.

How could they escape? The King's officers locked them up in prison for disobeying the law; yet they would not let them leave the land. No one could sail away from England without a licence from old Lord Treasurer Burghley. And he refused to give licences to Pilgrims. So, if they went at all, they must by hook or crook go in stealth by secret ways, like smugglers.

If they decided to run the gauntlet and try to escape, how were they even to reach the coast? There were no good roads; indeed only a few rough tracks crossed the land, and even the tracks were sloughs of mud in wet weather. And in all places in England in that day, the flat land of the undrained fens of Norfolk and Lincolnshire was the most desperately hard to cross.

There were shaky paths across bottomless morasses and over quaking bogs.[1]

Gracious God, draw close today, to those who are finding the going tough; anyone who is struggling along the pathway of faith and pilgrimage. Visit them on their journey, I pray, and encourage them. Protect them in the difficult times by shielding their hearts against pitfalls of discouragement and despair.

---

1   From *The Argonauts of Faith*.

"WHY DO YOU LOOK AT THE SPECK OF SAWDUST IN YOUR BROTHER'S
EYE AND PAY NO ATTENTION TO THE PLANK IN YOUR OWN
EYE? HOW CAN YOU SAY TO YOUR BROTHER, 'LET ME TAKE THE
SPECK OUT OF YOUR EYE,' WHEN ALL THE TIME THERE IS A PLANK IN
YOUR OWN EYE? YOU HYPOCRITE, FIRST TAKE THE PLANK OUT OF
YOUR OWN EYE, AND THEN YOU WILL SEE CLEARLY TO REMOVE THE
SPECK FROM YOUR BROTHER'S EYE."

(Matthew 7:3–5)

Browne refused to accept Calvin's doctrine that the "true" Church should embrace the entire baptized population.[1] He objected to such a sweeping inclusion of communicants "without regard to personal character". His was to be a "priesthood of believers", a church of "saincts",[2] from which the irreligious were to be excluded, whether baptized or not. And the lives of the Saints, naturally, were to be subject to the closest scrutiny and to continuous review, for every act and word, and even every thought, weighed in the balance. Sharp and constant criticism both of oneself and others was enjoined as a positive religious duty. From this sprang that sometimes fruitful searching of soul and that often mean-spirited prying into the most intimate details of one another's lives which marked the Separatist churches without exception and caused almost all to founder – even Browne's, which was shattered within two years by bitter recriminations and dissensions.[3]

Oh Lord! This level of introspection and interference sounds pretty dreadful!
Help me to find that happy balance of minding my own business while also
taking an interest in the spiritual wellbeing of my fellow Christians. Help me to
pray much more often that I pry! Bless me with the Christ-like proportion of
concern and criticism.

---

1   See Footnote 1, February 1st.
2   From the Old French *saint*, with the "c" added because of the "c" in Latin *sanctus*.
3   From *Saints and Strangers*.

THY WORD IS A LAMP UNTO MY FEET, AND A LIGHT UNTO MY PATH.
(Psalm 119:105 *KJV*)

To be caught in the darkness of night on one of the narrower paths across that land [Lincolnshire and Norfolk] was to have little chance of seeing the morning alive, save by remaining quite still through the cold and wet of the long black hours. For a single footstep might throw a man into the horrible, dragging, choking slime against which not even a Hercules could fight. So evil were the paths that, in those days, on the old tower of the church at Boston every night a great lantern was lighted so that its beams across the fens might by chance lead the feet of some lost travellers from the bogs to the first streets of the town.[1]

> I pray for any today, Lord, who are walking in darkness – especially anyone known to me personally: family members, friends, colleagues, neighbours. In your mercy, Heavenly Father, shine your light around their way and lead their feet into ways of truth and faith. Hear my prayer.

---

1   From *The Argonauts of Faith*.

THEN ONE OF THE TWELVE – THE ONE CALLED JUDAS ISCARIOT –
WENT TO THE CHIEF PRIESTS AND ASKED, "WHAT ARE YOU WILLING
TO GIVE ME IF I DELIVER HIM OVER TO YOU?" SO THEY COUNTED
OUT FOR HIM THIRTY PIECES OF SILVER. FROM THEN ON JUDAS
WATCHED FOR AN OPPORTUNITY TO HAND HIM OVER.

(Matthew 26:14–16)

In spite of perils of King's officers and of bogs and fens, however, they decided to go to Holland – pilgrims in search of freedom.

We do not know by what ways many of them ever reached the coast, or, having reached it, were able to sail to Holland…

Some of the Pilgrims went by stealth down to the coast. They secretly arranged with the British captain of a ship to take them aboard under cover of the darkness, and to sail with them across the North Sea to Holland. All went well till they reached the sea. Then they rowed out in boats and climbed aboard the ship. They soon hid themselves away below deck, and waited, expecting to hear the anchor weighed and the sails hoisted. But no such thing happened.

They heard instead the "clunk" of oars; men climbed aboard. There were the voices of these men aboard.

"Who are they?" questioned the Pilgrims.

They were not to stay long in doubt. The dastardly captain, having taken their money to convey them to Holland, had betrayed them to the King's officers, who were now on board.[1]

Father, forgive.

---

[1] From *The Argonauts of Faith*.

PAUL AND BARNABAS APPOINTED ELDERS FOR THEM IN EACH
CHURCH AND, WITH PRAYER AND FASTING, COMMITTED THEM TO
THE LORD, IN WHOM THEY HAD PUT THEIR TRUST.

(Acts 14:23)

Every day there were new prosecutions and persecutions, for the bishops were in a violently angry mood, occasioned by the appearance of a series of tracts addressed to the "proud, Popish, presumptuous, profane, paultrie [sic], pestilent, and pernicious Prelates"... No pamphlets were ever more eagerly snatched up and avidly read, and none ever caused a greater uproar. They brought Puritanism out of the closet into the market place, and stripped it of its sectarian air. Here was the ... inspired literature of the reform movement, and it struck deep...

A Puritan, one William Fulke,[1] published a short defence of three simple propositions, all of which the Pilgrims later embraced – every congregation had the right to (1) choose its own pastor and other officers, (2) discipline its own members, and (3) control all actions of its officers by approving or rejecting their decisions.[2]

Lord, I pray for my own church fellowship today, and specifically questions of leadership. I pray for my minister, and all those responsible for appointing elders and leaders. Grant them wisdom in their decision making, that your purposes may be accomplished at local level.

---

1 William Fulke (1538–89), English Puritan divine.
2 From *Saints and Strangers*.

... YEA, I HAVE A GOODLY HERITAGE.
(Psalm 16:6 *KJV*)

To ecclesiastics appointed from above this [the Puritan system of church government] was, of course, very disturbing doctrine, and Dean Bridges of Salisbury[1] took it upon himself to expose its fallacies and silence for ever the champions of such subversive nonsense. His self-dedication was roundly applauded by churchmen and schoolmen, for his scholarship was regarded as scarcely inferior to that of the learned Thomas Bilson, subsequently Bishop of Winchester,[2] who had recently proved so eloquently and with such a multitude of citations that the church had *always* been just what it was. The Anglican bishops had their authority directly from the Apostles and the Holy Ghost – indeed, from Adam, who had governed the Church for precisely 930 years, with Seth as his assistant for the last five centuries. Seth had then gone on alone for 112 years, and from him the mantle of authority had descended, through Moses, directly to Archbishop Whitgift.[3] [4]

> This is quite an astonishing claim, Lord! Nevertheless, whether it be accurate or
> not, I thank you today for my spiritual ancestors; those who paved the way for
> me to believe, and those who kept the faith in my own denomination. Thank you
> for their faithful witness. I pray to be a worthy successor to those gone before. So
> help me, God.

---

1   John Bridges (1536–1618), appointed Dean of Salisbury in 1577.
2   Thomas Bilson (1547–1616), Bishop of Worcester and Bishop of Winchester who oversaw the final edit of the *King James Bible*.
3   See Footnote 9, January 9th.
4   From *Saints and Strangers*.

> *"'... Love the Lord your God with all your heart and with all your soul and with all your strength and with all your mind...'"*
>
> (Luke 10:27)

Dean Bridges hoped to do at least as well as Dr. Bilson, and at last he was ready after almost incredible labours. His reply to Fulke's pointed argument of less than forty pages was a massive quarto volume of 1,500 pages, now remembered only because it brought down upon his addled pate the cool contempt, scathing wit, broad learning, and deep human sympathies of Martin Marprelate.[1] Citing chapter and verse in charging them with greed, malice, ignorance, and corruption, he stung the bishops to the quick, to the delight of many; the hierarchy replied with a roar of rage that grew louder as their bailiffs frantically rushed about in a vain effort to discover the author of the tracts and his secret wandering press. Whitgift had the Queen issue a proclamation against such "diffamatorie and fantasticall" writings aimed at promoting reform – or, as she called it, "monstrous and appaurant Innovation" [*sic*].[2]

I can't help feeling, Lord, that so much of this squabbling was a waste of time that could have been used in much better ways, for the furtherance of your kingdom. My prayer today, therefore, is for scholars and people of intellect, that they would return their academic gifts back to you, for those skills to be employed in ways that will edify and enrich. I thank you for them, Lord – theologians, teachers, writers, and lecturers – and I ask you to guide them as they unlock the Scriptures and share their knowledge. Help me, I pray, for my part, to study well.

---

1   Martin Marprelate (or Martin Mar-prelate or Marre–Martin), the *nom-de-plume* of the anonymous author(s) of tracts illegally circulated in England, attacking the episcopacy of the Anglican Church.

2   From *Saints and Strangers*.

... SIMON THE ZEALOT ...
(Matthew 10:4)

These men [the Separatists] were fanatics, but it is through its fanatics that the world progresses. They clung to their doctrines of a separation between Church and State, and their support of ministers by voluntary contributions and not by tithes. How great a debt both England and America owe to them, and to the men about them in the Netherlands whose influence shaped their character, the modern world is just beginning to appreciate...

One of the Separatist congregations... in the reign of James I, settled in Leyden,[1] and afterwards founded the famous American colony of Plymouth. The men of the congregation, whom Americans delight to call the Pilgrim Fathers, have played an important part in history, their theology having largely affected that of all New England. But they were few in number, and their direct influence on the world at large has not been great as compared with that exerted by some other Christian bodies which also originated among the English Separatists who settled in Holland.[2]

Fanatics and zealots, Lord – not easy people to deal with! Movers and shakers, Lord – not always comfortable company! Thank you, though, for those who disturb the status quo, when it leads to progress and development within the church. Help those of us who like our comfort zones, to appreciate the worth of people who speak loudly and with passion.

---

1   See Footnotes 1, January 12th.
2   From Douglas Campbell, *The Puritan in Holland, England and America*, Volume II, Harper, 1893.

I AM REMINDED OF YOUR SINCERE FAITH, WHICH FIRST LIVED IN
YOUR GRANDMOTHER LOIS AND IN YOUR MOTHER EUNICE AND, I
AM PERSUADED, NOW LIVES IN YOU ALSO.

(2 Timothy 1:5)

A close resemblance existed between the principles advanced by the English Separatists and those held long before by the Anabaptists, or Mennonites,[1] of Holland. When now these Separatists were driven from their homes to find a refuge in Holland, it was but natural that they should be attracted by the teachings of men to whom they owed so much. The city of Amsterdam became the headquarters of the English refugees, and here they found great numbers of the Mennonites. Distracted in their own congregations, some of the English Separatists left their brethren, accepted a new baptism at the hands of the Mennonites, and openly avowed many of their doctrines.[2] [3]

Heavenly Father, although the outcome of this particular situation wasn't ideal, I thank you, nevertheless, for those upon whose shoulders the Church now stands – those giants of Christian history who paved the way for the religious freedoms I now enjoy. Oh that I might be such a person!

---

1   See Footnotes 2 & 3, February 1st.
2   A number of websites exist, outlining Mennonite and Anabaptist doctrine.
3   From *The Puritan in Holland, England, and America*.

February 13TH

"BUT AS FOR YOU, BE STRONG AND DO NOT GIVE UP, FOR YOUR
WORK WILL BE REWARDED."
(2 Chronicles 15:7)

The [King's] officers ordered the Pilgrims on deck, drove them – men, women, and children – into open boats, rowed [the Pilgrims] back to the coast and cast them into prison in Boston, where they were brought before the magistrates, and finally sent back to their homes in the depth of one of the most dreadful winters of snow and ice that England has ever known. Their desperate attempt had failed; but they were not daunted...

They made another attempt.

Nearby Scrooby ran... the sluggish river Idle, a shallow and slow stream. Down the river went flat-bottomed boats, half-punt, half-barge. The women and the children were put aboard some of these boats, and with them were the packages holding their clothes and the clothes of the men, together with the things they valued. They steered slowly down the lazy stream till the Idle ran smoothly into the broader waters of the Trent.[1] This bit of country is where King Canute[2] used to live, and they say it was on the bank of this tidal river that the King's couriers urged him to command the tide to stop. King James was in these very days trying to stop the tide of freedom from flowing in the world.[3]

> He who would valiant be 'gainst all disaster,
> Let him in constancy follow the Master.
> There's no discouragement shall make him once relent
> His first avowed intent to be a pilgrim.[4]

---

1 The third longest river in the United Kingdom.
2 995–1035.
3 From *The Argonauts of Faith*.
4 From John Bunyan's hymn "He Who Would Valiant Be" (*The Pilgrim's Progress*), modified by Percy Dearmer* for *The English Hymnal*. Bunyan wrote these words during his twelve years in prison for his refusal to conform to the state church. *Percy Dearmer (1867–1936), priest and liturgist.

... A TIME TO LAUGH ...

(Ecclesiastes 3:4)

"The Puritans are angry with me," Marprelate[1] admitted, hastily adding, "I mean the Puritan preachers. And why? Because I am too open; because I jest." These preachers had been upset by his wit and broad humour. He had committed the mistake, said one, of making "sin ridiculous, whereas it ought to be made odious". This solemn and pompous view has had its advocates in all ages. Most of the Pilgrims shared it, but Marprelate would have none of it. He had chosen his course deliberately, he said, because only thus could he get the great majority of men to read.

"Aye," he exclaimed, "for jesting is lawfull by circumstances, even in the highest matters... The Lord being the author both of mirth and gravity, is it now lawfull in itself for Truth to use either of these ways?" [*sic*].[2]

Oh Lord! Teach me, I pray, when and how to use the lovely gift of humour! Keep me sensitive in doing so, only ever to lighten the mood or to lift another's spirits. Thank you, Heavenly Father, for such a precious facet of human nature – the ability to laugh and to take delight in that which is funny.

---

1   See Footnote 1, February 10th.
2   From *Saints and Strangers*.

AND THE BROTHER SHALL DELIVER UP THE BROTHER TO DEATH…
(Matthew 10:21 *KJV*)

Another of Brewster's contemporaries at Cambridge, John Greenwood,[1] had gone to the gallows, together with Henry Barrow,[2] one of the greatest of the early leaders of the Separation. Condemned for "devising and circulating seditious books", they had been granted a reprieve at the insistence of Lord Burghley, who protested that the blood of reformers who were essentially in agreement with the Protestant tenets of the Anglican Church should not be the first to flow "in a land where no Papist has been touched for religion by death". But Archbishop Whitgift was "very peremptory" and demanded their immediate execution. Burghley flared up and gave Whitgift and the bishops "some round taxing words", subsequently carrying the matter to Elizabeth. But as no one seconded him in the Privy Council, the Queen's venomous "little black husband"[3] finally had his way with Penry,[4] Greenwood, and Barrow, immediately taking steps to jail hundreds of others.[5]

> Heavenly Father, I pray for those whose convictions bring them into deadly collision with powerful authorities. I pray for those who, today, stand for Christ, even in the face of potential execution. Stand with them, Lord Jesus.

---

1 John Greenwood (1556–93), Puritan divine and Separatist.
2 Or Barrowe (c. 1550–6 April 1593), Separatist Puritan.
3 Archbishop Whitgift had dark skin, and was unmarried. This nickname was some kind of racist insult, but also a veiled threat, insofar as Queen Elizabeth I demanded absolute loyalty from Whitgift.
4 John Penry (1559–93), Welsh Protestant martyr.
5 From *Saints and Strangers*.

"SO IN EVERYTHING, DO TO OTHERS WHAT YOU WOULD HAVE THEM
DO TO YOU, FOR THIS SUMS UP THE LAW AND THE PROPHETS."
(Matthew 7:12)

Determined to crush all resistance, the bishops pushed through a reluctant Parliament the most nefarious act of Elizabeth's reign, aimed at the Brownists and "other Sectaries and disloyal persons". By this act ... any persons who absented themselves from the orthodox service for more than a month, or who attempted in any way to persuade others to do so, or who attended "any unlawful assemblies, conventicles, or meetings under colour or pretence of any Exercise of Religion", were to be imprisoned without bail until they pledged themselves to conform. If submission were not made within three months, they were to quit the realm on pain of death without benefit of clergy. If they ever returned, they were to be summarily executed.[1]

Lord, I pray for dictators and tyrants, who cannot abide any opinions other than their own. Have mercy and speak to their hearts, I pray. I ask you to help those who live in places where totalitarian regimes operate, where all kinds of freedoms and rights are ignored or suppressed. Grant them courage, and enable them to look with pity, and not anger. Give me a heart that respects different points of view.

---

1   From *Saints and Strangers.*

"... I WILL BUILD MY CHURCH, AND THE GATES OF HADES WILL NOT
OVERCOME IT."
(Matthew 16:18)

Reporting the passage of [Queen Elizabeth's] measure, Morice the Decipherer[1] attributed it to the "malice of the Bishops... which hath procured them much hatred of the common people", adding details on the execution of Penry and "two of the principal Brownists, Barrow and Greenwood... so as that Sect is in effect extinguished".

But Morice, for all his talents, was not apt at deciphering the future, for this was the beginning, not the end, of the Brownist movement and the Separation.[2]

"The fight is not over yet; the brunt of the battle is yet to come. They dreamed that the old gospel was dead, but they digged [*sic*] its grave too soon."[3]

---

1 John Morice, also known as Peter Halins, who served Queen Elizabeth as some kind of spy. He would run secret errands for the Queen, including the interception of correspondence she desired to read if she suspected it would hand her any political advantage. As much of this correspondence was either in French, or in scrawled handwriting, his task of deciphering was not an easy one. He was part diplomat and part intelligence-gatherer.

2 From *Saints and Strangers*.

3 From Charles H. Spurgeon, *The Complete Works of C.H. Spurgeon, Volume 32*, Delmarva Publications, 2013 (Kindle edition).

> "WHEN YOU COME TO THE LAND THAT THE LORD YOUR GOD IS
> GIVING YOU, AND YOU POSSESS IT AND DWELL IN IT AND THEN
> SAY, 'I WILL SET A KING OVER ME, LIKE ALL THE NATIONS THAT ARE
> AROUND ME,' YOU MAY INDEED SET A KING OVER YOU WHOM THE
> LORD YOUR GOD WILL CHOOSE."
> (Deuteronomy 17:14–15 *ESV*)

In the history of English Puritanism, the reign of James I[1] stands between the seed-time and the harvest. Under Elizabeth,[2] the soil was tilled and planted…

Something of the change in the feeling of the English people towards the monarchy began to manifest itself in the latter days of Elizabeth. She had been for a long period, and especially just after the destruction of the Invincible Armada,[3] the idol of the nation. But fifteen years had rolled around since that event, and in those years the people had been afforded time to find her out. Much of her popularity was due to the light calls she had made upon the public purse. Once launched into a war with Spain, these calls became frequent and onerous…

Had the English people at this time been cut off from the Continent, and left only to their own traditions; had they been without the example of a republic across the Channel, where all such oppressions were unknown, no one can tell how long they would have borne their accustomed yoke with meekness and content. But the last days of Elizabeth witnessed a great change. She died… friendless and unwept, as befitted the utter selfishness of her whole life. Within a week she seemed to be entirely forgotten.[4] [5]

How horribly sad, Lord – the decline and rejection of a leader, bereft of
authority and "friendless and unwept". Whatever the pros and cons of individual
situations, I pray for those who have fallen from grace. May it also be the case
that, in your mercy, they fall into grace.

---

1 James VI and I (1566–1625), King of Scotland as James VI from 1567 and King of England and Ireland as James I from the union of the Scottish and English crowns in 1603.
2 Elizabeth I (1533–1603), Queen of England and Ireland from 1558 until her death.
3 See https://www.historic-uk.com/HistoryUK/HistoryofEngland/Spanish-Armada/
4 King James forbade public and court mourning for Elizabeth, effectively signalling an oblivion of her reign.
5 From *The Puritan in Holland, England and America*.

"Now here is the king you have chosen,
the one you asked for…"
(1 Samuel 12:13)

For years before the death of Elizabeth, all parties in the State had been turning their eyes towards the rising sun in Scotland. Never was a monarch more cordially welcomed to a throne than was James I, the son of Mary Stuart,[1] to that of England. His title was probably defective at law, but no one thought of disputing its validity. The queen on her death-bed had recognized him as her successor, and all factions gladly acquiesced. The Catholics saw in him the son of a Catholic martyr, and his secret emissaries had held out hopes to them of a special indulgence in case of his succession to the throne. The Puritans saw in him the son of the Scottish Kirk, to which he had professed a devoted adherence. The High-Church party, perhaps better than either of the others, knew their man. Thus it came about that his accession raised not a breath of opposition.[2]

This brings to mind, Lord, the "honeymoon period" experienced by many church ministers! In the early days of their ministry, they can do no wrong, yet, over time, criticism raises its ugly head, as does discouragement. Help me, I pray, within my own church fellowship, to encourage and support to the best of my ability.

---

1   Mary, Queen of Scots (1542 – Executed 1587), or Mary I, Queen of Scotland from 1542 to 1567.
2   From *The Puritan in Holland, England and America*.

SHE SAID TO HER HUSBAND, "I KNOW THAT THIS MAN WHO OFTEN
COMES OUR WAY IS A HOLY MAN OF GOD."
(2 Kings 4:9)

Quietly settling down at Scrooby, obviously resigned to spending the remainder of his life there, Brewster soon won the friendship and respect of his neighbours and lived in "good esteeme" among them, "espetially the godly & religious" [sic]. As the Pilgrims used the phrase, this meant that he frequented reformist circles. He did much to forward the cause by his example and by his tireless efforts in providing the villages round about with good preachers, persuading others to assist in the work, he himself usually being "deepest in ye charge & sometimes above his abilitie" [sic].

Though a strong and zealous Puritan, Brewster was far from being sour of mien, solemn in manner, or harsh and intolerant in his views. On the contrary, he was "of a very cherfull spirite, very sociable & pleasante amongst his friends" [sic].[1]

Assist me, Lord, today, to live among my neighbours in such a way that I too may make this kind of favourable impression. In doing so, your Spirit helping me, may I positively enhance my witness as a follower of Christ. Guide me, I pray, in all I say and do, to that end. This is my prayer.

---

1 From *Saints and Strangers*.

"NOW THEN, PLEASE SWEAR TO ME BY THE LORD THAT YOU WILL
SHOW KINDNESS TO MY FAMILY…"
(Joshua 2:12)

Unlike so many of his brethren, who were apt to be contentious and stridently opinionated, [Brewster] was peaceable by nature and soft-spoken, "of an humble and modest mind", given to depreciating his own ability and overrating that of others. Towards the poor and unfortunate he was "tender-harted", with an always open purse to ease their sufferings. Only those offended him who put on airs and carried themselves haughtily when they had nothing to "commend them but a few fine cloaths, or a little riches more than others" [sic]. Altogether a wise, discreet, and extraordinarily gentle man, Brewster did more in a year to advance the Christian faith and spread the even broader gospel of simple human kindliness than most men in a lifetime, patiently "doeing ye best he could, and walking according to ye light he saw, till ye Lord reveiled further unto him" [sic].[1]

Gracious God, make me a kind person.

---

1   From *Saints and Strangers*.

... I HAVE LEARNED TO BE CONTENT WHATEVER THE
CIRCUMSTANCES. I KNOW WHAT IT IS TO BE IN NEED, AND I KNOW
WHAT IT IS TO HAVE PLENTY. I HAVE LEARNED THE SECRET OF BEING
CONTENT IN ANY AND EVERY SITUATION, WHETHER WELL FED OR
HUNGRY, WHETHER LIVING IN PLENTY OR IN WANT. I CAN DO ALL
THIS THROUGH HIM WHO GIVES ME STRENGTH.
(Philippians 4:11–13)

Although some seventy merchants subscribed money, the Common Stock was not big enough to send all the brethren to America. The majority had to stay in Holland. Those who chose, or were chosen, to go, left Leyden for Delft Haven,[1] where they went aboard the ship *Speedwell*, of 60 tons, which had been bought and equipped in Holland... The *Speedwell* sailed for Southampton.

At Southampton, the emigrants found waiting for them the ship *Mayflower*, of 180 tons. She was a London ship, chartered for the occasion. In her were other emigrants, some of them labourers, some of them Separatists eager to leave England. With them was the chief adventurer, Mr. Thomas Weston, who had come to ask the leaders of the party to sign the contract... As the leaders did not like the terms of the contract they refused to sign it. There was an angry dispute. In the end Mr. Weston went back to London, with the contract not signed.

It had been agreed that he was to advance them another sum of money before the ships set sail. As the contract was not signed, the pilgrims had to manage without this money. Without it, they found it difficult to pay the charges of the ships and crews. They were forced to sell sixty pounds' worth of provisions to obtain money for the discharge of these claims. In those days... passengers across the Atlantic lived upon supplies of food laid in and prepared by themselves. The Western passage was seldom made in less than two months. The pilgrims could not hope for any fresh supply of food before the next year's harvest in the New World. A considerable lessening of their stock of provisions might well lead to the ruin of the settlement.[2]

Lord Jesus, teach me the grace of contentment.

1   A borough of Rotterdam on the river Nieuwe Maas, South Holland, Netherlands.
2   From *Chronicles of the Pilgrim Fathers*.

FOR MANY ARE CALLED, BUT FEW ARE CHOSEN.

(Matthew 22:14 *KJV*)

The two ships [*Speedwell* and *Mayflower*] put to sea in company, carrying in all about 120 emigrants. After eight days, the captain of the *Speedwell* complained that his ship had sprung a leak. The expedition put back into Dartmouth to refit. On setting sail again, the ships beat a hundred leagues to the west of Land's End, when they were forced, by stress of weather, to put back into Plymouth. The captain of the *Speedwell* declared that his ship was too much battered to keep the seas. Though the man was lying in order to escape from the fulfilment of his charter, his word was taken.[1] The *Speedwell* was abandoned, the pilgrims in her were bidden to come aboard the *Mayflower* to take the places of some who could endure no more. About twenty of the pilgrims left the expedition at Plymouth. They were discouraged by hardship and seasickness, two doctors which never fail to teach the unfit that though many are called to the life of pioneers, very few are chosen.[2]

Help me, Lord, not to turn back, even though crosses come. Help me, Lord, not to turn back, even though my commitment to your call upon my life may cost me dearly. Help me, Lord, not to turn back, even when shadows fall across the path of duty. Grant me such daily graces, I pray.

---

1   It is possible some of the passengers on this voyage had changed their minds about the adventure. There is the possibility that, as their commitment waned, they persuaded (or bribed) the captain to exaggerate the extent of the damage the *Speedwell* had suffered.

2   From *Chronicles of the Pilgrim Fathers*.

IN ALL THE TRAVELS OF THE ISRAELITES, WHENEVER THE CLOUD
LIFTED FROM ABOVE THE TABERNACLE, THEY WOULD SET OUT; BUT
IF THE CLOUD DID NOT LIFT, THEY DID NOT SET OUT – UNTIL
THE DAY IT LIFTED. SO THE CLOUD OF THE LORD WAS OVER THE
TABERNACLE BY DAY, AND FIRE WAS IN THE CLOUD BY NIGHT, IN THE
SIGHT OF ALL THE ISRAELITES DURING ALL THEIR TRAVELS.
(Exodus 40:36–38)

[In Leiden] the Pilgrims [had] found much that was strange in the houses… They were mostly strong and fair to look at, with clean windows and their doors and shutters nicely painted. Arched brick passages led into bright courtyards and into gardens where tulips and daffodils and other flowers grew…

In the gardens they could see the young Dutch mothers in their gowns of black with lovely neck-ruffs of spotless muslin and over their heads a coif of fine white linen. The little children ran about and played; and the girls had on their heads little linen caps something like their mothers. Most of them looked plump, and this was partly because, for two of their meals in the day, they ate simply butter and cheese. The Pilgrim children soon got to know some of these Dutch boys and girls; but, to a large extent, they kept to themselves.[1]

> Lord, the Pilgrims had embarked upon their pilgrimage; from England to Holland and eventually to America, with any number of twists and turns along the way. My prayers today are for those who are seeking to discover the journey their life should take. Help them, I pray, especially when that journey includes strange customs, different languages, and unexpected cuisine. Bless those who travel for the kingdom's sake. May they know your steady presence throughout every twist and turn.

---

1 From *The Argonauts of Faith.*

AND GOD SAID, "LET... BIRDS FLY ABOVE THE EARTH ACROSS THE
VAULT OF THE SKY."
(Genesis 1:20)

[When they were in Leiden] the Pilgrim boys and girls would be sure to see the heavy
nests of the storks [on the top of some of the chimneys] ... They would see the long-
legged storks come flying to the city from far countries. The mother stork laid her
eggs in the old nest, while the father stork stood on one leg on "sentry go" on the roof
or stalked stiffly up the street, looking as proud as though no mother stork had ever
laid an egg before. The people thought one was very lucky if a stork made a nest on
one's house. The Pilgrim boys and girls soon learned that no one must ever throw a
stone at a stork or touch a stick of his nest. Very funny it was, some weeks later, to see
the quaint, long-legged baby storks trying to fly. And the father stork would be very
busy then hunting on the banks of the canal for frogs with which to feed his family.[1]

Creator God, open my eyes this day, to see the marvels of nature all around me;
even, perhaps, common sparrows and everyday sights, which can be reminders
of your creative energy. Remind me to look up, and to look around, so that I too
may catch sight of your handiwork in my daily routines. These sights will reassure
me of your good works, and of your love.

---

1   From *The Argonauts of Faith*.

HE HAD NO BEAUTY OR MAJESTY TO ATTRACT US TO HIM, NOTHING
IN HIS APPEARANCE THAT WE SHOULD DESIRE HIM.
(Isaiah 53:2)

If [King] James had been blessed by nature with a kingly bearing and endowed with a little common-sense, and had he exhibited even moderate ability as a statesman, the eclipse of his predecessor's fame might have been of long continuance.[1] He had shown, as is admitted on all sides, considerable skill in his management of affairs at home, and in preparing the way for his own succession to the English crown. But he had worked so hard and so long to obtain the prize that, when it was obtained, all his energies seemed to be exhausted. Although born and bred in the same island, he was always a foreigner in England, and never understood, nor cared to understand, the people over whom he came to rule.

From the outset everything told against his popularity. Coming from a nation which laid great stress on outward show, he excited ridicule by his rickety legs, his shambling, awkward gait, his slobbering mouth, and soiled, ill-fitting garments... He, probably from congenital causes, could not bear to look upon a naked sword, always wore a quilted doublet thick enough to turn a dagger, slept in a barricaded bedroom, and when he drove out surrounded his carriage with a swarm of running footmen to keep off possible assassins.[2]

> Lord Jesus, you are the King of kings, yet you came to us as a lowly man. This
> is grace. You allowed your features to be violently beaten, slapped, punched,
> and marred. This is love. You were deeply humiliated, mocked and ridiculed in
> public, all for my sake. This is mercy. You bled, you were tortured and butchered,
> and hung out to die. This is my God.

---

1   See Footnote 4, February 18th.
2   From *The Puritan in England, Holland and America.*

THERE IS A TIME FOR EVERYTHING ... A TIME TO BE SILENT ...
(Ecclesiastes 3:1, 7)

Elizabeth had ever flattered the common people – showed herself constantly in royal pageants, delighted in crowds, and was to the populace always affable and easy of access. James, when he came from Scotland, was greatly annoyed at the presence of the multitude who flocked about him, drove them away with curses, and issued orders for them to stay at home.

The men around the throne, who saw more of its new incumbent, were no less affected than the people at large by his personal characteristics. He possessed some natural capacity, had been educated by the celebrated George Buchanan,[1] and, in a few departments, was, for his time, no mean scholar. But his learning, which he aired on all occasions, ran to pedantry, and he was steeped in that self-conceit which makes a man of ordinary ability more hopeless than a fool.

The pedantry and conceit of James, especially as to theological questions, made him ridiculous at home and abroad.[2]

"Teach thy tongue to say, 'I do not know.'" (Maimonedes)[3]

---

1 George Buchanan , or Bochanan (1506–82), historian and scholar.
2 From *The Puritan in Holland, England and America.*
3 Moses ben Maimon, or Maimonedes, 1135 or 1138–1204. Rabbi, physician, and philosopher.

… DOMINION BELONGS TO THE LORD AND HE RULES
OVER THE NATIONS.
(Psalm 22:28)

Sir James Harrington,[1] in one of his confidential letters, gives an amusing account of his first interview with James, who, having heard of his scholarship, sent for him shortly after arriving in London. James examined him in Latin and Greek, as if he had been an applicant for the position of royal tutor, corrected his mistakes, paraded and boasted of his own superior learning, discoursed about witchcraft and tobacco, offered his services in elucidating the dark problems in theology and the classics which might perplex his visitor, and finally dismissed him with a request that the scholars about the court should be made acquainted with the attainments of their new sovereign…

Harrington, in another letter… gives an admirable description of the tact and cunning of Elizabeth, who, in all her personal characteristics, formed so marked a contrast to the man that after her death occupied the throne.[2]

Oh Lord! How awful to think that the fate of the Puritans rested largely in the hands of Elizabeth and James! Thankfully, you overruled, and you continue to do so. I pray for Christians today whose witness and wellbeing appears to be governed by unsympathetic and ignorant people in positions of power. Almighty God, may they, nevertheless, see your hand at work in their circumstances.

---

1 Sir James Harrington (c. 1430–1485), politician, soldier, and at times a member of the royal household.
2 From *The Puritan in Holland, England and America.*

REMEMBER HOW THE LORD YOUR GOD LED YOU ALL THE WAY IN
THE WILDERNESS THESE FORTY YEARS, TO HUMBLE AND TEST YOU
IN ORDER TO KNOW WHAT WAS IN YOUR HEART, WHETHER OR NOT
YOU WOULD KEEP HIS COMMANDS.

(Deuteronomy 8:2)

The expedition left Plymouth for [another] attempt. In the existing records little is said about the voyage; but it must have been a strange and terrible adventure to most of the party. The ship was very small, and crowded with people. Counting the crew, she must have held nearly a hundred and fifty people, in a space too narrow for the comfort of half that number. The passengers were stowed in the between decks, a sort of low, narrow room, under the spar deck, lit in fine weather by the openings of hatchways and gun-ports, and in bad weather, when these were closed, by lanterns. They lived, ate, slept, and were sea sick in that narrow space. A woman bore a child, a man died there. They were packed so tightly, among all the belongings and stores, that they could have had no privacy. The ventilation was bad, even in fine weather. In bad weather, when the hatches were down, there was none.[1]

> The Christian pilgrimage, Lord, is not often glamorous! Help me, therefore, to see you in what can sometimes be the ordinary footslog of discipleship, and to sense your abiding presence even when times are grim. Remind me, from time to time, that I follow a homeless carpenter! Help me not to flinch in the face of love's sacrificial demands.

---

1 From *Chronicles of the Pilgrim Fathers*.

YEA, THOUGH I WALK THROUGH THE VALLEY OF THE SHADOW OF
DEATH, I WILL FEAR NO EVIL: FOR THOU ART WITH ME; THY ROD
AND THY STAFF THEY COMFORT ME.

(Psalm 23:4 *KJV*)

In bad weather the pilgrims lived in a fog, through which they could see the water on the deck washing from side to side, as the ship rolled, carrying their pans and clothes with it. They could only lie, and groan, and pray, in stink and misery, while the water from the ill-caulked seams dripped on them from above. In one of the storms during the passage, the *Mayflower* broke her main beam. Luckily one of the passengers had a jackscrew, by means of which the damage was made good. But the accident added the very present fear of death to the other miseries of the passage.[1]

In one sense, Lord, I should expect death at any moment, insofar as I have no idea at all when I might die. In another sense, there are those times of accident or illness when my passing from this world into the next seems closer to hand. Help me at all times to trust in the words of today's text. Help me now, today, to make my soul ready for that day, whenever it might actually come to pass.

---

1   From *Chronicles of the Pilgrim Fathers.*

BUT NOW YE ALSO PUT OFF ALL THESE; ANGER, WRATH, MALICE...
(Colossians 3:8 *KJV*)

Among Brewster's earliest allies was Richard Clyfton,[1] the rector at Babworth,[2] a village about six miles to the south-east. A "forward" preacher of the Puritan school, for years the only one in the district, he had been labouring in this unpromising corner of the vineyard... and exerted considerable influence throughout the countryside, attracting followers from miles around. Early every Sabbath morning and occasionally during the week the Brewsters... wound their way down the lane to sit at the feet of the "grave & reverend" Clyfton, a notable and long-neglected figure in Pilgrim history... Enemies in later years pronounced him "a most simple and pietous [*sic*] teacher... weak in the Scriptures, unable to convince his gainsayers, and careless to deliver his doctrine pure, sound, and plain". But this was largely malice, it appears, for Bradford and others testified that this "paines & dilligens" [*sic*] had been a means of converting many.[3]

"Envy, jealousy, malice and pride – they must never in my heart abide." Lord Jesus, I pray that the words of that old Sunday school chorus may be true in my life. Help me, Lord, to put them into practice today.

---

1 Richard Clyfton, or Clifton (d. 1616), Brownist minister at Scrooby, Nottinghamshire, and subsequently in Amsterdam.
2 Babworth, in the Bassetlaw district of Nottinghamshire, England.
3 From *Saints and Strangers*.

RELIGION THAT GOD OUR FATHER ACCEPTS AS PURE AND
FAULTLESS IS THIS: TO LOOK AFTER ORPHANS…

(James 1:27)

Here one first glimpses, as a sickly and somewhat precocious boy, probably the ablest and certainly the most diversely gifted of the Pilgrim Fathers. Born at Austerfield… just across the River Idle in Yorkshire, William Bradford was the son and namesake of a prosperous yeoman who tilled many broad acres of his own, and others leased from the local gentry and the Crown. His wife was Alice Hanson, daughter of an enterprising local shopkeeper and farmer. Shortly after the birth of his son in 1589, the father died. Three years later the widow remarried and sent her young four-year-old to live with his grandfather, another William Bradford. Upon the latter's death in 1596 and his mother's the following year, the boy was taken in hand by his paternal uncles, Robert and Thomas, "who devoted him, like his ancestors, unto the affairs of husbandry".[1]

I thank you today, Lord, for those who devote their lives to looking after others.
Thank you for those who are willing to "sacrifice" their own lifestyle for the
benefit of those in their care: foster parents, those who adopt, and so on. Bless
them in that calling. Bless, too, children who are fostered or adopted.

---

1   From *Saints and Strangers*.

> But we have this treasure in jars of clay, to show that the surpassing power belongs to God and not to us.
>
> (2 Corinthians 4:7 *ESV*)

It is the usual manner of the dispensation of the majesty of heaven, to work wonderfully by weak means for the effectuating of great things, to the intent that he may have the more glory to himself. Many instances hereof might be produced, both out of the sacred Scriptures, and common experience; and amongst many others of this kind, the late happy and memorable enterprise of the planting of that part of America called New England, deserveth to be commemorized [*sic*] to future posterity...

Divers godly Christians of our English nation... being studious of reformation, and therefore not only witnessing against human interventions, and additions in the worship of God, but minding most the positive and practical part of divine institutions, they entered into covenant to walk with God, and one with another, in the enjoyment of the ordinances of God, according to the primitive pattern in the word of God.[1]

> Heavenly Father, how often do we notice your great works being executed and administered through ordinary people! This seems to be a favourite tactic of yours – to entrust spiritual work to the least, the lowest, and the most unassuming. You chose ordinary people such as the Pilgrim Fathers to bring about spiritual revolution, just as you selected unremarkable men and women time and again, in Scripture. I don't have much to give you, Lord, but all I have is yours, in your service.

---

1   From *Chronicles of the Pilgrim Fathers*.

A BISHOP THEN MUST BE BLAMELESS, THE HUSBAND OF ONE WIFE,
VIGILANT, SOBER, OF GOOD BEHAVIOUR, GIVEN TO HOSPITALITY,
APT TO TEACH...
(1 Timothy 3:2 *KJV*)

Finding by experience they could not peaceably enjoy their own liberty in their native country, without offence to others that were differently minded, they took up thoughts of removing themselves and their families into the Netherlands, which accordingly they endeavoured to accomplish, but met with great hindrance; yet after some time, the good hand of God removing obstructions, they obtained their desires; arriving in Holland, they settled themselves in the city of Leyden... enjoying much sweet society and spiritual comfort in the ways of God, living peaceably amongst themselves, and being courteously entertained and lovingly respected by the Dutch, amongst whom they were strangers, having for their pastor Mr. John Robinson, a man of learned, polished, and modest spirit, pious and studying of the truth, largely accomplished with suitable gifts and qualifications to be a shepherd over this flock of Christ; having also a fellow helper with him in the eldership, Mr. William Brewster, a man of approved piety, gravity, and integrity, very eminently furnished with gifts suitable to such an office.[1]

I thank you today, Lord, for good church leaders; men and women whose conduct is exemplary and whose gifts are inspirational. I pray once again for the leaders of my own church, asking you to bless them according to their daily needs. Bless their families too, who very often share some of the pressures of leadership.

---

1   From *Chronicles of the Pilgrim Fathers.*

... AS STRANGERS AND PILGRIMS ...
(1 Peter 2:11 *KJV*)

Notwithstanding their amiable and comfortable carrying on... although the church of Christ on earth in Holy Writ is sometimes called heaven; yet there is always, in their most perfect state here in this lower world, very much wanting as to absolute and perfect happiness, which is only reserved for the time and place of the full enjoyment of celestial glory; for, although this church was at peace, and in rest at this time, yet they took up thoughts of removing themselves into America, with common consent. The proposition of removing thither being set on foot, and prosecuted by the elders upon just and weighty grounds; for although they did quietly and sweetly enjoy their church liberties... they foresaw that Holland would be no place for their church and posterity to continue in comfortably, at least in that measure that they hoped to find abroad.[1]

> Heavenly Father, my heart goes out in prayer to those who feel as though they don't belong; as though they are in the wrong place. It's a horrible feeling, Lord; one that leads to disorientation, wandering, and unhappiness. Guide any such people, I pray, so that they may soon be able to make the very best of this life here on earth, awaiting their truest home, in heaven.

---

1 From *Chronicles of the Pilgrim Fathers.*

"Watch and pray so that you will not fall into temptation.
The spirit is willing, but the flesh is weak."
(Matthew 26:41)

[Reasons given for the failure of the pilgrims to settle in Holland]...

Because themselves were of a different language from the Dutch where they lived, and were settled in their way... whilst their church sojourned amongst them, they could not bring them to reform the neglect of observation of the Lord's day as a Sabbath, or any other thing amiss among them...

Because the countrymen, who came over to join with them, by reason of the hardness of the country, soon spent their estates, and were then forced either to return back to England, or to live very meanly...

Many of their children, through the extreme necessity that was upon them, although of the best dispositions and graciously inclined, and willing to bear part of their parents' burdens, were oftentimes so oppressed with their heavy burdens, that although their spirits were free and willing, yet their bodies bowed under the weight of the same, and became decrepit in their early youth, and the vigour of nature consumed in the very bud. And that which was very lamentable, and of all sorrows most heavy to be borne, was that many by these occasions and the great licentiousness of youth in that country, and the manifold temptations of the place, were drawn away by evil examples into extravagant and dangerous courses, departing from their parents. Some became soldiers, others took upon them far voyages by sea, and other some worse courses, tending to dissoluteness and the destruction of their souls, to the great grief of their parents, and the dishonour of God.[1]

Heavenly Father, my prayers this day are for those who are battling fierce
temptations of one kind or another. I ask you, Lord, in your mercy, to strengthen
them by your Holy Spirit. I pray that you would impart enabling grace. Help
them in their hour of weakness. Grant them victory.

---

1   From *Chronicles of the Pilgrim Fathers.*

HE HAS FILLED THEM WITH SKILL TO DO ALL KINDS OF WORK AS
ENGRAVERS, DESIGNERS, EMBROIDERERS IN BLUE, PURPLE AND
SCARLET YARN AND FINE LINEN, AND WEAVERS – ALL OF THEM
SKILLED WORKERS AND DESIGNERS.
(Exodus 35:35)

When the Pilgrims were in Leyden a little boy with a mop of curly hair lived in the big mill-house on the Western Rampart of the city on the river-bank...

The boy's name was Rembrandt of the Rhine [born in Leyden].

Rembrandt painted again and again the face of his old mother... He painted the stories that she told him out of the Bible. She must have told them wonderfully, for he painted them so really that you seem to see the very stories come alive again.

But he painted, too, the very things that the Pilgrim boys and girls saw as they went about the streets – the beggars whining on crutches from door to door, the cosy housewives in the market-place buying food; the meandering Old Rhine River creeping along between its strong banks; the steeples where the bells clanged on festival day; the network of canals up and down which the barges slowly nosed their way; the low, far-stretching land covered with thin grass; the waving arms of the windmills turning in the misty, amber-coloured air; the gale blowing the storks about the cloud-strewn sky, driving too the ships that scudded wildly by the shore in search of harbourage.[1]

Lord, you gift some people with their use of colour, enabling them to bless the world with their art. Thank you for those who add blues and purples and reds and golds to the landscape of life. I pray today for those who consecrate their creative skills to your service, that you might use them to tell others of your love where words might not suffice. Inspire them.

---

1   From *The Argonauts of Faith*.

IN EVERYTHING SET THEM AN EXAMPLE BY DOING WHAT IS GOOD.
(Titus 2:7)

The Pilgrims earned their living by doing many things while they were at Leyden. William Bradford was a *vastijnwerker* (i.e. a fustian-worker – fustian is a strong, coarse, cotton stuff). Others wove baize, made serge, carded wool, knitted stockings, engraved pictures, constructed trunks, cast metal into bells, or hammered gold into rings and brooches. They manufactured twine and string, chiselled stone and built it into houses, worked with chisel and saw and hammer and screw-driver at the carpenter's bench. William Brewster, being a scholar from Cambridge, taught the Dutchmen, Danes, and Germans to speak and write the English language, and was so clever at doing this that many men sent their boys to him. He taught the sons of the great men of the State.

Then William Brewster did something that was of still greater importance. It made King James I of England stretch out his arm across the sea, and try to imprison him even though he lived in another land. Brewster bought a printing press and set it up in a house in the *Choor-steeg* – Choir-lane, as we should say. A friend named Thomas Brewer helped him in this. So they printed and sent home books defending their wish to worship God in freedom – books such as were not allowed to be printed in England. But the King of England failed to get William Brewster into his clutches, though he sent messengers over to Holland to take him prisoner.[1]

Thank you, Lord, for your provision whereby you enable us to earn a living while also devoting some of our time to mission, one facilitating the other. Help me, I pray, to successfully allocate my time each day. All I do is for the Master, of course, but there is that sense of "paid" employment and that which is carried out voluntarily, for the church. Use all my days, and all my hours.

---

1   From *The Argonauts of Faith*.

How good and pleasant it is when God's people live together in unity! It is like precious oil poured on the head, running down on the beard, running down on Aaron's beard, down on the collar of his robe. It is as if the dew of Hermon were falling on Mount Zion. For there the Lord bestows his blessing, even life forevermore.

(Psalm 133)

The most famous of the houses that the Pilgrims had in Leyden was called "The House with the Green Door". It stood in the *Klooksteeg* (that is, Bell Lane) near the *Pieterskerk* (St. Peter's Church)... In the upstairs rooms of the house lived John Robinson, the wise and good pastor of the Church of the Pilgrims.

He knew that men who loved liberty as his people did were often ready to fight for it over trifling things. He was a very learned man, and knew the great books of Ancient Greece and Rome, and Christian writers of all the centuries. Yet his heart was simple and kind. The boys and girls loved him, and they thought of him with reverence. We can well believe that the reason why the people in the Church of which he was the minister quarrelled very little was due more than anything else to the gentle, brave spirit of good John Robinson. Under his leadership they certainly were a "happy band of Pilgrims". A man who joined them when they were at Leyden... said, "I persuade myself never people upon earth lived more lovingly together and parted more sweetly than we the Church of Leyden did."[1]

A happy church! What a blessing! Fill my church, I pray, with such a spirit of unity and fellowship as this. Furthermore, make me a part of that!

---

1   From *The Argonauts of Faith*.

March 12th

MAY HE GIVE YOU THE DESIRE OF YOUR HEART AND MAKE ALL YOUR
PLANS SUCCEED.

(Psalm 20:4)

[Reasons given for the failure of the pilgrims to settle in Holland] ...

[The concern that] their posterity would in a few generations become Dutch, and so lose their interest in the English nation; they being desirous rather to enlarge his Majesty's dominions, and to live under their natural prince ...

A great hope and inward zeal they had of laying some good foundation, or at least to make some way thereunto for the propagating and advancement of the gospel of the kingdom of Christ in those remote parts of the world, yea, although they should be but as stepping-stones unto others for the performance of so great a work.

These and such like were the true reasons of their removal, and not as some of their adversaries did, upon the rumour thereof, cast out slanders against them; as if the state were weary of them, and had rather driven them out ... than that it was their own free choice and motion ...

The reasons of their removal above named being debated first in private, and thought weighty, were afterwards propounded in public; and after solemn days of humiliation[1] observed both in public and private, it was agreed, that part of the church should go before their brethren into America, to prepare for the rest; and if in case the major part of the church did choose to go over with the first, then the pastor to go along with them; but if the major part stayed, then he was then to stay with them.[2]

Heavenly Father, my prayers this day are for those whose plans have had to change. Bless them, I pray, as they explore new opportunities and options. Draw close to them in days of uncertainty, and show them the way forward. Calm them as they wait upon you for guidance.

---

1   Humility before God in prayer, not humiliation as in embarrassment or belittling.
2   From *Chronicles of the Pilgrim Fathers.*

"THE LORD BLESS YOU AND KEEP YOU; THE LORD MAKE HIS FACE
SHINE ON YOU AND BE GRACIOUS TO YOU; THE LORD TURN HIS
FACE TOWARD YOU AND GIVE YOU PEACE."
(Numbers 6:24–26)

The time being come that they must depart, they were accompanied with most of their brethren out of the city... where the ship lay ready to receive them, so they left that goodly and pleasant city, which had been their resting-place... but they knew that they were pilgrims and strangers here below, and looked not much on these things, but lifted up their eyes to heaven, their dearest country, where God hath prepared for them a city, Heb. Xi. 16, and therein quieted their spirits.[1]

Lord of my comings and goings, I offer a prayer today for those who are leaving home and saying goodbye to loved ones. Bless them, I pray, in the midst of homesickness, when parting tugs at the heartstrings. Reassure them of your loving presence, in a way that will lift their spirits.

---

1   From *Chronicles of the Pilgrim Fathers.*

DO NOT PUT YOUR TRUST IN PRINCES, IN HUMAN BEINGS, WHO
CANNOT SAVE.
(Psalm 146:3)

It is estimated... that at the accession of James there were fifteen hundred Puritan ministers in England...

They desired now simply a purer form of worship within the Church, the abolition of what they regarded as superstitious usages, and the awakening of the clergy to a more earnest religious life and teaching...

The Queen [Elizabeth I]... cared little for their opinions, provided there was no open denial of her supremacy. The prelates, being in doubt as to the position which would be assumed by her successor, treated them with comparative indulgence.

To the new monarch their eyes were naturally turned with great hopes of the future. James had been bred a strict Calvinist and a Presbyterian... and had over and over again promised to maintain the Kirk in all its purity, his last promise being made just as he was leaving Scotland for his new throne. Not only had he made these promises to Scotland, but he had praised its Kirk as "the sincerest in the world," and denounced the Anglican service as simply "an evil-said mass in English."

But all this was what historians call "kingcraft." James, in this department, as in most others, could not approach Elizabeth, who as a kaleidoscopic and bewildering juggler with the truth has had few equals in history.[1]

Thank you, Lord, for leaders who are trustworthy, and people of their word.
I pray for those who work within the corridors of power, that they would resist
temptations towards duplicity, double-speak, and the equivalents of "kingcraft"
in their professional life.

---

1   From *The Puritan in Holland, England and America.*

**"I AM SENDING YOU OUT LIKE SHEEP AMONG WOLVES. THEREFORE
BE AS SHREWD AS SNAKES AND AS INNOCENT AS DOVES."**
(Matthew 10:16)

On the eve of his departure for England [King James] gave public thanks to God, in the Kirk of Edinburgh, "that he had left both Kirk and kingdom in that state which he intended not to alter anyways, his subjects living in peace"...

However, the Puritans, not being statesmen, but plain country parsons, merchants, manufacturers, and artisans, knew as little of this trait of their future monarch as of the other traits which he developed in the servile air of an English court... They believed in him, and had for years anticipated his coming to the throne as the day of emancipation for the Church.

Acting upon this belief... they presented to James, upon his journey from Scotland, what is known as the "Millenary Petition"... It fully recognized the system of Episcopacy, but asked, in the spirit of the early Reformers, for some changes in the ritual, and, in addition, that the better observance of the Lord's day should be enforced; that none but men able to preach should be admitted to the ministry; that pluralities should be abolished, and the revenues of the Church devoted to religious purposes; that ministers be, by law, permitted to marry; that they be compelled to subscribe, as required by statute, only to the Articles of Religion[1] and the king's supremacy, and that persons should not be excommunicated for trifling matters.[2]

Grant me, Lord, I pray, a heart that trusts, and always prefers to see the best in others. Help me, though, also to proceed with wisdom. Teach me to avoid cynicism, but teach me too, to be wary of naivety. Help me in my dealings with those who may not prove to be honourable.

---

1   The *Thirty-nine Articles of Religion*, the defining statements of doctrines and practices of the Church of England.
2   From *The Puritan in Holland, England and America*.

THUS SAITH THE LORD...
(Isaiah 45:1 *KJV*)

For six months James took no notice of the Puritans' position. The time was long enough to turn the head of a much stronger man than this ill-balanced alien pedant. He came from a poor, bleak, and sterile kingdom, where, amid the strife of warring factions, his royal authority had been constantly disputed. He came to an *El Dorado*,[1] where the fountains of wealth and honour seemed perennial, and where, from greedy courtiers and servile churchmen, he heard of nothing but of his absolute power and superhuman wisdom...

He announced that he would hear the Puritans in a formal disputation with their adversaries... The famous disputation took place in the royal palace at Hampton Court. The king, who acted as judge, also selected the disputants. He chose four divines from the Puritan ranks, men of ability and learning, their opponents were eighteen in number... The farcical results of such an argument were, of course, a foregone conclusion. The Puritan representatives were dismissed with ignominy, while the High Church party... declared that his "majesty spake [*sic*] by inspiration of the Spirit of God."[2]

Oh, Lord! How easy it is for someone to claim to have spoken in your name when they have done nothing of the sort! How easily misled we can be, by such claims. Teach me your voice, I pray, and grant me discernment this day. Guard my heart as I seek to follow you and your will. By the same token, Lord, guard my tongue, that the words I speak may carry your approval.

---

1   "The Golden One" in Spanish – the mythical tribal chief of the Muisca native people of Colombia. Legends surrounding this chief moved from being a man, to a kingdom, to an empire. "The Golden One" was sometimes referred to, in legend, as "The Golden King".
2   From *The Puritan in Holland, England and America*.

"MAN SHALL NOT LIVE ON BREAD ALONE, BUT ON EVERY WORD
THAT COMES FROM THE MOUTH OF GOD."
(Matthew 4:4)

The English-speaking world, through the efforts of the Puritans, received one gift from the Hampton Court conference, for his share in which due credit should be given to King James. Dr. Reynolds,[1] of Oxford, the leader of the Puritan disputants, and probably the most learned man in England, raised serious objections to the existing translations of the Bible, and proposed that a new and more correct translation should be made. Bancroft,[2] the spokesman of the prelates, objected; but here the scholarship of the king stood the nation in good stead. He adopted the suggestion of Dr. Reynolds, and shortly afterwards appointed a commission of fifty-four of the first scholars in the universities to undertake the task. Under wise instructions, requiring them, so far as possible, to follow the old translations, and to refrain from the use of sectarian words or comments, men of all shades of opinion were enabled to work together.[3] [4]

Thank you, Heavenly Father, for the Bible; that living word you have graciously given, to inspire, convict, guide, and teach. Help me, I pray, to feed my soul on what the Bible has to say to me each day. Speak to me this day, a word in season.

---

1 John Reynolds, or Reinolds (1549–1607), academic and churchman of Puritan views.
2 Richard Bancroft (1544–1610), Archbishop of Canterbury from 1604 until his death.
3 A number of Puritans were placed on this commission.
4 From *The Puritan in Holland, England and America*.

BUT BE YE DOERS OF THE WORD, AND NOT HEARERS ONLY...

(James 1:22 *KJV*)

In 1611, they gave to the world that noblest monument of the English language as it existed in the middle of the sixteenth century, when the early translations were made, King James's version of the Bible – a version which, after nearly three centuries, still holds its place, representing to untold millions of Protestants of all denominations, as recent experience has proved, the inspired Word of God much more faithfully than any Hebrew or Greek original.[1]

But this is all for which posterity has to thank King James in these early years. When leaving the conference at Hampton Court he told the Puritans that unless they conformed he would harry them out of the land, or else do worse and hang them. Well, he did keep his promise at the outset. A few weeks after the conference, Whitgift, the venerable archbishop, died. The king chose as his successor Bancroft,[2] the steady upholder of the divine right of kings and of Episcopacy. His career it is unnecessary to trace in any detail. It followed, almost exactly, although on a larger scale and with some exaggerations, the career of Whitgift, when he was first made archbishop. Elizabeth, at that time... gave orders to exterminate the Puritans. James now... gave the same orders to his facile bishops. They, in the main, obeyed with cheerfulness, although on occasions requiring the royal spur.[3]

Lord, how strange this seems, how incongruous! That someone can be committed to translating the Bible one day, then threatening executions the next. Help me, I pray, not merely to be a hearer of the word, but a doer also, lest its impact upon my life and behaviour is only ever superficial. In your mercy, speak to my heart as well as my head.

---

1   In 1582, the Jesuits had published, at Rheims, France, their English version of the New Testament.
2   See Footnote 2, March 17ᵗʰ.
3   From *The Puritan in Holland, England and America.*

THE WEAPONS WE FIGHT WITH ARE NOT THE WEAPONS OF
THE WORLD. ON THE CONTRARY, THEY HAVE DIVINE POWER TO
DEMOLISH STRONGHOLDS.

(2 Corinthians 10:4)

On Sunday morning the men and women of the Pilgrim Church at Leyden used to come to the House with the Green Door. They would walk to the door quietly, and, lifting the latch, enter the large room on the ground-floor which was their meeting-room for worship. John Robinson, as he sat in the minister's seat, would see the people he loved and whose lives he knew come in and take their places.

Here was young William Bradford... Then came the sturdy and clever William Brewster, who taught "great men's sons" in Leyden to speak English and learned from them how their land was governed. The strong, stalwart figure of Captain Miles Standish[1] would fill the doorway, for he cast in his lot with the Pilgrims while they were in Leyden, though he did not join the Church; and Miles and his wife would take their places in the room. Standish was a great fighter; a soldier of fortune who took part in many a tussle in the Netherlands... He had a quick temper that flamed up into anger, yet a warm heart that made him a good friend. He was so brave that he did not know what fear was, and was always at his best in a tight corner and in a stiff fight, for he could cut or contrive a way out when nine men out of ten would fail.[2]

I pray, Lord, for anyone who is fighting a battle today, particularly spiritually, or mentally. I ask you to draw alongside them and grant them victory in conflicts of the mind, heart, and soul. Protect and strengthen those who are coming under spiritual attack, and who are tormented with all kinds of temptations and discouragements. Help them to be like Captain Miles Standish, and to stand in the strength of your grace.

---

1   See Footnote 3, January 12ᵗʰ.
2   From *The Argonauts of Faith.*

... LET YOUR LIGHT SHINE BEFORE OTHERS, THAT THEY MAY SEE
YOUR GOOD DEEDS AND GLORIFY YOUR FATHER IN HEAVEN.
(Matthew 5:16)

So happily did they live together in Leyden that many others were drawn to join them. People in England living in Kent and Essex, Lincolnshire and Northamptonshire, went out to Leyden to escape persecution in their own land. After some years, the community had grown from just over a hundred to as many as three hundred. And so honest and straight were they in their dealing that, after living in Leyden for twelve years, the magistrates of the city could actually say, "These English have lived among us these twelve years, and yet we never had any suit or accusation against any of them."[1]

What a challenging example, Lord! Gracious Spirit, dwell within me so that others may be drawn to you. Be the guest of my soul this day.

---

1   From *The Argonauts of Faith*.

... MY DEAR BROTHERS AND SISTERS, STAND FIRM. LET NOTHING
MOVE YOU.
(1 Corinthians 15:58)

[King James issued] new decrees commanding the use of the Book of Common Prayer, full and unreserved acceptance of the Thirty-Nine Articles, suppression of all private religious meetings, and obligatory communion in the Anglican church at least three times a year. Within twelve months, more than three hundred clergymen were deprived of office for their obvious reluctance or flat refusal to obey these decrees. Again the tide of reform began to ebb under heavy pressure from above.

But Brewster and his friends... were not intimidated. For "sundrie years, with much patience", they had borne the silencing of "godly & zealous preachers". Now their patience was exhausted. The time for half measures had passed, and they began looking "further into things by the light of ye word of God". The deeper they probed... the more apparent it became that the Anglican church was "a prophane mixture of persons & things", none having any "warrante in ye word of God, but the same that were used in poperie & still retained" [sic]. That was why the church was filled with "base and beggarly ceremonies". Let the bishops follow them if they wished. As for themselves, they would not "become slaves to them & their popish trash".[1]

This is a dreadful state of affairs, Lord, and deeply regrettable. However, it leads me to pray for any today who are at the end of their tether, and whose patience is exhausted. Help them, Lord, in their days of frustration and despair. Help them especially not to make rash decisions in the heat of the moment. Guide them towards good solutions and decisions.

---

1   From *Saints and Strangers*.

"ISN'T THIS THE CARPENTER?"
(Mark 6:3)

The religious rebels were, for the most part, quite definitely "lower class", not only socially but in actual legal status. And their masters were not disposed to allow them to forget this for a moment, contemptuously asking who gave a tinker's dam what "Symon the Saddler, Tomkins the Tailor, or Billy the Bellows-maker" might have to say on any subject. Their duty was plain and simple enough – to do and believe precisely what they were told. Let them leave thinking to their "betters"![1]

Jesus the carpenter, my God and King.

---

1   From *Saints and Strangers*.

IN ALL THE TRAVELS OF THE ISRAELITES, WHENEVER THE CLOUD
LIFTED FROM ABOVE THE TABERNACLE, THEY WOULD SET OUT...
(Exodus 40:36)

In spite of all, things went slowly forward... The adventurers chartered a large vessel of 180 tons, "a fine ship"... The group in Leyden bought a smaller vessel of sixty tons, the *Speedwell*, which was to transport part of the company and stay in the New World for use there in "fishing and shuch other affairs as might be for ye good & benefite of ye colonie" [*sic*]. As the ship was in bad condition, she had to be refitted at considerable expense. New and larger masts were stepped in, a new suit of sail was bought for her, and she was now lying at Delft Haven ready to depart for the rendezvous at Southampton. Preparations for the long, hazardous journey still left much to be desired, many problems were yet unsolved, but with the summer already upon them and passing rapidly, it was obvious that if the company was to go at all, it was a question of going without further delay.[1]

Heavenly Father, if only all our plans went smoothly! If only we could easily detect your will for our lives, and follow you without setback or concern! Help us each, I pray, as we do our best to navigate life's voyage in your service. Graciously steer us through every twist and turn, and keep us on track, so that your will might be fulfilled. Guide our steps today and forgive us when we stray.
Haul us back!

---

1   From *Saints and Strangers*.

FOLLOW MY EXAMPLE, AS I FOLLOW THE EXAMPLE OF CHRIST.
(1 Corinthians 11:1)

As the congregation usually did on important occasions, a "day of solleme [*sic*] humiliation" was proclaimed. Some time was spent in "powering out prairs to ye Lord with great fervencie, mixed with abundance of tears" [*sic*]. Then Robinson rose to speak, taking his text from Ezra viii.21 and devoting most of the day to it "very profitably". His departing brethren never forgot his sermon. "I charge you before God and his blessed Angels to follow me no further than I follow Christ," he told them in his modest way, "and if God shall reveal anything to you by any other Instrument of his, be as ready to receive it as ever you were to receive any truth by my Ministry... Be not loath to take another Pastor or Teacher, for the Flock that hath two Shepherds is not indangered [*sic*] but secured by it."[1]

Thank you, Lord, for humble and gracious leaders, and the blessings they impart. Thank you for those whose shepherding is gentle, and whose focus is on Christ. Thank you for those who are willing to step aside, in grace and humility, for the kingdom's sake. Today, I pray for everyone involved in the leadership of my own church. I lift each of them before you in prayer: my minister(s), elders, and council members.

1   From *Saints and Strangers*.

AND JESUS... SAW A GREAT MULTITUDE, AND WAS MOVED WITH
COMPASSION TOWARD THEM...
(Matthew 14:14 *KJV*)

The Pilgrims were thankful, in many ways, that they could live in Leyden in freedom. But Leyden was not and could never be really home. They desired strongly to be in England, which was their real home. That, however, could not be, for the Government there still persecuted men and women for wishing to be free in worship. So their thoughts roamed the world in search of some other place where they could make a New England that would still be attached to the Old Country and under the King, yet might be free, and might become a new home. John Robinson's thoughts often ran westward across the Atlantic ocean to the West Indies – the islands off the coast of America...

Those, however, were hard lands to live in. There was dreadful fever in many of them... and in none was there any settled, ordered and secure life. If they sailed west it would certainly mean that the older people and the weaker ones could not go, but must stay at home.[1]

Gracious Father, I pray for those today who are classed as refugees or economic migrants. They too, though not necessarily by choice, roam the world in search of some place they might call home. They too face fever and illness, bereavement and unimaginable struggles. Bless them, I pray, and grant governments compassion in terms of their response.

The Salvation Army in the United Kingdom and the Republic of Ireland offers a ministry of practical care and support to refugees. If you would like to know more about this modern expression of the love of Christ, please contact The Salvation Army as follows:

The Refugee Services Coordinator
The Salvation Army
Territorial Headquarters
101 Newington Causeway
London SE1 6BN

https://www.salvationarmy.org.uk/refugees

---

1   From *The Argonauts of Faith*.

THE LORD YOUR GOD HAS BLESSED YOU IN ALL THE WORK OF YOUR
HANDS. HE HAS WATCHED OVER YOUR JOURNEY THROUGH THIS
VAST WILDERNESS.
(Deuteronomy 2:7)

[The Pilgrims'] sons, however, were growing up, and the adventurous ones were joining the army of the Netherlands, or were sailing the world in Dutch merchant-ships, or were seeking to marry Dutch wives. The mothers and fathers wished very strongly that their children should go to a land where they would not be drawn away into a foreign life, but would build up one of their own. They desired above all to make their life where their boys and girls might grow in body and soul, breathing the air of a generous and bracing freedom.

Their eyes turned across the ocean to the west… to found in America a settlement that would be the beginning of a New England across the waters. At last they determined that they too would go and seek in the wilds a place where, at whatever cost to themselves, they could build a home… They were in spirit "Sea-rovers, conquerors, builders in the waste."[1] [2]

Tough decisions, Lord! Bless those today who are weighing up the pros and cons
of deciding what to do for the sake of their families – where to move, and what
factors to include in order to secure the best future. Help them as they discuss
every issue, and as they pray to you for guidance.

---

1   From Sir Henry Newbolt's poem "The Non-Combatant". Sir Henry John Newbolt (1862–1938), poet and government advisor with a particular interest in the history of the English.
2   From *The Argonauts of Faith*.

... I PROCLAIMED A FAST, SO THAT WE MIGHT HUMBLE OURSELVES
BEFORE OUR GOD AND ASK HIM FOR A SAFE JOURNEY...
(Ezra 8:21)

With pennons flying bravely at the mastheads, the *Speedwell* slipped her hawsers, unfurled her bright new sails, and moved slowly out into the broad channel of the Maas, her rails crowded with excited but heavyhearted passengers frantically waving a last farewell to those still lining the quay – many suspecting what proved to be the fact, that this was a final separation from their loved ones, that they had seen old friends for the last time, that never again in this life would they hold their wives and laughing children in their arms. A salvo of cannon boomed from the ship and the passengers fired a volley of small arms in parting salute as the vessel got underway. Having a "prosperous winde" [*sic*], they were soon past the Hook of Holland and out into the North Sea, where Captain Reynolds set his course WSW to round the chalk cliffs at Dover and follow the coast to Southampton. The first leg of the long voyage was accomplished in good time, though the *Speedwell* proved to be a cranky vessel, heeling far over and shipping water even in a moderate breeze, giving the skipper cause for concern and the passengers several good wettings.[1]

> Lord, I pray for anyone starting out today; on a journey, maybe, or in some other kind of way – a new job or business venture, a fresh relationship, first-time parenting, or even moving from one church to another. For every new start, I ask your blessing. Calm nerves, give your peace, and meet every need.

---

1   From *Saints and Strangers*.

"SUPPOSE ONE OF YOU WANTS TO BUILD A TOWER. WON'T YOU
FIRST SIT DOWN AND ESTIMATE THE COST TO SEE IF YOU HAVE
ENOUGH MONEY TO COMPLETE IT?"

(Luke 14:28)

Those on board constituted only a small part of the congregation... numbering less than fifty persons – and almost half of them were children...

Some had decided to split their families... Others had chosen to come with children and not with wives...

Putting in at Southampton, they dropped anchor alongside the *Mayflower*, which had been waiting here for some days, having sailed round from London about a week before with the emigrants recruited at large by the merchant adventurers. The two groups were not acquainted, but there was no time to stand on ceremony. After "mutuall congratulations, with other frendly entertainements, they fell to parley about their business" [*sic*], and they found a great deal to discuss...

They were desperately short of funds, largely because of expensive repairs to the *Speedwell*. To correct the faults she manifested in crossing from Holland, her rig had been changed, and now it was necessary to change it again. In addition to all else, this involved a loss of precious time, itself a source of deep concern... They would run into heavy equinoctial gales on the high seas and wintry weather at the far end of their voyage, which would dangerously increase their difficulties in getting settled.[1]

> Practical matters, Lord! Thank you for your interest in bills for repairs, the cost of living, church property expenses, running a car, paying for the shopping; nothing escapes your loving notice. I pray today for those who are "desperately short of funds", reliant on foodbanks, and running up debts. Help them, I pray, and bless those churches and charities who do their best to support and advise.

---

1   From *Saints and Strangers*.

"WOE TO YOU WHEN EVERYONE SPEAKS WELL OF YOU, FOR THAT IS
HOW THEIR ANCESTORS TREATED THE FALSE PROPHETS."
(Luke 6:26)

For some years the local reformers had been annoyed and harassed by the authorities. But these troubles were "but as flea-bitings" to those that now came upon them when they finally left the church… The whole countryside was soon aroused against them, which can be readily understood without subscribing to Cotton Mather's[1] usual extravagant nonsense in characterizing their neighbours as "most ignorant and licentious people". The simple truth is that most Englishmen, without really knowing much about either, hated and feared Puritans and Separatists[2] alike, for the pulpit, the press of the day, thundered continuously against them.[3]

Lord, grant your Church courage to swim against the tide whenever that might be necessary. Free your Church from the tyranny of inappropriate popularity.

---

1   Cotton Mather (1663–1728), New England Puritan minister, prolific author, and pamphleteer. He left a scientific legacy due to his hybridization experiments and his promotion of inoculation for disease prevention, though he is most frequently remembered today for his involvement in the Salem witch trials (extracted from https://en.wikipedia.org/wiki/Cotton_Mather).

2   Separatists were, in the main, more extreme than Puritans. They desired a complete break from the Church of England, whereas Puritans were keen to see Anglicanism reformed from within.

3   From *Saints and Strangers*.

THE DISCIPLES WERE CALLED CHRISTIANS FIRST AT ANTIOCH.
(Acts 11:26)

The name Puritan began to acquire new meanings, which have led to great confusion among historians. There were, in fact, four classes of persons to whom it was now applied, some belonging to all four, and others to but three, two, or only one of those classes.

First were the Ceremonial Puritans, the men to whom the name was first given, and who need no further description.

Second, the Civil or Political Puritans. These were the men who, whether they cared for forms and ceremonies or not, were resolved to maintain the principles of civil liberty...

Third, the Doctrinal Puritans. This was a new application of the word... Until this time... the whole English Church was united on the doctrine of predestination as laid down by Calvin.[1] The king himself was one of the most ardent advocates of this doctrine, and plumed himself greatly on the theological learning which he displayed in its defence...

Against these three classes of Puritans there stood opposed: the prelatists,[2] with their celestial origin of the Established Church; the courtiers,[3] with their divine right of kings; and the Arminians,[4] with their anti-Calvinistic theology.[5]

Lord, make my focus only ever to be known as a Christian.
Help me in that witness.

---

1   John (Jean) Calvin (1509–64), French theologian, pastor, and reformer, after whom Calvinism is named.
2   One who supports and advocates church government by bishops and ecclesiastical authorities.
3   Those in attendance at the courts of kings and monarchs, believing them to have been divinely appointed.
4   Protestantism based around the teaching of the Dutch theologian Jacobus Arminius (1560–1609).
5   From *The Puritan in Holland, England and America*.

LIVE SUCH GOOD LIVES AMONG THE PAGANS THAT, THOUGH
THEY ACCUSE YOU OF DOING WRONG, THEY MAY SEE YOUR GOOD
DEEDS AND GLORIFY GOD.
(1 Peter 2:12)

There was still another class in the community to the members of which the name Puritan was now popularly applied... This was made up of all persons, whatever their political or theological opinions, who by their conduct protested against the flood of corruption and immorality which threatened to ingulf [sic] the nation. The mass of Englishmen... were living a life of practical heathenism. The man, outside the ranks of the avowed Catholics, who lived a life of chastity and sobriety, avoided gambling and profanity, especially if he maintained family devotions, kept the Sabbath, and attended church with regularity, was, by the people at large, regarded as a "Puritan." Never was a higher tribute than this paid to the members of any political or religious party. Better than volumes of testimony, it evidences the moral work that the Puritans were doing.[1]

What a wonderful "mistake", Lord – to be labelled a Puritan on account of good works! Help me, I pray, to earn such a tribute today. It doesn't matter whether or not I am made aware of it, so long as my life reflects your indwelling presence.

---

1   From *The Puritan in Holland, England and America.*

... ONE OFFICIAL IS EYED BY A HIGHER ONE, AND OVER THEM BOTH
ARE OTHERS HIGHER STILL.

(Ecclesiastes 5:8)

[The Pilgrims] decided to send to England to ask King James for a charter to allow those who could endure the hardships of the voyage and of the difficult and dangerous life to go across the Atlantic and settle on the east coast of America. To get that charter settled and then signed by the King was more difficult than winning any obstacle race. There were the hurdles of religious persecution to get over; the slippery pole of jealousy to clamber along; the pond of greed to jump, and the gorse-bushes of prejudice to force. But at last, through a band of Merchant-adventurers – called the London Virginia Company[1] – they received their charter... They had permission to settle in America.[2]

Bureaucracy, Lord! Forms to fill in and protocols to be observed! I pray today, Heavenly Father, for church administrators and those whose ministry is to keep paperwork and documentation in order. Theirs is often an unsung ministry, yet one which is crucial if churches are to run well, in keeping with the law of the land. Bless them as they work for the wellbeing of others. Bless those especially who lift these responsibilities from church ministers.

---

1   The London Company was an English joint-stock company established in 1606 by royal charter by King James I with the purpose of establishing colonial settlements in North America (from https://en.wikipedia.org/wiki/London_Company).

2   From *The Argonauts of Faith*.

YOU HAVE… PUT MY TEARS IN YOUR BOTTLE. ARE THEY NOT IN
YOUR BOOK?
(Psalm 56:8 *ESV*)

Early on a bright midsummer morning… the Pilgrims all met together in the great room which was the meeting-place of the Pilgrim Church in John Robinson's house with the green door…

Then they passed out of the shadow of the room into the open street to the Nuns' Bridge, opposite the Robinson's house. Barges were moored near the bridge by the street side. All who were sailing in the *Speedwell* – as well as some like John Robinson himself who were travelling as far as Delfshaven to see them off – went down into the barges; mothers and fathers, young men and women, boys and girls, and one or two babies who would blink unconcernedly at the sunshine and not know at all that they were going out into a life that was as new as themselves.

The barges were loosed and started. Those who were left behind waved farewell from the bank – though indeed some of them could not see for the tears that blurred their eyesight. The barges crept quietly along the Vliet, the canal that runs from Leyden to Delft.[1]

> Liquid emotion, Lord – those tears that fall at times of parting and separation.
> Draw close to those for whom today will include crying and heartbreak; those
> who will be bereaved this day, or who will part from loved ones for one reason
> or another. Even in a positive context, such times can induce real heartache.
> Strengthen them with your loving presence. Thank you, Lord, that no falling tear
> goes unnoticed.

---

1   From *The Argonauts of Faith*.

HE CHANGES TIMES AND SEASONS; HE DEPOSES KINGS AND RAISES
UP OTHERS.
(Daniel 2:21)

[The Pilgrims] passed between the houses inside the city; then they came to the water-gate that guarded Leyden so that no enemy might be able to enter. In front of them rose the northern walls of the town. The barges passed under the shadow of the tunnel through the walls and out into the open country. Looking back, they could see the turrets standing above the Cow-gate and the glitter of the helmet of a sentry. It was their last look at Leyden.

"They lefte," says William Bradford, "the goodly and pleasante citie which had been ther resting-place... but they knew that they were prilgrimes" [sic].

Out across the low pasture lands they could see the quiet cows and sheep grazing and the windmills lazily turning in the breeze of the summer morning. For nine miles the barges butted their way to a bend to the left under the Hoorn Bridge by the Hague. Then for five miles the canal-boats went on till they came to the city of Delft. Going in under the walls, they passed through the centre of the city. Over them, they saw the tall tower, leaning out of the straight, of the Old Kirk of Delft. Opposite to it was the red-tiled house in which the great soldier and statesman of freedom – William the Silent[1] – had been assassinated by the dagger of Balthazar Gerard.[2][3]

History moves and has its way, Lord, and as the centuries unfold, we look back and see your hand at work. You shape the destinies of people and of nations. Grant me, I pray, the ability to see your plans for my life in the light of "the bigger picture". I may not realize every detail, but help me to trust that what I do today will matter in the future. Grant me that perspective.

---

1 Or William the Taciturn, or William of Orange, William I, Prince of Orange (1533–84), the leader of the Dutch Revolt against the Spanish Habsburgs, in the cause of Dutch independence. He was assassinated by Balthazar Gerard.

2 Balthazar Gérard, or Gerards, or Gerardts (c. 1557–84). He was tried and executed.

3 From *The Argonauts of Faith.*

... THOUGH THE RIGHTEOUS FALL SEVEN TIMES, THEY RISE AGAIN...
(Proverbs 24:16)

All things being got ready, and every business despatched, they... chose a governor, and two or three assistants for each ship, to order the people by the way, and to see to the disposing of the provision, and such like affairs; all which was not only done with the liking of the masters of the ships, but according to their desires; which being done, they set sail from Southampton... But alas, the best enterprises meet oftentimes with many discouragements; for they had not sailed far, before Mr. Reynolds, the master of the lesser ship [*Speedwell*], complained that he found his ship so leaky, he durst not put further to sea... Mr. Jones, the master of the bigger ship [*Mayflower*], likewise putting in there with him, and the said lesser ship was searched and mended, and judged sufficient for the voyage, by the workmen that mended her; on which both ships put to sea the second times, but they had not sailed above an hundred leagues, ere the said Reynolds again complained of his ship being so leaky, that he feared he should founder in the sea, if he held on; and then both ships bore up again, and went in at Plimoth [*sic*]; but being there searched again, no great matter appeared, but it was judged to be the general weakness of the ship.[1]

Gracious and understanding God, I pray today for any who are struggling with what seems like repeated failure. I pray for those whose best efforts never seem to succeed, that you would protect them against the dreadful pitfalls of frustration and despair. Bless them, I pray, with the grace of perseverance, and grant them faith to keep trying, if they feel that what they are doing is right. Most of all, I pray, help them not to adopt the label "failure".

---

1   From *Chronicles of the Pilgrim Fathers*.

MULTITUDES, MULTITUDES IN THE VALLEY OF DECISION!
(Joel 3:14)

The true reason of the retarding and delaying of matters was not as yet discerned; the one of them respecting the ship (as afterwards was found), was, that she was overmasted, which, when she came to her trim, in that respect she did well; and made divers [sic] profitable and successful voyages. But secondly, and more especially by the deceit of the master and his company, who were hired to stay a whole year in the country; but now fancying dislike, and fearing want of victuals, they plotted this stratagem to free themselves, as afterwards was known, and by some of them confessed; for they apprehended that the greater ship being of force, and in whom most provisions were bestowed, that she would retain enough for herself, whatsoever became of them and them and the passengers. But so strong was self-love and deceit in this man, as he forgot all duty and former kindness, and dealt thus falsely with them. These things thus falling out, it was resolved by the whole company to dismiss the lesser ship and part of the company with her, and that the other part of the company should proceed in the bigger ship; which when they had ordered matters thereunto, they made another sad parting, the one ship, namely, the lesser, going back for London, and the other, namely, the *Mayflower*, Mr. Jones being master, proceeding on the intended voyage.[1] [2]

How awful this must have been, Lord – dreadful overcrowding, with every possibility of fever and disease, not to mention the practical issues of personal space and the absence of fresh air. I pray for those who are living in such conditions today: families who know only squalor and whose daily lives are blighted by suffocating conditions; those who live in crowded refugee camps, those whose homes are abandoned storage containers, or buildings that are unsafe and unsuitable. Lord, have mercy.

---

1   From *Chronicles of the Pilgrim Fathers*.
2   This "doubling up" meant that the *Mayflower* was seriously overcrowded for the remainder of the voyage.

... WEEP BITTERLY FOR HIM WHO IS EXILED, BECAUSE HE WILL
NEVER RETURN NOR SEE HIS NATIVE LAND AGAIN.
(Jeremiah 22:10)

Few of the Pilgrims went to sleep in that... night. They talked of the adventure that lay before them... They did not know how to part from one another. For they had lived twelve years together. Fathers were saying "Goodbye" to their sons and mothers to their daughters. William Bradford tells us:

Truly dolfull was the sight of that sad and morunfull parting; to see what sighs and sobs and praires did sound amongst them, what tears did gush from every eye, and pithy speeches peirst each harte; that sundry of the Dutch strangers refraine from tears... But the tide (which stays for no man) called them away that were thus loath to depart [sic].[1]

Be with those, Lord, who are separated against their will, whatever the reasons behind such separations: military personnel, perhaps, who are obliged to spend months apart from their loved ones; married couples, maybe, who need to live separately after decades together; people sent to prison, and their families left behind. Have mercy, Lord.

---

1   From *The Argonauts of Faith*.

BROTHERS, PRAY FOR US.
(1 Thessalonians 5:25 *ESV*)

John Robinson fell upon his knees and asked for God's blessing on all the Pilgrims. The friends went ashore. The sails were hoisted. The sailors cast loose the ship. The *Speedwell* swung away from the quay-side. There was a crack and a blaze, followed by a hollow roar. The men on the ship fired a volley from their muskets into the air; three of the ship's five cannon then boomed a salute.

Soon the fluttering of kerchiefs on the quay-side grew less and less. The little ship began to feel the heave and fall of the swell of the tide in the open sea. She ran south-west through the Channel between Dover and Calais, and, passing the harbour of Folkestone and the long flats of Romney Marsh, was driven by the fair wind westward... until, sighting the Isle of Wight, she ran in the narrow channel past Portsmouth to Southampton.[1]

Thank you, Lord, for those who have prayed for me. Thank you, Lord, for those who devote themselves to prayer on behalf of others. Thank you, Lord, for the blessings I enjoy as a result of intercessory prayer. Today, I ask you to bless those who have faithfully held me in their prayers over many years, and spent time on their knees with my name on their lips. As they have been a blessing, may they, in turn, receive a blessing.

---

1   From *The Argonauts of Faith*.

THIS IS WHAT THE LORD SAYS ... HE WHO FORMED YOU
"DO NOT FEAR, FOR I HAVE REDEEMED YOU; I HAVE SUMMONED
YOU BY NAME; YOU ARE MINE. WHEN YOU PASS THROUGH THE
WATERS, I WILL BE WITH YOU ..."
(Isaiah 43:1–2)

On board the two ships, crowding the rails for a last glimpse of the green shores of their homeland, were about 120 passengers, with perhaps ninety of these on the *Mayflower*. There was a governor on each ... "to order ye people by ye way, and to see to ye disposing of their provvisions and shuch like affairs" [*sic*]. The vessels went scudding along under a good stiff breeze, but after a few days at sea the *Speedwell* was "open and leakie as a sieve" [*sic*]. At one place "ye water came in as at a mole hole".[1] After a conference, Captains Reynolds and Jones decided to turn back, the two ships putting in at Dartmouth – and just in time ... for if the *Speedwell* had "stayed at sea but 3 or 4 howers more, she would have sunke right downe" [*sic*]. As the company worried and fretted, the vessel was again searched and mended "to their great charge and losse of time and a faire wind" [*sic*], which did nothing to improve the dispositions of either passengers or crew.[2]

How wonderful, Lord, that in the midst of all life's circumstances – good, bad or indifferent – you know each of us individually. In every circumstance of life, you do not count us as numbered groups, be that 120 or ninety. In your sight, we are precious individuals. Thank you, Heavenly Father, that you know us each by name, and that you love us individually.

---

1   A hole below the waterline.
2   From *Saints and Strangers*.

WISDOM'S INSTRUCTION IS TO FEAR THE LORD, AND HUMILITY
COMES BEFORE HONOUR.
(Proverbs 15:33)

These men, self-expatriated for their religion, came from a district of England where agriculture was the only pursuit, and agriculture, as followed by them, had been an industry in its rudest form...

Of the original emigrants two, and two only, were scholars. One was William Brewster. He for a time supported himself, and perhaps laid away something, by teaching English to the Dutch... The other scholar was John Robinson, the minister, who was a man of no mean acquirements... He was admitted to the University of Leyden, being enrolled as a student of theology...

The other Pilgrim Fathers were of a different class... Men who, as Bradford says, were "used to a plaine country life and ye innocent trade of husbandry" [*sic*].[1]

Lord, in your service there is a place for all! Whether we've been up to college, or we haven't had formal education, we are loved, and of immense value to your kingdom. Help me, I pray, never to judge anyone by their qualifications, or their lack of them. Likewise, help me never to judge someone by what they do for a living. Christ died for one and all, lords and labourers alike! Let that glorious truth be my only yardstick.

---

1   From *The Puritan in Holland, England and America.*

BUT SEEK FIRST HIS KINGDOM AND HIS RIGHTEOUSNESS, AND ALL
THESE THINGS WILL BE GIVEN TO YOU AS WELL.
(Matthew 6:33)

The Pilgrims were forced – before they could sail away – to pay their harbour dues out of the money they had with them. They sold sixty pounds' worth of their provisions on board ship to pay the dues before leaving. They were in difficult straits after reducing their provisions; but they were not daunted.

"We have," they wrote… "scarce any butter, no oyle, not a sole to mend a shoe, nor every man a sword to his side, wanting many muskets, much armoure, etc. And yet we are willing to expose ourselves to such eminente providence of God rather than His name and truth should be evil spoken of for us" [*sic*].[1]

Lord, this is a very challenging example – to maintain a sense of kingdom
perspective even when times are difficult. Help me, I pray, to bear this in mind
when I too am being tested.

---

1   From *The Argonauts of Faith*.

THE LORD SAID TO GIDEON, "WITH THE THREE HUNDRED MEN
THAT LAPPED I WILL SAVE YOU AND GIVE THE MIDIANITES INTO
YOUR HANDS. LET ALL THE OTHERS GO HOME."

(Judges 7:7)

These delays took the heart out of all but the bravest and most determined of the Pilgrims. They were in the Slough of Despond. Eighteen of them – like Mr. Pliable in *The Pilgrim's Progress*[1] – were so discouraged that they decided not to go at all. They turned back. As William Bradford, who was among the valiant ones who would not turn back, said, "Like Gedion's armie, this small number was devided, as if the Lord by this worke of His providence thought these few to many for the great worke He had to doe" [*sic*].[2]

We rely not on our numbers!

---

1   John Bunyan.
2   From *The Argonauts of Faith*.

MAY THE LORD REPAY YOU FOR WHAT YOU HAVE DONE.
(Ruth 2:12)

It was decided not to take the little *Speedwell* with them at all. The Pliables and their Captain went aboard her, and she sailed back along the coast of Hampshire, Sussex, and Kent up the estuary of the Thames, and so to inglorious safety determined to sail in spite of all. The good, stout-hearted Devon folk of Plymouth were very kind to the brave Pilgrims who were going forward, and helped them to stock their ship for the voyage. The Pilgrims, many years after, spoke of that kindness done to them in their dark time.

So they walked for the last time on Plymouth Hoe where Drake had played his game of bowls. The twelve extra Pilgrims left over from the *Speedwell* went aboard the *Mayflower*. There were now one hundred and two men, women, boys, and girls on board the ship. Thirty-four of them were grown men, eighteen were wives. There were twenty boys on board and eight girls. Nineteen of the travellers were men-servants, and three were maid-servants.[1]

Help me this day, Lord Jesus, to be kind.

---

1   From *The Argonauts of Faith*.

... LET US BE GIVEN VEGETABLES TO EAT AND WATER TO DRINK.

(Daniel 1:12 *ESV*)

The Mayflower once again put out to sea and headed westward, favoured by a "fine small gale" [sic]. The roar of the wind in the rigging, the steady roll of the ship as she swung along at six or seven knots were reassuring but certainly not a pleasure at first, for, "according to ye usuall manner, many were afflicted with seasickness" [sic].

As the ship had only the crudest of conveniences and no sanitary facilities of any kind except the traditional bucket, as there was no provision for bathing or even cursory washing (even if it had been a practice of the time to indulge), the air in the narrow, crowded quarters below deck must have been nauseating at best and at worst simply staggering. The North Atlantic is always cold, and the passengers found it almost impossible to keep warm and dry. Except for an occasional hot bath, they lived on a monotonous and upsetting diet of hard tack,[1] "salt horse",[2] dried fish, cheese, and beer.[3]

> Father God, I pray today for those who are deprived of the privilege of making their own choices: those who have little say in what food (if any) they will eat this day. Help me never to take a warm house and a comfortable bed for granted. I pray that you will help those who suffer deprivations in practical ways. I pray too for churches, charities, and agencies who do their best to restore dignity and wellbeing. Bless their efforts.

---

1   A type of biscuit, or cracker, made to be long-lasting and durable. It was commonly known as "Ship's Bisket".
2   A nautical term for salted beef.
3   From *Saints and Strangers*.

THE ARK IS TO BE THREE HUNDRED CUBITS LONG, FIFTY CUBITS
WIDE AND THIRTY CUBITS HIGH.
(Genesis 6:15)

The *Mayflower*, apple-cheeked, broad of beam, double-decked, with high superstructures – "castles" – fore and aft, was a fine ship… She was also a "sweet" ship, having been engaged since 1616 in the Mediterranean wine trade, though she undoubtedly retained about her some trace of the years she had spent hauling fish, timber, turpentine, tar, and other smelly products from Norway. A stout chunky vessel of 180 tons, she was far above the average in size… Yet any ocean voyage three centuries ago was a trial and an heroic adventure in itself.[1]

> **Lord, you are the God of detail. You gave Noah specific instructions for the dimensions of his ark, and I derive from that, that you are interested in the details of my life. Nothing is random with you, or left carelessly to chance. You are my God.**

---

1   From *Saints and Strangers*.

I WOULD FLEE FAR AWAY AND STAY IN THE DESERT; I WOULD HURRY
TO MY PLACE OF SHELTER, FAR FROM THE TEMPEST AND STORM.
(Psalm 55:7–8)

Sails were hoisted to a good breeze that was with them. They swung out to sea, and, with their bows toward the sunset, went bowling merrily and swiftly into the west. For day after day in fine weather and with a strong favouring wind they ran on their journey. They looked forward to reaching their journey's end without further adventure.

But their delays had brought them to the time of the equinoctial gales. These are the storms that come each year at the time… when in Britain and North America the days and nights are equal in length.

The wind began to whistle through the cordage. "White horses," crested the waves. The seamen went aloft to furl the sails. The waves were lashed into fury by the wind, which grew more and more violent until a gale was raging. The gale increased to a tempest.

The great Atlantic rollers swept seething and hissing across the streaming decks of the little ship. She shivered from stem to stern as the waves struck her. She climbed the giddy heights of one wave only to be slung dizzily down its slopes into dark chasms of water that threatened to swallow her up and sink her into the depths.[1]

Father, have mercy on those whose lives are beset by storms, and whose daily existence is a struggle. Let them know that you will hold them tight. May they discover you to be their place of shelter in the tempest.

---

1   From *The Argonauts of Faith.*

... GOD SHOWS HIS LOVE FOR US IN THAT WHILE WE WERE STILL
SINNERS, CHRIST DIED FOR US.

(Romans 5:8 *ESV*)

The *Mayflower* was packed to the gunwales,[1] for 102 passengers had been crammed on board with their goods and supplies. No impression is more deeply imbedded in the popular mind, nothing is more firmly woven into the American *mythos* than the notion that these first Pilgrims were a homogeneous and united group, all from Scrooby by way of Leyden, closely knit by family and personal ties, by the hardships and dangers they had suffered together, the hearts of each and all fired with a burning zeal to found a church of their own in the wilderness. It is a pleasing fantasy, but the Pilgrims would have exploded it in the name of "ye trueth" [*sic*]. Only three of the company were from Scrooby – William and Mary Brewster and William Bradford – and little more than a third of those on board came from Leyden – forty-one, to be exact, made up of seventeen men, ten women, and fourteen children.

The others, the great majority, were "Strangers", largely from London and south-eastern England. They were not Brownists; neither were they Separatists of any rival school. On the contrary, they were good members of the Church of England – not from reasoned choice or any strong conviction perhaps, but simply because they had been born and baptized in that faith. They were content, like most of us, to accept the beliefs handed down to them by their fathers... A few others belonged to the Puritan wing of the church, it appears, but most of them were as orthodox in their uncritical way as any Anglican bishop. They had no intention of breaking with their cultural past and religious faith. What they were seeking in the New World... was not spiritual salvation but economic opportunity, a chance to better their worldly lot, and for a time resisted all attempts to convert them to "ye trueth" [*sic*].[2]

> How awkward and tense this must have been, Lord! A mixed bag of passengers!
> Yet, how wonderful it is, that you love us while we are still sinners. You do not
> wait for anyone to deserve your love. Rather, you extend it to one and all – the
> whole crew, as it were! This leads me to pray today for Christians whose daily
> life, or working life, is spent among similar company. Bless them, I pray, as they
> endeavour to make a good witness.

---

1   A gunwale is the upper edge of a boat or ship. The word is derived from "gun walls", the fortified parts of a ship's body which help support guns or cannon.
2   From *Saints and Strangers*.

DO NOTHING FROM SELFISH AMBITION OR CONCEIT, BUT
IN HUMILITY COUNT OTHERS MORE SIGNIFICANT THAN
YOURSELVES.
(Philippians 2:3 *ESV*)

The passengers had one thing in common. All were lower class, "from the cottages and not the castles of England", a strong cohesive force at a time when society was still rigidly stratified, with rights and privileges concentrated at the top. There was not a drop of blue blood to be found anywhere among them in the *Mayflower*, as these Pilgrims were all too acutely aware from the poverty and other disabilities they suffered. They were of the common people and in conscious revolt against the aristocratic principle so called, a fact which seems to have escaped some of their descendants with their proofs of "blood" and pathetic interest in coats of arms.[1]

Heavenly Father, hear my prayers today for those around the world who suffer from class bias and prejudice, and whose status is regarded as lowly, or even worthless. I think, Lord, of cultures in which people are treated as second-class citizens simply by accident of birth, and whose lives are spent in poverty and deprivation. Be with those people, Lord, as they are often condemned to years of menial labour and hardship. May they know your loving presence.

---

1   From *Saints and Strangers*.

... I SAW THAT UNDER THE SUN THE RACE IS NOT TO THE SWIFT,
NOR THE BATTLE TO THE STRONG, NOR BREAD TO THE WISE,
NOR RICHES TO THE INTELLIGENT, NOR FAVOUR TO THOSE WITH
KNOWLEDGE, BUT TIME AND CHANCE HAPPEN TO THEM ALL. FOR
MAN DOES NOT KNOW HIS TIME.

(Ecclesiastes 9:11–12 *ESV*)

The Saints and Strangers [were not] the only two distinct and often antagonistic groups on board. A third consisted of the hired men, five in all, under contract to remain in the colony for a year. They were not regarded as settlers or members of the company, sharing neither the rights nor responsibilities of the latter. In addition to Alden, the cooper, there were two ordinary seamen and two master mariners, Thomas English, who was to captain the long boat or shallop[1] which the *Mayflower* was carrying between decks, and John Allerton... having been hired to return to Leyden and help bring over those left behind. It was a major blow a few months later when both master mariners died.[2]

> Lord of life and death, I pray for any today who are embarking on the road of bereavement. I pray for those whose loved ones have died, as they begin to try to come to terms with the "major blow" of a final parting. However strong one's faith, Lord, grief is still dreadful. In your mercy, please draw alongside those who need you in this way.

---

1   A light sailing boat used mainly for coastal fishing. It could also be used to transport supplies from larger, ocean-going vessels to the mainland.
2   From *Saints and Strangers*.

April 19th

FEARING THAT WE WOULD BE DASHED AGAINST THE ROCKS, THEY
DROPPED FOUR ANCHORS FROM THE STERN AND PRAYED...
(Acts 27:29)

The great Atlantic rollers swept seething and hissing across the streaming decks of the little ship. She shivered from stem to stern as the waves struck her. She climbed the giddy heights of one wave only to be slung dizzily down its slopes into dark chasms of water that threatened to swallow her up and sink her into the depths.

The Pilgrims were crowded down in the stifling air between decks. The hatches of the deck were closed. The boys and girls were flung about as the ship rolled and tossed in the waves. The gun port-holes were screwed tight. The dim yellow light of a lantern that hung from a beam, shone fitfully on the Pilgrims. Many were ill. The close air and the stench were poisonous. Yet the hatches could not be opened.

The Pilgrims heard the *Mayflower* creak and groan in every timber as she reeled before the storm. The sea crept in through the stringing planks, and washed sullenly across the floor, soaking their clothes and their luggage. There was a silence among them all as they heard a wrenching sound, as though the ship herself were breaking up.[1]

Lord, it is hard to read this account without one's thoughts turning to the dreadful experiences inflicted upon slaves in years gone by, as they were brutally transported from one country to another in horrendous conditions. Lord, in your mercy, forgive humankind for such atrocities; treating fellow human beings as mere objects in pursuit of wealth or power. Forgive me personally, I pray, for any occasions on which I have exploited anyone for my own advantage, especially if I have done so knowingly.

---

1   From *The Argonauts of Faith*.

> ... I AM WITH YOU; DO NOT BE DISMAYED, FOR I AM YOUR GOD. I
> WILL STRENGTHEN YOU AND HELP YOU; I WILL UPHOLD YOU WITH
> MY RIGHTEOUS RIGHT HAND.
> (Isaiah 41:10)

The main beam of the ship had been bowed and cracked by the storm. The beam was amidships. The captain examined it. He and his seamen could see at once that there was serious danger of the ship breaking up if her beam were wrenched so that it could not hold out the sides of the ship and keep her taut, and help her to resist the battering of the waves.

As the captain with serious face talked it over with his officers, Brewster and Bradford and some other Pilgrims joined the group.

"Would it not be better even now to turn back and sail for home?" suggested one of the Pilgrims.

"No," replied the captain, "that would be of no use. We are half-way across the Atlantic now. It is as far to go back as it is to go on. We must get this beam back in her place again."[1]

**Lord Jesus, be with those today whose "props" and "supports" are falling away.
Be with them especially if they feel they have reached a point of no return.**

Abide with me, fast falls the eventide;
The darkness deepens Lord, with me abide.
When other helpers fail and comforts flee,
Help of the helpless, oh, abide with me.[2]

---

1   From *The Argonauts of Faith*.
2   From Reverend Henry Francis Lyte's hymn "Abide With Me".

DO NOT EXPLOIT THE POOR BECAUSE THEY ARE POOR ...
(Proverbs 22:22)

There was a fourth and much larger group sharply set off from all the others – the indentured servants. These were not servants in our sense of the word. They were not housemaids, butlers, cooks, valets, or general flunkeys to wait upon the personal needs of the Pilgrims. On the contrary, they were brought along to do the heaviest kind of labour. They were to fell trees, hew timbers, build houses, clear fields, and plough them, tend crops, gather the harvest, and do whatever their masters ordered. During the period of their indenture, which usually ran for seven years, they were fed, clothed, and housed by their masters, but received no wages, being virtually slaves, and were frequently bought, sold, and hired out as such.

Eleven of the eighteen servants on board were strong young men, a sixth of the adult company. For the most part, they belonged to the Leyden group, which suggest that if the Saints were poor, the Strangers were still poorer... Among the Strangers only three had the means to transport bondslaves... In this servant group were four small waifs... poor orphans of London... dragged off quite as if they were debtors or criminals sentenced. Encouraged by the Lord Mayor and the Bishop of London, this was a favoured means of relieving the pressure of population in the poorer quarters of the city.[1]

> This is shocking, Lord – the Church complicit in the exploitation and suffering of the poor. Sadly, Lord, honesty compels us to admit that this has all-too-often been the case across the centuries. We have failed you by our cowardice and silence, and a strange reluctance, sometimes, to speak up for the marginalized. Lord of the Church, forgive your people when we have acted in ways contrary to the laws of love. Send your Holy Spirit upon your Church afresh.

---

1   From *Saints and Strangers*.

"THE LORD DOES NOT LOOK AT THE THINGS PEOPLE LOOK AT.
PEOPLE LOOK AT THE OUTWARD APPEARANCE, BUT THE LORD
LOOKS AT THE HEART."
(1 Samuel 16:7)

On the pitching, rolling vessel there was still another group and quite as important as any – the ship's officers and crew. The latter numbered thirty or more seamen, by all accounts an ungodly and intemperate lot, who worked under the sharp eye of a tough old bosun given to mighty oaths which, though usually lost on the "monkeys" in the rigging, always made the Saints wince. Hailing from Rotherhithe, Surrey, Jones was close to forty and a rough sea dog, as all skippers of the day had to be, but under his quarterdeck manner he was really a kindly and reasonable person, and a more human master than most.[1]

> Lord, help me not to judge by appearances! In your grace, you look upon the heart, and even though surface matters might not meet with your approval, you see the persona – and the potential – within. Thank you for such grace. Help me, today, to look for the best in those I meet.

---

1   From *Saints and Strangers.*

TWO ARE BETTER THAN ONE, BECAUSE THEY HAVE A GOOD RETURN
FOR THEIR LABOUR:
IF EITHER OF THEM FALLS DOWN, ONE CAN HELP THE OTHER UP.
BUT PITY ANYONE WHO FALLS AND HAS NO ONE TO HELP THEM UP.
(Ecclesiastes 4:9–10)

Under [Skipper Jones] were four mates and a master gunner. The first officer, John Clarke, a man of many adventures and always a good friend of the Pilgrims, had been in the New World at least twice before. On his last voyage… he had gone to Virginia with a shipload of cattle from Ireland. The other mates were Andrew Williamson, John Parker, and Robert Coffin, usually referred to as the "pilot". Though the Pilgrims never once mentioned his name, it has been discovered recently that there was a ship's doctor on board, Giles Heale,[1] who later had a profitable practice in London. Perhaps Bradford and his brethren had no confidence in him, preferring the ministrations and mysterious potions of their own "chirurgeon & physition" [sic], Deacon Samuel Fuller.[2]

Thank you, Heavenly Father, for your gracious gift of those who travel life's
journey with me – family, friends, neighbours. Thank you for what they bring to
that journey – their experiences, their skills, and their love and acceptance of me.
We may not always see eye-to-eye, but even that can be a valuable learning curve.
Thank you.

1   History has bestowed upon Giles Heale the title "The Mayflower Surgeon".
2   From *Saints and Strangers*.

A BRUISED REED HE WILL NOT BREAK, AND A SMOULDERING WICK
HE WILL NOT SNUFF OUT.

(Isaiah 42:3)

It was fortunate that one of the Pilgrims – who must have been a man of strong good sense – had brought with him a powerful jack-screw. They placed this under the beam, and, pulling at the lever that turned the screw, they at length forced the bent main-beam straight again. Having thrust the great timber back into its place, in order to make it double secure, they got a strong post; this they stood upon the lower deck, and forced the top end in under the cracked beam and lashed it into place.

They found, however, that the severe wrenching of the ship had opened cracks in her timbers through which the sea was leaking into the hull. They soaked oakum in tar and caulked the timbers with it – that is, they rammed the tarred oakum firmly in between the edges of the planks to keep the water from rushing into the ship.[1]

Redeeming God, you specialize in taking that which is broken and, in the eyes of many, damaged beyond repair. You lovingly and faithfully pick up the pieces. You refuse to write off those whose lives are cracked and hurting. In your kingdom of love, there is no such thing as a scrapheap. You are my God.

---

1   From *The Argonauts of Faith*.

... THE LORD DELIGHTS IN THOSE ... WHO PUT THEIR HOPE IN HIS
UNFAILING LOVE.
(Psalm 147:11)

They felt safer now; but their troubles were not at an end. The wind sank for a little; but it soon began to rage again. They dared not spread an inch of sail. Night followed day and day night, yet still they scudded before the tempest under bare masts. The wind shrieked continuously through the rigging. Wave after wave came chasing across the ocean, like wolves hunting the little ship, and then flung themselves greedily over her as though to swallow her up. But the dauntless *Mayflower* shook herself free again and again, and plunged away westward.

In the midst of all this din and turmoil one day there mingled strangely with the roar of the seas the first cries of a little baby boy. He was born there between the upper and lower deck of the *Mayflower*. His mother[1] was the wife of Stephen Hopkins. They baptized the baby, giving him the name Oceanus, because he was born on the Atlantic.[2][3]

> Oceanus Hopkins! How wonderful, Lord, that even in the midst of "troubles", you should offer this beautiful glimmer of hope, in the form of "the first cries of a little baby boy"! Lord, I do not dismiss the very real problems of those experiencing problems and difficulties. Nevertheless, hope remains and can prevail even when life is challenging. Grant glimmers of hope today, I pray!

---

1   Elizabeth.
2   Oceanus Hopkins (1620 – c.1626), the only child born on the *Mayflower*. Sadly, he died in America, aged six. His name, Oceanus, is the Latin for 'ocean'.
3   From *The Argonauts of Faith*.

BUT GOD SAID TO HIM,
"YOU FOOL! THIS VERY NIGHT YOUR LIFE WILL BE DEMANDED
FROM YOU. THEN WHO WILL GET WHAT YOU HAVE PREPARED FOR
YOURSELF?"
(Luke 12:20)

The *Mayflower* was now in mid-Atlantic and making steady headway. But as week after week dragged on with nothing to break the monotony of the voyage, tensions began to rise on the crowded ship – between Saints and Strangers, masters and servants, passengers and crew. The sailors loathed Christopher Martin[1] and all about him, and could not stomach the pious ways of the Leyden group, "cursing them dayly with grievous execrations" [*sic*]. One of their worst tormentors, a huge brawny seaman, used to taunt the weak and sick by saying that he expected to bury half of them at sea and "make merry with what they had". When they reproached him, no matter how gently, "he would curse & swear most bitterly". But retribution was swift in coming. Stricken himself one morning, this "proud and very profane yonge man" [*sic*] was dead by afternoon and his body was the first to go over the side, to the great astonishment of his wicked cronies, said Bradford, and with a most salutary effect, for they saw that it was "ye just hand of God upon him".[2]

Lord Jesus, I pray today for friends and relatives who do not know you as their Saviour. In your mercy, I ask you to convict them of their sins, and to lead them gently towards repentance. Holy Spirit, I pray that you would work in their hearts and minds as I name them before you now. Make haste to save them, Lord.

---

1   An excellent and hugely informative article about Christopher Martin and his involvement with the voyage is available on https://en.wikipedia.org/wiki/Christopher_Martin_(Mayflower_passenger). This explains why there was such resentment towards him, in greater detail than space here allows.

2   From *Saints and Strangers*.

Rescue the perishing; don't hesitate to step in and help.
If you say, "Hey, that's none of my business," will that get
you off the hook?
(Proverbs 24:11–12 *The Message*)

The weather changed as fierce storms came roaring out of the west. For days at a time it was impossible to carry a yard of sail, the ship drifting under bare poles, with the helmsman desperately trying to hold her into the wind, as she wallowed through mountainous seas, which often had her lying on her beam-ends. The pounding of heavy seas opened up many seams in the... superstructure, letting cascades of icy water down upon the ill and frightened passengers curled up in their narrow bunks below. Unable to endure it any longer in the stuffy hold, John Howland[1] came on deck one day and was immediately swept overboard. The ship happened to be trailing some of the topsail halyards, and Howland managed to get hold of these and hang on, "though he was sundrie fadomes under water" [*sic*], till he was pulled in with a boat-hook. He was "something ill with it, yet he lived many years after, and became a profitable member, both in church & commone wealth".[2]

> *Rescue the perishing,*
> *Care for the dying,*
> *Snatch them in pity from sin and the grave;*
> *Weep o'er the erring one,*
> *Lift up the fallen,*
> *Tell them of Jesus the mighty to save.*[3]

---

1   John Howland (c. 1592–1673) was an indentured servant aboard the *Mayflower*.
2   From *Saints and Strangers*.
3   From Fanny Crosby's hymn "Rescue the Perishing".

AFTER FORTY DAYS NOAH OPENED A WINDOW HE HAD MADE IN THE ARK AND
SENT OUT A RAVEN, AND IT KEPT FLYING BACK AND FORTH UNTIL THE WATER
HAD DRIED UP FROM THE EARTH. THEN HE SENT OUT A DOVE TO SEE IF THE
WATER HAD RECEDED FROM THE SURFACE OF THE GROUND. BUT THE DOVE
COULD FIND NOWHERE TO PERCH BECAUSE THERE WAS WATER OVER ALL THE
SURFACE OF THE EARTH; SO IT RETURNED TO NOAH IN THE ARK. HE REACHED
OUT HIS HAND AND TOOK THE DOVE AND BROUGHT IT BACK TO HIMSELF IN THE
ARK. HE WAITED SEVEN MORE DAYS AND AGAIN SENT OUT THE DOVE FROM THE
ARK. WHEN THE DOVE RETURNED TO HIM IN THE EVENING, THERE IN ITS BEAK
WAS A FRESHLY PLUCKED OLIVE LEAF! THEN NOAH KNEW THAT THE WATER HAD
RECEDED FROM THE EARTH. HE WAITED SEVEN MORE DAYS AND SENT THE DOVE
OUT AGAIN, BUT THIS TIME IT DID NOT RETURN TO HIM.

(Genesis 8:6–12)

Eight weeks had now gone by since they had sailed… out of Plymouth Harbour. For many days they had been battened down below hatches, crowded close together in a little wooden ship far too small either for their number or for the perils of a journey across the Atlantic. Then one of the men… fell ill. He swiftly became worse and died. They buried him at sea, in the midst of the tossing waters. The Pilgrims felt as though everything was against them; and some of the bravest began to lose heart. "Being pestered nine weeks in this leaking, unwholesome ship, lying wet in their cabins; most of them grew very weak, and weary of the sea."

Three more days passed by. They were now able to be on deck. Suddenly the cry came from one of the clearest-sighted sailors, "Land ho!"

Immediately the Pilgrims rushed to the bows and strained their eyes westward. There, sure enough, was land. It was flat, like the country [Holland] to which they had been accustomed. But it was covered with trees…

"What bit of coast is this?" the Pilgrims asked Captain Jones.

"I think," said he, "that this is the eastern side of Cape Cod."

The faces of some of the leaders among the Pilgrims would grow serious when they heard this, for they were hoping to land on a far better part of the coast called Manhattan, by the river Hudson. Cape Cod was some distance north of Manhattan.[1]

What a voyage! Lord, there will come that Great Day when we safely cross
Jordan and arrive in that heavenly land! When we all get to heaven – what a
time of rejoicing that will be! Thank you, Heavenly Father, for such a wonderful
prospect, when this life is over and the life to come has come. Thank you.

---

1   From *The Argonauts of Faith*.

MY PEOPLE WILL LIVE IN PEACEFUL DWELLING PLACES, IN SECURE
HOMES, IN UNDISTURBED PLACES OF REST.
(Isaiah 32:18)

Their course had brought them to the wrist of Cape Cod, apparently to a point off the high bluffs at Truro. The ship stood in toward shore, but after a conference with the skipper they tacked about and stood off to the south'ard, for the Pilgrims were still ostensibly bent on finding "some place aboute Hudson's river for their habitation" [sic]. Running close to shore, they followed this course till noon, when, at the sharp elbow of the Cape... they suddenly "fell amongst deangerous should and roring breakers" [sic]. They had stumbled into... treacherous waters... The *Mayflower* seemed to be "in great danger, & ye wind shrinking upon them withal" [sic], the helm was put hard over and they headed back up the coast, "happy to get out of those dangers" before nightfall. With a gentle breeze blowing, the ship lay to in the open sea all night, and early the next morning – sixty-six days out of Plymouth, ninety-eight out of Southampton, almost four months out of Delft Haven – the Pilgrims rounded the curved tip of the Cape, into what is now Princetown harbour, as fine and fair as any on the continent, large enough to shelter a fleet of a thousand sail.[1]

Lord, how tricky and how difficult the journey "home" can sometimes be;
the wanderer looking to return to Jesus after years away. How many obstacles
and disappointments the devil will place in that person's way – diversions,
distractions, and disappointments. Lord Jesus, please guide such wanderers
safely into harbour. Be with them and honour their intention to repent.

Softly and tenderly Jesus is calling...
Calling, O sinner, come home.[2]

---

1   From *Saints and Strangers*.
2   From Will Lamartine Thompson's hymn.

I WILL GIVE THANKS TO YOU, LORD, WITH ALL MY HEART...
(Psalm 9:1)

They arrived at Cape Cod[1]... and being brought safe to land, they fell upon their knees, and blessed the God of heaven, who had brought them over the vast and furious ocean, and delivered them from many perils and miseries...

They made the land... and on the same day they landed 15 or 16 men well-armed, to procure wood and reconnoitre the place. They found neither house nor person; but laded their boat with juniper (red cedar).[2]

Teach me to list today, Lord, those things for which I can give you grateful thanks. Help me to note the priority of the Pilgrims, who "blessed the God of heaven" before they set about their work. May I be found to do likewise.

---

1   So named by Bartholomew Gosnold (1571–1607), English explorer who visited that shoreline in 1602 and caught "great store of codfish". Gosnold led the first recorded European expedition to Cape Cod.
2   From *Chronicles of the Pilgrim Fathers*.

GOD CALLED THE DRY GROUND "LAND," AND THE GATHERED
WATERS HE CALLED "SEAS." AND GOD SAW THAT IT WAS GOOD.
(Genesis 1:10)

As the anchor went down with a rattle of chains and the decks under foot became stable again, "no marvell if they were thus joyefull, seeing wise Seneca[1] was so affected with sailing a few miles on ye coast of his owne Italy that he affirmed he had rather remain twentie years on his way by land than pass by sea to any place in a short time, so tedious and dreadfull was ye same" [*sic*].[2]

Each to their own, Lord! Some prefer the sea; others prefer dry ground! Thank you, Heavenly Father, for the precious gift of diversity, without which this would be a very boring existence. Help me to appreciate the differences I see in others, and the way in which those differences can enrich my life.

---

1   Seneca the Younger (c. 4 BC–AD 65), Lucius Annaeus Seneca, Roman stoic philosopher, statesman, and dramatist.
2   From *Saints and Strangers*.

... THESE PIONEERS WHO BLAZED THE WAY...
(Hebrews 12:1 *The Message*)

Some of the Pilgrims were falling ill with scurvy and other diseases, through being cramped so long in between decks, and through lack of fresh vegetables and other food and water...

With a splash the anchor was dropped. The Pilgrims fell on their knees and said their prayers of thanks to God who had brought them safely over the vast waste of waters through the tempest. They had been sixty-five days crossing the Atlantic Ocean. It was... the dawn of a new day for freedom in all the world.

The great crossing was ended. But the end of the voyage was only the beginning of the adventure.

All the past we leave behind;
We debouch upon a newer, mightier
World, varied world;
Fresh and strong the world we seize,
World of labour and the march,
Pioneers! O Pioneers!
Till with sound of trumpet,
Far, far off the daybreak call – hark! How
Loud and clear I hear it wind;
Swift! To the head of the army! – swift!
Spring to your places,
Pioneers! Pioneers![1] [2]

Thank you, Lord, for those whom you have gifted as pioneers – those who blaze the trail in church life, those who seek out and create openings. Theirs can sometimes be a thankless task – a lonely one, even – as they break new ground. Grant them courage and vision as they plan to extend your kingdom in creative ways.

---

1   Extracted from Walt Whitman's much longer poem "Pioneers! O Pioneers!" Walt Whitman (1819–92), American poet, essayist, and journalist. He greatly admired the American spirit of pioneering.

2   From *The Argonauts of Faith*.

May 3rd

So God created the great creatures of the sea and every
living thing with which the water teems and that moves
about in it, according to their kinds ...
(Genesis 1:21)

The Pilgrims, as they looked out from the deck of the *Mayflower* to the coast, were glad because the perils of the tempest were over, and the horrors of the long voyage in the dark between decks had passed.

The boys, gazing out over the bulwarks, saw that their ship was floating safely on the quiet waters of a splendid natural harbour. There was room for all the navies of the world of that day to come to anchor in Cape Cod Harbour. Outside glittered the wider waters of Cape Cod Bay running away south and west as far as eye could see.

Suddenly a boy saw a curious fountain of water rise from the sea in a white spray, and fall back into the water; then another and another went up.

"The whales are spouting," said the sailors.

The Pilgrims and the sailors were very sorry that they had no whaling harpoons with them, for they could have hunted and killed some of the giant whales and boiled down the blubber. Thus they could have made oil to send home to England – enough to pay over and over again for all the cost of the voyage in the *Mayflower*. They reckoned that the whales that they saw would have brought them over three thousand pounds' worth of oil.[1]

Not quite a modern, politically correct response to the sight of those majestic
whales, Lord! However, as this is a prayer book and not a political manual, I
shall simply thank you today for the astonishing wonders of nature and creation.
These speak of your marvellous handiwork. Help me to appreciate what I see all
around me today – probably not spouting whales, but plenty to admire – and to
praise you. You are my Creator God!

---

1   From *The Argonauts of Faith*.

ONCE SAFELY ON SHORE, WE FOUND OUT THAT THE ISLAND WAS
CALLED MALTA. THE ISLANDERS SHOWED US UNUSUAL KINDNESS.
THEY BUILT A FIRE AND WELCOMED US ALL BECAUSE IT WAS
RAINING AND COLD.

(Acts 28:1–2)

Before we pass on, let the reader, with me, make a pause, and seriously consider this poor people's present condition, the more to be raised up to admiration of God's goodness towards them in their preservation; for being now passed the vast ocean, and a sea of troubles before them in their preparation, they had no friends to welcome them, no inns to entertain or refresh them, no houses, much less towns, to repair to seek for succour. The barbarians that Paul the apostle fell amongst in his shipwreck, at the isle Melita,[1] showed him no small kindness, Acts xxviii., but these savage barbarians, when they met with them (as after will appear), were readier to fill their sides full of arrows, than otherwise.[2]

> Thank you so much, Lord, for those whom you have gifted with the special grace
> of generous hospitality; those who gladly open their homes to welcome people
> in need of lodging, food, and company, counting it no inconvenience. Thank you
> too for those who are sensitive to the needs of others; those who invite students
> home for hot meals, or who take the time and trouble to invite lonely people for
> dinner, making friends of strangers. Bless them in this lovely ministry.

---

1   Malta.

2   From *Chronicles of the Pilgrim Fathers*.

O GIVE THANKS UNTO THE LORD, FOR HE IS GOOD: FOR HIS MERCY
ENDURETH FOR EVER. LET THE REDEEMED OF THE LORD SAY SO,
WHOM HE HATH REDEEMED FROM THE HAND OF THE ENEMY;
AND GATHERED THEM OUT OF THE LANDS, FROM THE EAST, AND
FROM THE WEST, FROM THE NORTH, AND FROM THE SOUTH. THEY
WANDERED IN THE WILDERNESS IN A SOLITARY WAY; THEY FOUND
NO CITY TO DWELL IN. HUNGRY AND THIRSTY, THEIR SOUL FAINTED
IN THEM. THEN THEY CRIED UNTO THE LORD IN THEIR TROUBLE
AND HE DELIVERED THEM OUT OF THEIR DISTRESSES.
(Psalm 107:1–6 KJV)

What could they see but a hideous and desolate wilderness, full of wild beasts and wild men? And what multitudes of them there were, they then knew not; neither could they, as it were, go up to the top of Pisgah, to view from this wilderness a more goodly country to feed their hopes; for which way soever they turned their eyes (save upward to heaven), they could have little solace or content in respect of any outward object... All things stand in appearance with a weather-beaten face, and the whole country full of woods and thickets, represented a wild and savage hue; if they looked behind them, there was the mighty ocean which they had passed, and was now as a main bar and gulf to separate them from all the civil parts of the world...

Ought not, and may not the children of these fathers rightly say, our fathers were Englishmen, which came over this great ocean, and were ready to perish in this wilderness; but they cried unto the Lord, and he heard their voice, and looked on their adversity. Let them therefore praise the Lord, because he is good, and his mercy endureth for ever; yea, let them who have been redeemed of the Lord, show how he hath delivered them from the hand of the oppressor.[1]

Gracious God, how lovely and how easy it would be, if this life was all sweetness and light! It is not, however, not by any means, and we need you in our times of wandering – our desert experiences, as it were. I thank you this morning that you do indeed look upon us in days of adversity. As you were with the Pilgrims in their season of difficulty, I pray you will be with your people today, wherever and however they might be struggling. May they too sense your mercy in their midst.

---

1   From *Chronicles of the Pilgrim Fathers*.

"Be still, and know that I am God ..."
(Psalm 46:10)

In the year 1620, divers godly Christians of our English nation, in the north of England, being studious for reformation ... entered into covenant to walk with God, and one with another, in the enjoyment of the ordinances of God, according to the primitive pattern in the word of God. By finding by experience, they could not peaceably enjoy their own liberty in their native country, without offence to others that were differently minded, they took up thoughts of removing themselves and their families.[1] [2]

> **Lord of my days, teach me to pause, to "be still", sometimes, before moving forward. Release me from perpetual motion! Teach me the benefit and worth of doing so, in order that my soul may catch up with my body.[3]**

---

1 I have inserted this excerpt here, at this stage of the general narrative, in order to provide some sort of "interlude" for personal reflection and devotion. The Pilgrims have sailed the seas, and have landed in America. This offers us each the opportunity to reflect upon our own pilgrimage with God, from when that journey first began, and why it commenced, to where (and how) we find ourselves this day. These reflections, placed here for that specific purpose, will enable us to ponder, to consolidate spiritual matters, and then to continue. My prayer is that you will find such a "pause" beneficial. Sometimes, we look back in order to look forward! I will use the next few pages to recap, almost as a resting place along the way.

2 From *The Pilgrim Fathers at Plymouth August and September 1620*, published by City of Plymouth, 1957.

3 You are invited to link this prayer with the pages that will follow.

NEVER BE LACKING IN ZEAL, BUT KEEP YOUR SPIRITUAL
FERVOUR, SERVING THE LORD.
(Romans 12:11)

Not only did [the Pilgrims] want to carve out a colony in the new world where they could live as they liked – they wished to proselytize. They had "which was not the least, a great hope and inward zeal… for the propagating and advancement of the gospel of the Kingdom of Christ in those remote parts of the world."[1] [2]

Lord, as I pause to reflect, help me to include this question as part of my personal meditations: do I have enough zeal for you, and for your kingdom? How am I doing, Lord? Speak to my heart, I pray, as I wait upon you, and release any latent passion which might currently lie dormant. Thank you for an opportunity to quietly consider important spiritual questions such as this one.

---

1 See Footnotes 1 & 3, May 6th.
2 From *The Pilgrim Fathers at Plymouth.*

TEST ME, LORD, AND TRY ME, EXAMINE MY HEART AND MY MIND...
(Psalm 26:2)

At Plymouth... the *Speedwell* was thoroughly examined. No specific trouble was found, beyond what the shipwrights described as "a general weakness". This examination took time... and this time the *Mayflower* sailed alone. The *Speedwell* returned to London with her unwilling master and those for whom the *Mayflower* had no room – about a sixth of the expedition.[1]

Heavenly Father, in these "interlude" days of contemplation,[2] I pray for your gentle and gracious examination of my spiritual life, my relationship with you. As "the *Speedwell* was thoroughly examined", may it also be that I welcome your inspection of my life as a Christian. Help me, I pray, to discern your voice in this context. Holy Spirit, speak to me and advise me of anything that may need to be jettisoned and left behind if I am to move forward and keep going as a follower of Jesus.

Search me, O God, and know my heart today,
Try me, O Saviour, know my thoughts, I pray;
See if there be some wicked way in me;
Cleanse me from every sin, and set me free.[3]

---

1   From *The Pilgrim Fathers at Plymouth*.
2   See Footnotes 1 & 3, May 6ᵀʰ.
3   From James E. Orr's hymn "Search Me, O God".

THEN SAMUEL TOOK A STONE AND SET IT UP BETWEEN MIZPAH
AND SHEN. HE NAMED IT EBENEZER, SAYING, "THUS FAR
THE LORD HAS HELPED US."

(1 Samuel 7:12)

The two ships turned back and limped into Plymouth...

Plymouth... became an important place in the memories of the Pilgrims. It was first of all a place of haven after danger, a place where they were "kindly used and courteously entertained" by people of much the same opinion as themselves – one last place of comfort and familiarity on a voyage to the unknown. Plymouth was also the testing-place of many of them. About twenty persons had to turn back, for whom there was no room – the doubters, those whose courage failed them – "either out of some discontente or fear they conceived of ye ille success of ye voyage, seeing so many crosses befallen" [sic], and those with large families of young children accompanying them, who had already tested to the full the conditions they were likely to get on the voyage. Plymouth to some must have been a place of heart-searching and disappointment. To others, about whose constancy there was no doubt, a place of strengthening of purpose.[1]

Lord, as I walk this earthly pathway, there are certain places along the route that have come to carry a special spiritual significance – a particular church, maybe, or the house in which I grew up; a country or a town, perhaps, where I have felt your loving touch. I thank you for such locations – a walk in the woods, or a scene in nature, all conducive to the edification of my soul. Thank you for your grace in meeting me in such places and at such times. In these days of reflection, as I retrace some of my footsteps, I am reminded of your great faithfulness over many years. Thank you for my important places.

---

1   From *The Pilgrim Fathers at Plymouth*.

LET YOUR SERVANT RETURN, THAT I MAY DIE IN MY OWN TOWN
NEAR THE TOMB OF MY FATHER AND MOTHER.
(2 Samuel 19:37)

Plymouth stayed in their minds, long after the *Mayflower* had put out to sea and headed westward… When the Pilgrims reached New England… they settled in a place called Thieves' Harbour[1]… The "Thieves Harbour" name disappeared, but the Pilgrims, although none of them were West Country men, instead of taking some nostalgic place-name from their own native north or east, kept to the name of "Plymouth". This kinship with the old Plymouth persisted.[2] [3]

> *When we asunder part,*
> *It gives us inward pain;*
> *But we shall still be joined in heart,*
> *And hope to meet again.*[4]

The ties of home, Lord! How strong they can be! Likewise, the privilege of lovely memories of one's home town and district, with all its comfortable familiarity. Heavenly Father, as I conclude these few days of reflection, I give thanks for that place I call home. By the same token, though, I ask you to help me in my resolution to serve you in the future. Grant me that grace whereby I may move forward in obedience, even if it means leaving my comfort zones and loved ones.

---

1   A bay close to Cape Cod had previously been called "Thievish Harbour", on account of the fact that "one of the wild men" with whom previous sailors had come into contact "stole a harping iron (harpoon) from them" there.
2   From *The Pilgrim Fathers at Plymouth*.
3   This page concludes this brief "interlude" – a resting-place on our journey, as it were – a time to take stock, to consider one's destination, before pressing on. I hope this has been helpful.
4   From John Fawcett's hymn "Blest Be the Tie That Binds".

IN THOSE DAYS WHEN THE NUMBER OF DISCIPLES WAS
INCREASING, THE HELLENISTIC JEWS AMONG THEM COMPLAINED
AGAINST THE HEBRAIC JEWS BECAUSE THEIR WIDOWS WERE
BEING OVERLOOKED IN THE DAILY DISTRIBUTION OF FOOD. SO
THE TWELVE GATHERED ALL THE DISCIPLES TOGETHER AND SAID,
"IT WOULD NOT BE RIGHT FOR US TO NEGLECT THE MINISTRY OF
THE WORD OF GOD IN ORDER TO WAIT ON TABLES. BROTHERS AND
SISTERS, CHOOSE SEVEN MEN FROM AMONG YOU WHO ARE KNOWN
TO BE FULL OF THE SPIRIT AND WISDOM. WE WILL TURN THIS
RESPONSIBILITY OVER TO THEM AND WILL GIVE OUR ATTENTION
TO PRAYER AND THE MINISTRY OF THE WORD." THIS PROPOSAL
PLEASED THE WHOLE GROUP. THEY CHOSE STEPHEN, A MAN FULL
OF FAITH AND OF THE HOLY SPIRIT; ALSO PHILIP, PROCORUS,
NICANOR, TIMON, PARMENAS, AND NICOLAS FROM ANTIOCH,
A CONVERT TO JUDAISM. THEY PRESENTED THESE MEN TO THE
APOSTLES, WHO PRAYED AND LAID THEIR HANDS ON THEM.

(Acts 6:1–6)

As they talked of the future, one man said that they must do this thing, and one man another; some were for going off on their own account and dividing up. But, as the leaders heard this talk, they knew that in a wild land, in which savage Indians lived, it would be death to divide. They must stay together; and they must work together. Therefore, they said to one another, "We must have a government."

But what government could they have – just a hundred people, and only thirty-four of them grown men? King James and his Government were three thousand miles away across the trackless ocean. So they made up their minds that they would themselves form a government in which all would freely join together. It was simple and easy to do this; yet the hour when, in the cabin of the *Mayflower*, the heroic thirty-four men signed the paper to say that they joined in one commonwealth was a great birthday of what men call "democracy" – "government of the people, by the people, for the people."[1]

Lord of the Church, my thoughts and prayers today turn towards questions
of church government and leadership. I pray for any forthcoming parochial
elections, and for those whose names are under consideration. Bless and guide
any such deliberations, so that the right people are elected, according to your
will. I pray for my own church in this respect.

1   From *The Argonauts of Faith*.

AND I WILL GIVE YOU PASTORS ACCORDING TO MINE HEART, WHICH
SHALL FEED YOU WITH KNOWLEDGE AND UNDERSTANDING.
(Jeremiah 3:15 *KJV*)

Just as in a scout troop or a football or a baseball team there must always be someone who is in authority, and can tell others what to do – so the Pilgrims knew that... they also must have one man to be head of them all. So they elected John Carver[1] their Governor for the first year.[2]

> Lord God, my prayers today are for leaders – male and female – of major
> Christian denominations. They carry huge responsibilities, as well as enjoying
> great privileges. Strengthen them, I pray, and guard them against temptations,
> that they may lead well, and successfully. I pray especially for the senior leader(s)
> of my own denomination. Bless them and honour them. Where I see the name
> "John Carver" here, I insert the names of church leaders for whom I pray today.

---

1   John Carver (before 1584–1621).
2   From *The Argonauts of Faith*.

"CHOOSE FOR YOUR TRIBES WISE, UNDERSTANDING, AND
EXPERIENCED MEN, AND I WILL APPOINT THEM AS YOUR HEADS."
(Deuteronomy 1:13 *ESV*)

Another matter had to be attended to before the historic first Pilgrim assembly adjourned. As it was now a "civill body politik" [*sic*], the company had to have officers duly authorized to act and speak for it. For the time being it was decided that one would suffice – a governor, to be chosen by popular election of the freemen, just as it had long been the custom of the Saints to choose a pastor. Apparently there was no electioneering by the rival factions, and the unanimous choice fell upon John Carver, "a godly man & well approved amongst them," whose real title to fame is not that he was the Pilgrims' first governor, but rather the first colonial governor in the whole New World, perhaps the first of history, to be named by themselves in a free election. The pattern set here on the *Mayflower* on the day of her arrival continued throughout the life of the Plymouth colony, which from first to last chose to govern itself through officers named at regular annual elections, though it should be remembered that narrow limitations upon the right to vote denied many a voice in the direction of affairs.[1]

I pray, Lord, for the process of political democracy, wherever it is in place around the world. I thank you for it, as imperfect as it is. I pray for fairness and justice in elections. My prayers are also with those nations who know little of such electoral freedom; people whose lives are lived under totalitarian regimes. I pray for the many who are still, even today, denied a voice. Lord, have mercy.

---

1   From *Saints and Strangers*.

May 14th

I WILL BE LIKE THE DEW TO ISRAEL; HE WILL BLOSSOM LIKE A LILY.
LIKE A CEDAR OF LEBANON
HE WILL SEND DOWN HIS ROOTS; HIS YOUNG SHOOTS WILL GROW.
HIS SPLENDOUR WILL BE LIKE AN OLIVE TREE, HIS FRAGRANCE LIKE
A CEDAR OF LEBANON.
(Hosea 14:5–6)

The first party ashore consisted of sixteen armed men, under orders to reconnoitre the neighbourhood, and bring back badly needed supplies of wood and water. With muskets primed and ready, the party marched inland several miles, for enough to learn that they were on a slender hook of land between Cape Cod and the ocean. It reminded them of the sand dune country in parts of Holland. Only this was better, they reported, for it had a topsoil of "excellent black earth", and was well wooded, though in most spots "open and without underwood, fit either to go or ride in". They met no Indians and, more surprising, saw no signs of habitation. Nor did they find any fresh water. Returning soon to the beach, they pushed off for the *Mayflower* with a boatload of juniper, which, as it burned on the comforting fires, "smelled very sweet and strong", like frankincense itself to those who had lived for months in the smelly hold.[1]

> Thank you, Lord, for this lovely word-picture of your life-changing grace, in today's Bible text. Thank you that your love enters our lives as a sweet fragrance, refreshing our souls against what is sometimes the stagnant condition of a fallen world. Enable me to sense your fragrance this day, in the midst of the mundane and ordinary, for that will do me good.

---

1   From *Saints and Strangers*.

THE LORD WILL GUIDE YOU ALWAYS; HE WILL SATISFY YOUR NEEDS
IN A SUN-SCORCHED LAND...
(Isaiah 58:11)

Their shallop being ready, they set out a second time for a more full discovery of this place, especially a place that seemed to be an opening as they went into the... harbour some two or three leagues off, which the master judged to be a river; about thirty of them went out on this second discovery, the master of the ship going with them; but upon the more exact discovery thereof, they found it to be no harbour for ships, but only for boats. There they also found two... houses covered with mats, and sundry... implements in them; but the people ran away and could not be seen. Also there they found... corns and beans of various colours...

Having thus discovered this place, it was controverted amongst them what to do, touching their abode and settling there. Some thought it best for many reasons to abide there

1st   Because of the convenience of the harbour for boats, though not for ships.

2nd   There was good corn ground ready to their hands, as was seen by experience in the goodly corn it yielded, which again would agree with the ground, and be natural seed for the same.

3rd   Cape Cod was likely to be a place for good fishing, for they daily saw great whales of the best kind for oil.

4th   The place was likely to be healthful, secure, and defensible.[1]

> Heavenly Father, at times of important decision-making in my life, bless me with your guidance. Thank you for the gift of common sense and intelligence, whereby I may weigh up all the factors to hand, pray, and then make my best decision. Correct me, I pray, if I get things wrong.

---

1   From *Chronicles of the Pilgrim Fathers*.

FOR THE LORD YOUR GOD IS BRINGING YOU INTO A GOOD LAND...
(Deuteronomy 8:7)

It has been supposed by some that our ancestors were not fortunate in the selection of their plantation, and that they would have found better land on the other side of the bay. But this is a mistake, for no part of Massachusetts could be better suited to their condition. Had they settled down upon a hard and heavy, though rich soil, what could they have done with it? They had no ploughs, nor beasts of the plough, and yet their chief subsistence was to be derived from the ground. The Plymouth lands were free, light, and easy of tillage, but hard enough for poor pilgrims to dig and plant. And there is perhaps no place in New England where Indian corn could have been raised to better advantage with the same labour. The land yielded well, being new and unworn. And for fish, they could scarcely have been better supplied; and the forests were as well supplied with game as elsewhere... And, moreover, Divine Providence seems to have opened the door to the pilgrims at Plymouth by removing the native inhabitants, so as to make a place for their settlement there.[1]

My prayers today, Heavenly Father, are for farmers, farm labourers, and agricultural workers. How often they are taken for granted, when fruits and vegetables just seem to appear in supermarkets! Thank you for those who work so hard to produce good food. Theirs can often be a precarious existence, Lord, with profits cut to the finest margins. Help them, I pray, and especially those organizations seeking to improve the lot of farmers all over the world, working for a fairer market-place.

---

1   From *Chronicles of the Pilgrim Fathers*.

HE GUIDES THE HUMBLE IN WHAT IS RIGHT AND
TEACHES THEM HIS WAY.
(Psalm 25:9)

Surprise is sometimes expressed that the attempt at self-government on a Puritan basis… proved successful in New England. The explanation is very simple…

It was the exceptional character of the men who founded New England that made their experiment of self-government succeed… But there was something about these men… which must be kept in mind if we would understand their history, and the development of the United States, upon which they made so marked an impress.

Modern English writers often criticise their countrymen for an unwillingness to accept ideas from other nations, explaining by this fact many of the defects which appear in the England of today. Whether this criticism is just or not, as regards recent times, the reader can determine for himself. It certainly does not apply to the… stretch of years… in which were laid the foundations of the American Republic. This whole period was marked by the phenomenal exhibition of two human faculties…

One was a many-sided, indomitable energy, the other was an unparalleled power of assimilation.[1]

Oh, Lord! Help me, I pray, to be ever-willing to assimilate new ideas and concepts. Preserve me from any form of complacency, or even xenophobia, whereby my thoughts become stuck in a rut. Teach me that grace of never being defensive when unfamiliar concepts are aired. Grant me a teachable spirit.

---

1 From *The Puritan in Holland, England and America.*

INSTRUCT THE WISE AND THEY WILL BE WISER STILL; TEACH THE
RIGHTEOUS AND THEY WILL ADD TO THEIR LEARNING.
(Proverbs 9:9)

The English Reformers take their Calvinistic theology from Geneva, the Puritans take their system of church government from Scotland or Holland, and the nation at large takes from the Netherlands its lessons in manufactures, agriculture, and commerce.

It would be strange, indeed, if a people so receptive in every other department had not exhibited the same spirit when it came to the question of social, legal, and political reforms...

Turning now to New England, we find this receptive faculty equally developed among her thinkers; and here they fortunately ruled the State. These men loved their native land, but they did not love its limitations. They left their homes just at a time when the dwarfing, crippling, insular English spirit had temporarily lost its force. Hence it was that reforms which were impossible in the mother country... became settled facts in America...

Such were the Puritan settlers of New England... exceptional in their willingness to entertain new ideas. Their latter characteristic has, however, been little noticed by historians, who usually regard them as transplanted Englishmen carrying English institutions to America.[1]

Lord, I can but repeat yesterday's prayer, asking that, day-by-day, I will keep my heart and mind open to learning more about life and love: how to live, and how to love!

---

1   From *The Puritan in Holland, England and America.*

"REMEMBER THE SABBATH DAY BY KEEPING IT HOLY."
(Exodus 20:8)

No work was done [on the] Sabbath, which was quietly spent on board [the *Mayflower*] in prayer and meditation. The Pilgrims had much to be thankful for, and one and all, Saints and Strangers alike, "fell upon their knees & blessed ye God of heaven, who had brought them over ye vast & furious ocean, and delivered them from all ye periles & miseries thereof, againe to set their feete on ye firme and stable earth, their proper elemente" [*sic*]. Yet as they looked about them, the prospect had little to assure even the most sanguine and stout of heart. It was clear from a casual glance or two that they had not come to an earthly paradise... All things bore "a weatherbeten face, and ye whole countrie, full of woods & thickets, represented a wild & savage heiw" [*sic*].[1]

Almighty God, in an ever-changing world, when trading standards vary and High Street opening hours encroach upon any possibility of a day of rest, I pray for Christian employees who are sometimes obliged to work when they would rather be at church or at home with their families. Help them through what can sometimes be a tricky modern maze, I pray. Grant them wisdom and the ability to make a credible witness in a secular setting.

---

1   From *Saints and Strangers*.

MAY THE FAVOUR OF THE LORD OUR GOD REST ON US; ESTABLISH
THE WORK OF OUR HANDS FOR US – YES, ESTABLISH
THE WORK OF OUR HANDS.
(Psalm 90:17)

The women were early put ashore under an armed guard to do the family "wash, as they had great need". While they were beating, scrubbing, and rinsing heaps of dirty clothes and bedding, the children ran wildly up and down the beach under the watchful eye of the sentries. The men brought in the long boat stowed between decks on the *Mayflower* and beached her for repairs, for she had been badly battered and bruised by the storms at sea, and her seams had been badly opened up with "the people's lying in her". As a gang went to work on the shallop, under the direction of Francis Eaton,[1] the ship's carpenter from Bristol, the rest prowled the beach and tidal flats in search of shellfish. Ravenous for fresh food, they made a great feast on tender soft-shell clams and succulent young quahogs[2] ... and also put away many large mussels, "very fat," which was a grave error, as many another visitor to the Cape has since discovered, for the mussels made them deathly sick.[3]

Times may have changed, Lord, regarding the distribution of jobs by gender, but the fact remains that the work still has to be done! Thank you for the privilege of employment and all its benefits. The alternative, Lord – the sheer boredom and misery of unemployment and having nothing much to do all day – is awful, and I pray for those whose days are empty. Guide them back into the workplace.

---

1 Francis Eaton (c. 1596–1633), a *Mayflower* passenger.
2 A hard-shelled clam.
3 From *Saints and Strangers*.

FOR LOOK, THE WICKED BEND THEIR BOWS; THEY SET THEIR
ARROWS AGAINST THE STRINGS TO SHOOT FROM THE SHADOWS AT
THE UPRIGHT IN HEART.
(Psalm 11:2)

They divided their company... some on shore and some in the boat, where they saw... Indians... and so they ranged up and down all that day; but found no people, nor any place they liked, as fit for their settlement; and that night they on shore met with their boat at a certain creek where they make a barricado[1] of boughs and logs, for their lodging that night, and, being weary, betook themselves to rest (this is thought to be a place called Namskeket).[2] The next morning, about five o'clock (seeking guidance and protection from God by prayer), and refreshing themselves, in way of preparation, to persist on their intended expedition, some of them carried their arms down to the boat, having laid them up in their coats from the moisture of the weather; but others said they would not carry theirs until they went themselves. But presently all of a sudden, about the dawning of the day, they heard a great and strange cry, and one of their company being on board, came hastily in, and cried, Indians! Indians! and withal, their arrows came flying amongst them; on which all their men ran with speed to recover their arms; as by God's good providence they did. In the meantime some of those that were ready, discharged two muskets at them, and two more stood ready at the entrance of their rendezvous, but were commanded not to shoot until they could take full aim at them; and the other two charged again with all speed, for there were only four that had arms there, and defended the barricado which was first assaulted.[3]

> **Lord, my prayers today are with Christian missionaries whose vocation leads them into dangerous or even life-threatening situations. I pray, too, for those nations where a Christian influence has not always been sensitive or as positive as it should have been, and where people may have suffered as a result. Forgive such intrusions, Lord, and grant your people sensitivity.**

And from the ground there blossoms red
Life that shall endless be.[4]

---

1   Archaic form of "barricade".
2   Near Namskeket Creek, Massachusetts.
3   From *Chronicles of the Pilgrim Fathers*.
4   From George Matheson's hymn "O Love That Wilt Not Let Me Go".

IN THE FEAR OF THE LORD IS STRONG CONFIDENCE...
(Proverbs 14:26 *KJV*)

The cry of the Indians was dreadful ("Woach, woach, ha hach woach"),[1] especially when they saw their men run out of their rendezvous towards the shallop, to recover their arms; the Indians wheeling about upon them; but some running out with coats of mail, and cuttle-axes in their hands, they soon recovered their arms, and discharged amongst them, and soon stayed their violence. Notwithstanding there was a lusty man, and no less valiant, stood behind a tree within half a musket shot, and let his arrows fly amongst them; he was seen to shoot three arrows, which were all avoided, and stood three shot of musket, until one taking full aim at him, made the bark or splinters of the tree fall about his ears; after which he gave an extraordinary shriek, and away they went all of them; and so leaving some to keep the shallop, they followed them about a quarter of a mile, that they might conceive that they were not afraid of them, or any way discouraged. We took up eighteen of their arrows, which we had sent to England, by Master Jones; some whereof were headed with brass, others with hart's horn, and others with eagle's claws.[2]

Frightening times, Lord! It is unlikely I will need to face bows and arrows today. Nevertheless, I pray for anyone known to me who is living in fear, whose nerves are shredded, and for whom each day is filled with anxiety. Help them, Lord, whatever the reasons for their fearfulness. May they come to know your healing presence in mind and body.

1   Most likely, a language now known as Wampanoag. This was one of many Native American languages, most common in the district of Massachusetts.
2   From *Chronicles of the Pilgrim Fathers.*

LET ALL THINGS BE DONE UNTO EDIFYING.
(1 Corinthians 14:26 *KJV*)

The settlement of America, to the world at large, has an importance far beyond that which attaches to it as an incident in the records of the English race. It marks the transference to an almost illimitable continent of all that was best, not only in the institutions and ideas of England, with her traditions of liberty, but those of Continental Europe which had been handed down from the matured civilization of the past...

Some suggestions have been made regarding the mode in which free schools, a free press, a free religion, and an enlightened prison and hospital system have worked into the American Commonwealth. But much more than this still remains to be considered. America has today other institutions of great value which were brought over by the early settlers, and which existed in the Netherlands two centuries and a half ago, while none of them were then known in England... We have traced a connection between Puritan England and the Dutch so intimate as to be sufficient alone to account for the subsequent history of the American colonies...

The... [Plymouth] settlers also came directly from Holland, and... all that was best in the new additions for several years came from the same country.[1]

Lord, history informs us that not every cultural import is a good one!
Nevertheless, many are, and bring great benefits to recipients. Help me today,
I pray, whether or not I actually travel anywhere, to only "import" that which
is edifying into the lives of those I encounter. At the end of this day, may I look
back and conclude that I offered "all that was best" to my friends, family, and
neighbours. By your grace, may this be so.

---

1   From *The Puritan in Holland, England and America.*

LET US DISCERN FOR OURSELVES WHAT IS RIGHT; LET US LEARN
TOGETHER WHAT IS GOOD.

(Job 34:4)

As they went up on to the deck and looked out again over the land, the most important question to decide was this: "Is this land, by the shore of which we are now anchored, a good land for us to live in, or must we sail on to find a better place?"

The boys looked at the shore, and wondered whether the Red Indians,[1] of whom they had heard, were lurking, tomahawk in hand, in the woods. For the woods came right down to the water's edge. There were spreading oak trees now dropping their acorns in the soil; tall, straight pines with dark green needles and brown pine cones; there were also junipers and many shrubs that would make a scent when they burnt – like sassafras.[2]

The sound of the whizzing of many thousand wings filled the air. Great flocks of wild duck and other wildfowl flew round and round in the air; more than could ever be counted, wheeling and forming and reforming like regiments in the sky.

The boys and girls on the *Mayflower* looked at the birds with excitement and joy. But the leaders of the expedition looked serious.[3]

We think we know, Lord, yet our understanding is actually very limited! You, on the other hand, know the beginning and the end. With that in mind, I pray for anyone who is choosing where to live – a new house, a career change, perhaps, with all the complexities of so many different factors. So many things can go wrong, with lasting consequences. Help them, Lord. Guide them by your Spirit. Grant discernment on important and expensive decisions.

---

1 I am aware of the fact that this description of Native American Indians is no longer acceptable, and is politically incorrect. Nevertheless, I have retained it here, not so as to cause offence, but to retain the authenticity of this narrative. This language captures a note in history, and for that reason I feel it to be a valid inclusion.

2 Trees native to North America and Asia.

3 From *The Argonauts of Faith*.

"… I MAY SAY TO YOU WITH CONFIDENCE ABOUT THE PATRIARCH
DAVID THAT HE BOTH DIED AND WAS BURIED, AND HIS TOMB IS
WITH US TO THIS DAY."
(Acts 2:29 *ESV*)

Coming out of the woods near the bay shore, they discovered several large clearings used by the Indians as cornfields. Here they noted several curious heaps of sand, and one in particular caught their eye. It was covered with grass mats, and had an arched piece of wood at one end, a half-buried earthen pot at the other. Their curiosity aroused, they dug into this, turning up several rotted arrows and an old bow, which they carefully put back and covered with sand, rightly surmising that the Indians had buried one of their braves here, and that "it would be odious unto them to ransack their sepulchres". Proceeding to the "river" which interested them, they were unable to determine from brief investigation whether it was a river or only a tidal inlet. Whatever it was, it had possibilities as a harbour and apparently would accommodate ships.[1]

Teach me to learn, Lord, from this story, a proper and appropriate respect for the dead, for souls who have passed on. Teach me to revere their memory, with gratitude. I pray, Lord, for anyone who is visiting the grave or final resting place of a loved one today, perhaps for an anniversary. Support them, I ask, as memories are stirred and tender feelings are exposed. Deal with them gently.

---

1 From *Saints and Strangers.*

... MAKE IT YOUR AMBITION TO LEAD A QUIET LIFE: YOU SHOULD
MIND YOUR OWN BUSINESS...
(1 Thessalonians 4:11)

The Pilgrims kept to the shore on their return and within a mile or two came to a high sandy hill rising steeply from the beach. At its base was a large meadow, and in it they again noted curious heaps of sand. One had been freshly made, and casting all scruples to the winds, they decided to excavate. A few feet down they came upon a large basket, "very handsome and cunningly made". It held three or four bushels and was filled to the top with corn, "some in eares, faire and good, of diverce colours, which seemed to them a very goodly sight (haveing never seen any such before)" [*sic*]. This they did not cover up and leave as they found it. First posting a guard to keep off any Indians who might object to their proceedings, they hauled the basket out of the ground.[1]

A simple prayer today, Heavenly Father: teach me to keep my nose out of that which needn't concern me! Help me only to have a healthy curiosity for that which will benefit me, and to leave other people's business well alone.

---

1   From *Saints and Strangers*.

ILL-GOTTEN TREASURES HAVE NO LASTING VALUE …
(Proverbs 10:2)

In their wanderings they had picked up a big iron kettle, obviously a ship's kettle "brought out from Europe", probably by some of the English or Breton fishermen who occasionally visited this coast. The Pilgrims filled up the kettle with corn and then stuffed their pockets with the yellow, red, and blue maize. Unable to carry all of it, they left the remainder in the basket and put it back in the ground, salving their consciences by saying that as soon as they met the Indians, they would "satisfie them for their corne" [sic]. On their way to the ship they soon tired of carrying the heavy kettle and tossed it away, salvaging some of its contents. Back on the *Mayflower* at last, after being three days out, they put the corn into the common store "to be kept for seed", which made everybody "marvelusly glad" [sic]. This was just plain larceny, of course, but the Pilgrims were inclined to regard it as another special providence of God.[1]

Oh dear – ascribing this light-fingered activity to you and your provision, Lord! Forgive us, I pray, if ever we are tempted to suggest that you collude with anything improper or underhand. Forgive us such self-seeking justifications.

---

1 From *Saints and Strangers.*

AND ASA DID THAT WHICH WAS RIGHT IN THE EYES OF THE LORD,
AS DID DAVID HIS FATHER.
(1 Kings 15:11 *KJV*)

The great majority of the settlers were Englishmen, who came directly from their native land. They were Puritans, the clearest-headed, and in many respects the most advanced, of their race. Thus, with the characteristics of their time, they could appreciate and appropriate the civil institutions of the Dutch Republic, which bore transplanting, but they had not absorbed sufficient from their neighbours to make them liberal in all directions.[1]

As I look back, Lord, I gratefully acknowledge the various influences that have shaped my life and, indeed, shaped me as a person. Thank you for those whose influence has been good, and whose impressions are lasting in a positive way. As the Pilgrims had imbibed certain characteristics of their Dutch hosts, may I adopt the characteristics of Christ within.

---

1   From *The Puritan in Holland, England and America*.

THEN SAID JESUS, FATHER, FORGIVE THEM...
(Luke 23:34 *KJV*)

Corn was carried to the *Mayflower*, the Pilgrims... having dug into several mounds which they knew to be graves. In one they found the skeletons of a child and a man, the latter's skull with "fine yellow hair still on it and some of the flesh unconsumed". It was wrapped in a sailor's canvas cassock and a pair of cloth breeches, and in the grave were many bowls, trays, trinkets, a knife, a pack needle, strings of fine white beads, and two or three old iron things. Still musing upon the mystery of the yellow-haired man, the Pilgrims closed the grave, having removed "sundrie of the prettiest things" [*sic*] to take away with them. In their meanderings they also stumbled upon several of the Indians' round huts, from which the occupants had evidently just fled. Nosing about, they found antlers, eagle claws, a piece of broiled herring, several chinks of venison, some tobacco seed, many wooden trays and dishes, thin and heavy mats, earthen pots, an English bucket without a handle, large baskets ingeniously made of crab shells, other baskets of fibre "curiously wrought with black and white in pretty works". Here, too, they took "some of the best things" away with them, making note of the fact that they "left the houses standing".[1]

This is so horribly disappointing, Lord – Pilgrims who made such a brave stand for righteousness, suddenly becoming thieves, and behaving in such an arrogant manner, as though their Christianity entitled them to plunder from the Indians. I don't know how to pray today, Lord, in response to this excerpt. Maybe I will just ask that you forgive your people when we get things so badly wrong.

---

1   From *Saints and Strangers*.

So Abram said to Lot, "Let's not have any quarrelling
between you and me, or between your herders and mine,
for we are close relatives. Is not the whole land before
you? Let's part company. If you go to the left, I'll go to the
right; if you go to the right, I'll go to the left."
(Genesis 13:8–9)

Many wanted to settle at "Corn Hill" immediately, arguing that it was a fertile, healthful, and easily defended site. It was close by, which would obviate the risks of exploring further afield... While the harbour there left much to be desired, it offered safe anchorage for boats and was "like to be a place of good fishing". No cod had yet been caught, but every day they saw "great whales of the best kind for oil and bone", and... with the proper gear they could have made £3,000 or £4,000 right here in the harbour, more than twice their debt to the merchant adventurers.

But others spoke against Corn Hill, citing its want of an adequate water supply. They would have to depend upon freshwater ponds, which might dry up in the summer. If their town were built on the top of the hill for better defence, they would have to haul water and all their supplies up its steep slopes... Some suggested sailing away to the far side of Cape Ann[1] ... having heard that the harbour, land, and fishing were good there.[2]

The art and skill of disagreement, Lord! Give me that grace of heart, and wisdom
of mind, to know how to disagree without causing offence. By the same token,
impart courage if and when I feel the need to disagree with a certain point of
view or a particular proposal.

---

1   North-eastern Massachusetts.
2   From *Saints and Strangers*.

PEOPLE WILL COME FROM EAST AND WEST AND NORTH AND SOUTH,
AND WILL TAKE THEIR PLACES AT THE FEAST IN THE KINGDOM
OF GOD.

(Luke 13:29)

The Leaders of the Pilgrims asked Captain Jones to cruise about along the shore in search of the best place for settling.

"No," said Captain Jones, "I will not do that. You have put your little sailing boat on board. You must put her together and the men must explore the coast for themselves. Then I will sail to the place you choose, and put you all ashore. You must decide at once. I have only just enough provisions for the voyage back to England, without any more delay"...

They began to walk southward along the shore.

Suddenly they all came to a halt. Ahead of them on the beach were other men. There were six of them. They had a dog with them. They were Red Indians.

The Pilgrim Scouts pushed on, hoping to be able to find out from the Indians what kind of land they were in. But, as they went on, the Red Indians turned and ran. They disappeared among the trees and were soon lost in the woods... [The Pilgrims moved on]; not to hunt the Indians, but to find their settlement, and try to make friends with them.

They pushed through the woods on the trail in Indian file up hill and down dale for mile after mile; but the Indians always kept well ahead of them. The sun came near the horizon. They had followed the trail for ten miles into the woods. Around them was the silence of the mysterious forests in which the Indians were hidden. Their friends were now far from them.[1]

What an adventure, Lord! An unexpected encounter with the Indian tribespeople; two very different cultures coming together. Thank you, Father, that your kingdom is for all; there is plenty of room for people from every tribe and every race. Thank you, Father, that men, women, and children from different nations and all ethnicities will embrace under the Lordship of Christ. You are an international God!

---

1   From *The Argonauts of Faith*.

JESUS REPLIED, "FOXES HAVE DENS AND BIRDS HAVE NESTS, BUT THE
SON OF MAN HAS NO PLACE TO LAY HIS HEAD."
(Luke 9:58)

They... began to erect the first house for common use, to receive them and their goods. And after they had provided a place for their goods and common store... they began to build some cottages for habitation, as time would admit; and also consulted of laws and order both for their civil and military government, as the necessity of their present condition did require.[1]

I pray for those in need of suitable accommodation, Lord; those who are homeless, and those who rely upon the goodwill of charities, family, and friends for somewhere to stay. Help me to play my part in supporting them. Grant me a heart of compassion, moved at the impulse of love towards those whose home is the pavement or a shop doorway.

---

1   From *Chronicles of the Pilgrim Fathers*.

THERE WERE STAYING IN JERUSALEM GOD-FEARING JEWS FROM
EVERY NATION UNDER HEAVEN. WHEN THEY HEARD THIS SOUND,
A CROWD CAME TOGETHER IN BEWILDERMENT, BECAUSE EACH
ONE HEARD THEIR OWN LANGUAGE BEING SPOKEN. UTTERLY
AMAZED, THEY ASKED: "AREN'T ALL THESE WHO ARE SPEAKING
GALILEANS? THEN HOW IS IT THAT EACH OF US HEARS THEM IN
OUR NATIVE LANGUAGE?"

(Acts 2:5–8)

The Indians… would show themselves afar off, but when they endeavoured to come near them they would run away. But… a certain Indian called Samoset, came boldly among them and spoke to them in broken English, which yet they could well understand, at which they marvelled; but at length they understood that he belonged to the eastern parts of the country, and had acquaintance with sundry of the English fishermen,[1] and could name sundry of them, from whom he learned his language. He became very profitable to them, in acquainting them with many things concerning the state of the country in the eastern parts, as also of the people here; of their names, number, and strength, of their situation and distance from this place, and who was chief among them. He told them also of another Indian called Squanto, alias Tisquantum, one of this place, who had been in England, and could speak better English than himself: and after courteous entertainment of him he was dismissed.[2]

Today, Lord, I thank you for linguists and Bible translators, and I thank you for their special gifting and ministry. They have a special vocation, translating the Scriptures into complicated minority languages, thereby enabling your Word to wing its way around the globe and into the hearts of many. Bless them as they pore over translations and as they consider dialects. Help them to get it right!

---

1   The coastline around Cape Cod was a particularly rich source of fish, and well worth the effort of English fishermen who would travel there in order to bring home huge hauls of seafood. This was a lucrative business. These fishermen, though, had no intention of settling in America.
2   From *Chronicles of the Pilgrim Fathers*.

... God gave us a spirit not of fear but of power and love
and self-control.

(2 Timothy 1:7 *ESV*)

For some time now the Indians had been causing the Pilgrims steadily increasing concern, being a source of constant nagging worry. Not because of anything they had done – but precisely because they had done nothing, which seemed very suspicious and aroused much uneasy speculation.

Had the savages withdrawn at sight of them, retreating into the wilderness to organize their forces and recruit allies with the intention of returning in force to fall upon New Plimoth [*sic*] some dark night with tomahawk and torch?... Or were the savages contriving some diabolical trap, skilfully laid ambush?

What puzzled the Pilgrims most was that weeks went by without sight of an Indian. Yet there were Indians in the neighbourhood, as was evident from the columns of smoke from their fires occasionally seen in the distance... So apprehensive were they, according to an old and probable tradition, that they secretly buried their dead at night... levelling out the graves and planting them with corns to hide their great and growing losses from the Indians... That unseen eyes were watching them from the dark rim of the forest was a profoundly disturbing thought and led the Pilgrims to keep stricter watch and look carefully to their muskets, "which with the moisture and raine were out of temper" [*sic*].[1][2]

> Real or imagined, Lord, fears and anxieties can become powerful enemies.
> Gracious God, draw alongside those whose horrible battles with mental health
> issues act as personal prisons – the paranoid and agoraphobic, and so on. Come
> with healing, Lord, to those whose lives are blighted in such ways.

---

1 A number of the Pilgrims, and other passengers from the *Mayflower* voyage, had succumbed to fevers and other illnesses that could largely be attributed to the difficulties of their journey (dreadful overcrowding and an inadequate diet on board, for example). The death toll was unfortunately high, as many struggled to adjust to the trying conditions of life in the settlement. It should also be remembered, though, that elderly people in the company would have died anyway, even if they had remained in England or Holland, simply because they had reached the natural sunset of their lives.

2 From *Saints and Strangers*.

AND HE TOOK BREAD, GAVE THANKS AND BROKE IT, AND GAVE IT
TO THEM, SAYING, "THIS IS MY BODY GIVEN FOR YOU; DO THIS IN
REMEMBRANCE OF ME." IN THE SAME WAY, AFTER THE SUPPER HE
TOOK THE CUP, SAYING, "THIS CUP IS THE NEW COVENANT IN MY
BLOOD, WHICH IS POURED OUT FOR YOU."
(Luke 22:19–20)

[Samoset] came again with some other natives, and told them of the coming of the great Sachem, named Massasoiet,[1] who (about four or five days after) came, with the chief of his friends and other attendants, with the aforesaid Squanto, with whom (after friendly entertainment and some gifts given him) they made a league of peace with him, which continued with him and his successors to the time of the writing hereof. The terms and conditions of the said league are as followeth:

1. That neither he nor any of his, should injure or do hurt to any of their people.
2. That if any of his did hurt to any of theirs, he should send the offender that they might punish him.
3. That if anything were taken away from any of theirs, he should cause it to be restored, and they should do the like to his.
4. That if any did unjustly war against him, they would aid him; and if any did war against them, he should aid them.
5. That he should send to his neighbour confederates, to inform them of this that they might not wrong them, but might be likewise comprised in these conditions of peace.
6. That when his men came to them upon any occasion, they should leave their arms (which were then bows and arrows) behind them.
7. Lastly. That so doing their sovereign Lord King James would esteem him as his friend and ally.[2]

Thank you, Lord Jesus, for that great covenant established by grace, whereby you offered humankind a contract written in red and sealed in love. Thank you, Lord Jesus, for a covenant ratified on Calvary. You are my God.

---

1   Or Massassowat, King of the Wompanaog Tribe. "Sachem" translates as "king".
2   From *Chronicles of the Pilgrim Fathers*.

I PUT SHELEMIAH THE PRIEST, ZADOK THE SCRIBE, AND A
LEVITE NAMED PEDAIAH IN CHARGE OF THE STOREROOMS AND
MADE HANAN SON OF ZAKKUR, THE SON OF MATTANIAH, THEIR
ASSISTANT, BECAUSE THEY WERE CONSIDERED TRUSTWORTHY. THEY
WERE MADE RESPONSIBLE FOR DISTRIBUTING THE SUPPLIES...
(Nehemiah 13:13)

[Massasoiet] gave unto them all the lands adjacent, to them and their heirs forever.

After these things he returned to his place called Sowams, about forty miles distant from Plimouth [*sic*, and hereafter], but Squanto[1] continued with them, and was their interpreter, and proved a special instrument sent of God for their good, beyond expectation; he directed them in planting their corn, where to take their fish, and to procure their commodities; and also was their pilot to bring them to unknown places for their profit, and never left them until his death.[2] He was a native of this place where Plimoth is, and scarce any left besides himself. He was carried away (with divers others) by one named Hunt,[3] a master of a ship, who thought to sell them for slaves in Spain, but he got away to England, and was entertained by a merchant in London, and employed to Newfoundland and other parts; and at last brought hither into these parts by one Mr. Dermer,[4] a gentleman employed by Sir Ferdinando Gorges[5] and others, for discovery and other designs in these parts.[6]

Thank you so much, Lord, for those who offer their services and skills as assistants; those who do not necessarily seek the limelight or high office, but are content to help "behind the scenes". I thank you for such people in my own church, whose contribution is essential, yet whose service often goes unnoticed. As I thank you for them, I ask you to bless them.

1   Subsequently known as Squantam or Tisquantam.
2   In his dying days, Squanto asked the Governor of the Pilgrims to pray with him, so that he might "go to the Englishman's God".
3   Possibly, Captain Henry Hunt or his brother William.
4   Thomas Dermer (born c. 1520), navigator and explorer.
5   Sir Ferdinando Gorges (1565–1647), English colonial entrepreneur, sometimes referred to as the "Father of English Colonization in North America", although he never actually set foot in America.
6   From *Chronicles of the Pilgrim Fathers*.

> "… NO WEAPON FORGED AGAINST YOU WILL PREVAIL, AND YOU
> WILL REFUTE EVERY TONGUE THAT ACCUSES YOU. THIS IS THE
> HERITAGE OF THE SERVANTS OF THE LORD, AND THIS IS THEIR
> VINDICATION FROM ME," DECLARES THE LORD.
> (Isaiah 54:17)

Let the reader take notice of a very remarkable particular, which was made known to the planters at Plimouth, some short space after their arrival, that the Indians, before they came to the English to make friendship with them, they got all the powaws[1] in the country, who, for three days together, in a horrid and devilish manner did curse and execrate them with their conjurations; which assembly and service they held in a dark and dismal swamp. But to no return.[2]

How Satan laboured to hinder the gospel from coming to New England! Bless your people everywhere, Lord, as and when they come up against opposition, especially when they are intent on seeking out new openings in evangelism.

---

1   Or pawaw, or powah, or pawau. A traditional social gathering of Native American communities, something akin to a district conference. The English equivalent is "pow wow", meaning a family discussion or something of that nature, in search of a communal decision.
2   From *Chronicles of the Pilgrim Fathers*.

... LEAD ME TO THE ROCK THAT IS HIGHER THAN I.
(Psalm 61:2 *ESV*)

[William Bradford and a group of sailors] came to the great decision that they would recommend to the company of Pilgrims on the *Mayflower* to settle ... "which did much comforte their harts" [*sic*]. This was the harbour that they called Plymouth Harbour, naming it after the great Devon [England] port from which they had sailed. And, as they set foot upon the great boulder by the side of which the boat was beached, they called it Plymouth Rock.

The words of Manito,[1] the Great Spirit, to the Red Indian tribes:

"I have given you lands to hunt in,
I have given you streams to fish in,
Why then are you not contented?
I am weary of your quarrels,
Weary of your wars and bloodshed,
Weary of your prayers for vengeance,
Of your wranglings and dissensions;
All your strength is in your union,
All your danger is in discord;
Therefore be at peace henceforward
And as brothers live together."[2] [3]

Gracious God, establish me in my faith today. Fix me firmly on the rock of that faith, namely, Jesus Christ. Let me, like the Pilgrims, "settle".

---

1   A Native American name for God or Deity. Some Native American Christian churches in Mexico, Canada, and America often use this term.
2   From Longfellow's "The Song of Hiawatha". Henry Wadsworth Longfellow (1807–82), American poet. Much of his work concentrates on American legend and history.
3   From *The Argonauts of Faith*.

MY FLESH AND MY HEART MAY FAIL, BUT GOD IS THE STRENGTH OF
MY HEART AND MY PORTION FOREVER.

(Psalm 73:26)

The Pilgrim-scouts joyfully turned the bows of the shallop northward to go back from the bay that they had discovered to the *Mayflower*. She lay at anchor twenty-five miles away.

The Pilgrims on board her kept an anxious lookout for the return of their men. William Bradford, looking out from the shallop as she ran toward the mother-ship, would try to catch the wave of her kerchief in the hand of his wife – Dorothy May – whom he had married… at Leyden… But he could see no wave of her hand. He and others climbed aboard the *Mayflower*. Then one of the Pilgrims took him aside and told how, during the storm, while he had been away, she had fallen overboard. They had been unable to rescue her; and she had drowned.

William Bradford could say at that hour what Oliver Cromwell was later to say at the loss of his son. "It went to my heart like a dagger indeed; it did."[1] But he took strong grip of himself, and gave his whole life to the great enterprise of clearing the waste for the Pilgrims and in that waste building the life of New England.[2]

What a dreadful shock, Lord. What a blow. Be with those who today have
suddenly lost a loved one, without the opportunity to say a last goodbye. At such
times of awful loss, please make haste to comfort and uphold the bereaved. May
they find themselves surrounded by a peace that only you can give.

---

1   In January 1632, Oliver Cromwell's son, James, died the day after his baptism. He recorded this sentiment in one of his letters.
2   From *The Argonauts of Faith*.

ALL THE BELIEVERS WERE ONE IN HEART AND MIND. NO ONE
CLAIMED THAT ANY OF THEIR POSSESSIONS WAS THEIR OWN, BUT
THEY SHARED EVERYTHING THEY HAD.
(Acts 4:32)

The shallop put out to the *Mayflower*. Food was put into that smaller vessel, and every man or boy who could work tumbled into her to come ashore and hasten on with the building.

Very quickly they set to work. Some of the strongest made the shore ring with the sound of their axes, and the grinding crash of falling trees. Others in parties lopped and dragged the timber to the building place.

Twenty men stayed ashore... on guard. The others went back to the *Mayflower*. The next day was Sunday. They all rested. The men ashore stayed on guard...

On the top of the hill they levelled a space... On it they built a timber gun-platform. They brought out in the shallop a cannon from the *Mayflower*, and with much toil dragged it up the hill and placed it on the platform...

All this time the work of building went rapidly forward. They decided first to put up a common house that all could use as shelter till each had his own separate home. This common-house they decided to use afterwards as a meeting-place – such as the House with the Green Door had been at Leyden.[1]

Community living, Lord! It's not for everyone! Some people choose it, and enjoy it, while others have no choice but to live among groups of relative strangers. Bless those who like that way of life, and help those who would prefer a home of their own – those whose accommodation is a hostel or something of that nature.

---

1   From *The Argonauts of Faith*.

... JESUS WENT OUT OF THE HOUSE AND SAT BY THE LAKE.
SUCH LARGE CROWDS GATHERED AROUND HIM THAT HE GOT
INTO A BOAT AND SAT IN IT, WHILE ALL THE PEOPLE STOOD ON
THE SHORE. THEN HE TOLD THEM MANY THINGS IN PARABLES,
SAYING: "A FARMER WENT OUT TO SOW HIS SEED. AS HE WAS
SCATTERING THE SEED, SOME FELL ALONG THE PATH, AND THE
BIRDS CAME AND ATE IT UP. SOME FELL ON ROCKY PLACES, WHERE
IT DID NOT HAVE MUCH SOIL. IT SPRANG UP QUICKLY, BECAUSE THE
SOIL WAS SHALLOW. BUT WHEN THE SUN CAME UP, THE PLANTS
WERE SCORCHED, AND THEY WITHERED BECAUSE THEY HAD NO
ROOT. OTHER SEED FELL AMONG THORNS, WHICH GREW UP AND
CHOKED THE PLANTS. STILL OTHER SEED FELL ON GOOD SOIL,
WHERE IT PRODUCED A CROP – A HUNDRED, SIXTY OR THIRTY TIMES
WHAT WAS SOWN.
(Matthew 13:1–8)

They now began to hasten the ship away, which tarried so long by reason of the necessity and danger that lay on them, because so many died both of themselves and the ship's company likewise; by which they became so few, as the master durst not put to sea until those that lived recovered of their sickness...[1]

They planted their first corn in new England, being instructed in the manner thereof by the forenamed Squanto; they likewise sowed some English grain with little success, by reason partly of the badness of the seed... or some other defect then not discovered.[2]

Lord of the harvest, I think of those churches where the gospel is preached, faithfully, week after week, and where a good consistent witness is made. Likewise, I think of those individual Christians who "sow seeds", as it were, into the lives of their loved ones, with their personal witness and with their prayers. May it be, Lord, under your good hand, that those churches and those individuals see success in their soul-winning.

---

1 See Footnote 1, June 3rd.
2 From *Chronicles of the Pilgrim Fathers*.

… I HEARD A VOICE FROM HEAVEN SAYING UNTO ME,
WRITE, BLESSED ARE THE DEAD WHICH DIE IN THE LORD FROM
HENCEFORTH: YEA, SAITH THE SPIRIT, THAT THEY MAY REST FROM
THEIR LABOURS; AND THEIR WORKS DO FOLLOW THEM.
(Revelation 14:13 *KJV*)

Their governor, Mr. John Carver, fell sick, and within a few days after he died, whose death was much lamented, and caused great heaviness amongst them, and there was indeed great cause. He was buried in the best manner they could, with as much solemnity as they were in a capacity to perform, with the discharge of some volleys of shot of all that bare arms. This worthy gentleman was one of singular piety, and rare for humility, as appeared by his great condescendency, [*sic*] when as this poor people were in great sickness and weakness, he shunned not to do very mean services for them, yea the meanest of them. He bare a share likewise of their labour in his own person, accordingly as their extreme necessity required; who being one also of a considerable estate, spent the main part of it in this enterprise, and from first to last approved himself not only as their agent in the first transacting of things, but also all along to the period of his life, to be a pious, faithful, and very beneficial instrument, and now is reaping the fruit of his labour with the Lord.

Gov. Carver was taken sick in the field, while they were engaged in their planting.[1]

What an impressive eulogy! What a challenge!

1   From *Chronicles of the Pilgrim Fathers.*

"BUT WHILE HE WAS STILL A LONG WAY OFF, HIS FATHER SAW HIM
AND WAS FILLED WITH COMPASSION FOR HIM; HE RAN TO HIS SON,
THREW HIS ARMS AROUND HIM AND KISSED HIM. THE SON SAID
TO HIM, 'FATHER, I HAVE SINNED AGAINST HEAVEN AND AGAINST
YOU. I AM NO LONGER WORTHY TO BE CALLED YOUR SON.' BUT THE
FATHER SAID TO HIS SERVANTS, 'QUICK! BRING THE BEST ROBE AND
PUT IT ON HIM. PUT A RING ON HIS FINGER AND SANDALS ON
HIS FEET. BRING THE FATTENED CALF AND KILL IT. LET'S HAVE A
FEAST AND CELEBRATE. FOR THIS SON OF MINE WAS DEAD AND
IS ALIVE AGAIN; HE WAS LOST AND IS FOUND.' SO THEY BEGAN TO
CELEBRATE."
(Luke 15:20–24)

"Welcome," said the Indian, greeting them in English, smiling as the Pilgrims stared at him in blank surprise.

His name was Samoset, he said, and from him the Pilgrims learned many things they wished to know. But before answering their flood of questions, he asked for some beer. Having none, they gave him "strong water" – brandy, perhaps, or Holland gin – and "bisket, and butter, and cheese, & pudding, and a peece of mallard, all of which he liked well" [*sic*]. Then they threw about him a long coat, a bright red horseman's coat – to keep him warm, they said, but rather to cool their own crimson blushes, it would seem, for he was stark naked except for a leather string about his waist "with a fringe about a span longe, or little more" [*sic*].[1]

What a welcome the Pilgrims gave to Samoset, Lord! And what a welcome you
give to the prodigal! Thank you so much for today's Bible text. It resounds with
the warmth of your Fatherhood. Help me, I pray, to always welcome strangers
and those returning to faith – those coming home
– and to do so warmly, without judgment.

---

1   From *Saints and Strangers*.

HE REMEMBERS HIS COVENANT FOREVER, THE PROMISE HE MADE,
FOR A THOUSAND GENERATIONS…
(1 Chronicles 16:15)

The story of our Pilgrim Fathers, and their settlement upon these shores, is as familiar to us as an oft-repeated tale. Still it is a tale of such Christian heroism, and grand achievement, that it will never lose its interest with mankind, and least of all to us their children. We owe so much to them, and to the God who raised them up, and inspired them with such sentiments, and guided them to this land, and guarded them through all their perils, and enabled them to plant here a pure church, and a Christian Commonwealth, that we shall never tire of recounting their deeds and God's mercies. Nor should we fail to instruct our children in this history, or to teach it to the world.[1][2]

Help me, Lord, to develop the devotional practice of deliberately pausing occasionally, every so often, to reflect upon past blessings. Prevent my heart from ever being so preoccupied with the here and now that I forget your goodness in days gone by. Teach me that skill. Minister to my memory.

---

1   I have placed this reflection here quite deliberately. As we have observed, the Pilgrims have survived their journey, and have begun to build houses, and to arrange the essential elements of their new life in America. It seems fitting, therefore, to pause briefly in order to contemplate the goodness of God in bringing them thus far.
2   From S. G. Buckingham, *A Memorial of the Pilgrim Fathers*, Springfield: Samuel Bowles & Company, 1867.

BUT THE ADVOCATE, THE HOLY SPIRIT, WHOM THE FATHER WILL
SEND IN MY NAME, WILL TEACH YOU ALL THINGS AND WILL REMIND
YOU OF EVERYTHING I HAVE SAID TO YOU.
(John 14:26)

Driven out from England because they could not conscientiously conform to the requirements of the Established Church, the Puritans went over to Holland and established themselves for a few years at Leyden. But finding it difficult, as they tell us, to support themselves in that country, and that few were willing to join them there, and that as they grew old, their company was in danger of becoming extinct, or at least of being scattered, and that their children were corrupted by the bad influences around them, and desiring also to live under the protection of England, and to retain the language and name of Englishmen, and on account of their inability to give their children such an education as they had themselves received, and owing to their grief at the profanation of the Sabbath around them, and having lastly (as they express it), "a great hope and inward zeal of laying some good foundation, or at least to make some way thereunto, for the propagating and advancing the gospel of the kingdom of Christ in these remote parts of the earth, though they should be but as stepping-stones unto others for performing of so great a work".[1] [2]

A wonderful reflection, Father God, of how you led your people from one place to another. What might my spiritual diary include? Were I to journal my personal pilgrimage in such a way as this, and were I to look back across the years, what blessings might I recall? Bring them to mind, Lord, I pray. They will encourage me to continue. They will remind me of your steadfast love.

Through many dangers, toils, and snares,
I have already come;
'Tis grace hath brought me safe thus far,
And grace will lead me home.[3]

---

1   See Footnote 1, June 13ᵗʰ.
2   From *A Memorial of the Pilgrim Fathers*.
3   From John Newton's hymn "Amazing Grace".

Now Elisha had been suffering from the illness…
(2 Kings 13:14)

[The Indian] Samoset… was not a native of these parts but a "foreigner", like the Pilgrims themselves, having come some months before on a visit from Pemaquid, far up the Maine coast, where he was chief or sagamore of a sub-tribe of the Abnaki, or Wabenake, "people of the dawn". From him the Pilgrims learned that the Indian name for New Plimouth was Patuxet, meaning Little Bay or Little Falls, and he explained the mystery of… why it was that no Indians had been seen for weeks. There were none to see, for a great tragedy had recently overwhelmed the Patuxet tribe… A devastating plague – probably smallpox – had swept the forests of New England, spreading rapidly from the trading posts operated along the Maine coast during the fishing season.[1] No part of the "white man's burden" has weighed more heavily upon the "dark" continents than his diseases – smallpox, tuberculosis, and syphilis, in particular.[2]

Two prayers today, Lord:

What a lovely name, "people of the dawn"! This speaks of new beginnings and fresh hope. Wouldn't it be marvellous, Lord, if your church adopted this title! Grant your church the grace to be "people of the dawn", offering such new beginnings and fresh hope to those in need of same.

I pray for doctors and nurses, Lord, giving thanks for the enormous strides of progress made in areas of vaccination and the curing of diseases. Bless those who study those crucial areas of medicine, I pray, and help them in their research.

1   See Footnote 1, June 2nd.
2   From *Saints and Strangers*.

... "LOVE YOUR NEIGHBOUR AS YOURSELF."
(Mark 12:31)

"Free in speech, so farr as he could expresse his mind, and of seemely carriage" [sic], Samoset spoke of the tribes round about, where they lived, how strong they were, and who ruled them. The overlord of the region, he said, was his friend Ousamequin (Yellow Feather), better known as Massasoit, the Big Chief, sachem[1] of the Wampanoag, who lived off the southwest on the shores of Narragansett Bay, about forty miles distant. Massasoit exercised vague dominion over all the tribes here in the southeastern corner of New England, including those on Cape Cod, the most powerful of whom were the Nauset, a hundred strong.[2]

Getting along with the neighbours, Lord! Make me a good neighbour, I pray, so that my witnessing for Jesus is outworked in the everyday matters of daily life.

---

1   See Footnote 1, June 4th.
2   From *Saints and Strangers*.

... THE LORD BLESSES HIS PEOPLE WITH PEACE.
(Psalm 29:11)

Their peace being well established with the natives about them, which was much furthered by an Indian named Hobamak, a Chief Captain of Massasoit, who continued to live with the English till his death, and gave some good hopes that his soul went to rest. He [was] a proper lusty[1] young man, and one that was in account amongst the Indians in those parts for his valour, continued faithful and constant to the English until his death. He, with the said Squanto, being sent amongst the Indians about business for the English, were surprised by an Indian Sachem named Corbitant, who was no friend to the English; he met with him at Namassaket, and began to quarrel with him, and offered to stab Hobamak, who, being a strong man, soon cleared himself of him; and with speed came and gave intelligence to the Governor of Plimoth, saying he feared that Squanto was slain, for they were being threatened, and for no other cause, but that they were friends to the English, and serviceable to them. On which it was thought meet to suffer them to be thus wronged, and it was concluded to send some men to Namassaket well armed, and to fall upon them; whereupon fourteen men being well prepared... and when they came thither... understood that Squanto was alive; so they withheld and did no hurt, save three of the natives, pressing out of the house when it was beset, were sorely wounded; which they brought home to their town with them, and were dressed by their surgeon and cured.[2]

God of peace and goodwill, my prayers today turn towards those parts of the world where intimidation and violence are the norm, where stabbings are relatively commonplace, and where gangs rule the roost. I think of streets, ghettos, and estates where gang warfare is a daily reality, and where families live in fear of their lives. Father, bless social workers, churches, community workers, and law enforcement officials in such places, so that people can come and go without the constant threat of muggings, abuse, and vandalism.

---

1   Lusty as in strong and capable of hard labour, not licentious.
2   From *Chronicles of the Pilgrim Fathers*.

HOPE DEFERRED MAKES THE HEART SICK ...
(Proverbs 13:12)

They espied a vessel at sea, which at the first they thought to be a Frenchman, but it proved one that belonged to Mr. Thomas Weston,[1] a merchant; which came from a ship which he and another had sent out on fishing...

This boat brought seven men, and some letters, but no provisions to them, of which they were in continual expectation from England, which expectations were frustrated in that behalf; for they never had any supply to any purpose after this time, but what the Lord helped them to raise by their injury among themselves; for all that came afterwards was too short for the passengers that came with it.[2]

Lord, how frustrating this must have been for the Pilgrims! Waiting for news and supplies from home, yet finding "no provisions". How disappointed they must have been. My thoughts and prayers, Lord, reach out towards those whose hopes have been dashed: bad news, perhaps, an unsuccessful interview for a job, a medical diagnosis. Answer their prayers, and mine, as they labour with heavy hearts today. I pray for any known to me personally.

---

1 See Footnote 1, January 26ᵗʰ.
2 From *Chronicles of the Pilgrim Fathers*.

THEN THEY CAST LOTS...
(Acts 1:26)

A stream ran down to the harbour. They decided to make that stream determine the line of their one street.[1] In order to keep the number of houses as low as possible all the Pilgrims were divided up into nineteen families. The unmarried men were attached to different households. Each family had to build its own house.

The plots for the houses and gardens were arranged down each side of the street by the stream. Exactly which family should have which plot of land was determined by drawing lots.[2]

> This seems a strange way of doing business, Lord, and somewhat alien to a
> modern way of thinking. It has an air of superstition around it. All the more
> reason, Lord, to thank you that you always meet us at our point of need.
> You don't wait for us to get everything right and proper before you agree to
> help us, such is your grace. Thank you for meeting me where I am today. My
> understanding of some matters of faith and theology may be incorrect, yet you
> do not hesitate to visit my life and come to my aid. You are my God.

---

1   The area around the stream became known as Townbrook, and the street was named Leiden Street. It ran from the gun-platform that had been established (see June 9th), to the beach.
2   From *The Argonauts of Faith*.

Do not forget to show hospitality to strangers, for by
so doing some people have shown hospitality to angels
without knowing it.

(Hebrews 13:2)

After the Big Chief had placed his mark upon the document[1] ... the Indians departed, being escorted with fitting ceremony as far as Town Brook where the governor and the sachem again embraced. Well pleased with the day's proceedings, the Pilgrims heaved a sigh of relief and relaxed, thinking the show was over. But upon his return ... the Big Chief sent his brother Quadequina and many of his men to sample the Pilgrims' hospitality. They "took kindlie" [*sic*] to their entertainment, several of the braves being so delighted, especially with the "strong water", that they announced that they would stay the night. The Pilgrims eventually got rid of them, allowing only Samoset and Squanto to remain, and at dusk Massasoit and his men, many with their squaws and children, moved off a short distance and encamped about a half mile away. During the night the Pilgrims "kepte good watch, but there was no appearance of danger" [*sic*].[2]

O, Lord! People who outstay their welcome! Give me the grace of being hospitable, I pray – especially if and when my hospitality is exploited and my patience is stretched.

---

1   See June 4ᵗʰ.
2   From *Saints and Strangers*.

DO NOT NEGLECT TO DO GOOD AND TO SHARE WHAT YOU HAVE,
FOR SUCH SACRIFICES ARE PLEASING TO GOD.
(Hebrews 13:16 *ESV*)

Early the next morning Massasoit's warriors came streaming into town,[1] eager to be wined and dined once more. The Pilgrims evaded the issue, and soon a messenger came from the Big Chief with an invitation to the Pilgrim leaders to visit his camp to be honoured and entertained... [They] went "venterously" [*sic*] and enjoyed "three or four ground nuts, and some tobacco" [*sic*]. Returning, they brought with them a large kettle which was filled with English peas and sent back to the Indians, "which pleased them very well, & so they wente their way" [*sic*].[2]

Thank you, Lord, for those friends I see from time to time, perhaps for a bite to eat or a coffee together. Thank you for the privilege of their company. Thank you for their conversation. Thank you for all that they give to my life. I pray your blessing upon that particular circle of people.

---

1   Note the use of the word "town" here, indicating the formation of a settled dwelling area, as opposed to simply a basic clearing in a forest.
2   From *Saints and Strangers*.

... OUR LIGHT AFFLICTION, WHICH IS BUT FOR A MOMENT,
WORKETH FOR US A FAR MORE EXCEEDING *AND* ETERNAL WEIGHT
OF GLORY...

(2 Corinthians 4:17 *KJV*)

They were all at work with a will. They hewed down trees with their axes; lopped the branches from the trunks with hatchets; sawed the trunks into logs of the right length, and split the logs into thick rough planks. They also brought down the withes for thatching the roofs. In four days from beginning to build, the timber-work of the common-house was finished, and a half of the roof was thatched.

Then began the darkest of all the days of the Pilgrims. First one and then the other fell ill with a strange and terrible sickness. For months they had lived on the very poor food that could be carried on ship. They could, in fact, get no fresh food, save the fish they might catch, until the next year's harvest. They had been crowded in the evil-smelling closeness of the under-deck of the *Mayflower*. The tempests had drained their remaining strength. Many of those who fell ill died.[1]

Lord Jesus, there are those days when, just as everything seems to be going well, and things are running smoothly, sudden calamity can strike. A car accident, maybe, or bad news within the family – an unexpected bereavement, even. Be near me, I pray, at such times, and draw close to those who are in shock today, their peaceful routine shattered. Hold us steady on days like that.

---

1   From *The Argonauts of Faith*.

SURELY HE WILL SAVE YOU... FROM THE DEADLY PESTILENCE.
(Psalm 91:3)

Dreadful pestilence swept them down. At one time, out of the hundred in the company, only six or seven could crawl about to take food to the others. The little heroic band in its Pilgrim's Progress was passing through the Valley of the Shadow of Death.

The strong, rough soldier, Captain Miles Standish,[1] in this time of plague became like the tenderest nurse. He and stalwart Brewster escaped the pestilence, and were great pillars of strength to all the others.

Quietly and in the darkness they carried those who died up the hill and buried them there.[2] They raised no monument then over the graves. They were even obliged to flatten the earth, so that no eye could tell that anyone lay there. For they knew that, if they left the mounds of the graves visible, the Indians would come by stealth, and, counting the graves, would thus discover how many of them had died.[3]

Heavenly Father, I barely know what to pray when I hear of villages or towns
that are struck with illness or disease. Sometimes I listen to news on the radio
or television, or I read about natural disasters which bring sickness and death in
their wake. Lord, I don't know how to pray, except to ask for mercy.

---

1 See Footnote 3, January 12th.
2 This area became known as "Burying Hill".
3 From *The Argonauts of Faith*.

EACH OF US SHOULD PLEASE OUR NEIGHBOURS FOR THEIR GOOD…
(Romans 15:2)

Mr. Thomas Weston, who had formerly been one of the merchant adventurers to the plantation of New Plimouth (but had now broken off and deserted the general concerns thereof), sent over two ships, the one named the *Sparrow*,[1] the other the *Charity*, on his own particular interest; in the one of them came sixty lusty men, who were to be put to shore at Plimouth, for the ship was to go with other passengers to Virginia; these were courteously entertained… at Plimouth aforesaid, until the ship returned from Virginia, by the direction of the said Mr. Weston, their master, or such as he had set over them, they removed into the Massachusetts Bay, he having got a patent for some part there, yet they left all their sick folks at Plimouth, until they were settled and fitted for housing to receive them. These were an unruly company, and no good government over them, and by disorder fell into many wants.[2]

I think today, Lord, of your people who live among unruly neighbours, and whose witness is made in rough or deprived neighbourhoods. Help them, I pray, when their faith is ridiculed, or if they see little reward for their efforts. Bless churches too, I pray, that are situated on "run down" estates and districts. May they shine like lights in the darkness.

---

1   In other accounts, the *Swan*.
2   From *Chronicles of the Pilgrim Fathers*.

... HALF OF MY MEN DID THE WORK, WHILE THE OTHER HALF
WERE EQUIPPED WITH SPEARS, SHIELDS, BOWS AND ARMOUR.
THE OFFICERS POSTED THEMSELVES BEHIND ALL THE PEOPLE OF
JUDAH WHO WERE BUILDING THE WALL. THOSE WHO CARRIED
MATERIALS DID THEIR WORK WITH ONE HAND AND HELD A
WEAPON IN THE OTHER, AND EACH OF THE BUILDERS WORE HIS
SWORD AT HIS SIDE AS HE WORKED.

(Nehemiah 4:16–18)

They built a fort with good timber, both strong and comely, which was of good defence, made with a flat roof and battlements; on which fort their ordnance was mounted, and where they kept constant watch, especially in time of danger. It served them also for a meeting-house, and was fitted accordingly for that use. It was a great work for them to do in their weakness, and times of want; but the danger of the time required it; there being continual rumours of the Indians, and fears of their rising against them, especially the Narragansets.[1][2]

To work and watch! Help me to learn that lesson!

---

1   Algonquian-speaking tribe from what is now the state of Rhode Island, west of Narragansett Bay.
2   From *Chronicles of the Pilgrim Fathers*.

FROM ONE MAN HE MADE ALL THE NATIONS, THAT THEY SHOULD
INHABIT THE WHOLE EARTH; AND HE MARKED OUT THEIR
APPOINTED TIMES IN HISTORY AND THE BOUNDARIES OF THEIR
LANDS. GOD DID THIS SO THAT THEY WOULD SEEK HIM AND
PERHAPS REACH OUT FOR HIM AND FIND HIM, THOUGH HE IS NOT
FAR FROM ANY ONE OF US.
(Acts 17:26–27)

Their relations with the Indians were almost too successful, the Pilgrims soon felt, for hungry braves kept dropping in on them at all hours of the day and night, often with their wives and children, and all had insatiable thirsts and appetites. They were such a nuisance that a mission was sent to Massasoit to stop this "disorderly coming"... Two Pilgrims arrived to find that the Big Chief was not at home. A messenger was sent for him, and upon his arrival the next morning the Pilgrims lifted their blunderbusses and greeted him with a salvo, which greatly frightened the Big Chief and all his people, especially the women and children. The Pilgrims always found it the very height of diplomacy to show off their firearms, which terrified the savages and held them in respectful awe for some time. [They] then presented the sachem with a red horseman's coat, doubtless the one that had been thrown about Samoset,[1] but now tricked out with a deal of lace. Donning it, the Big Chief strode up and down a good while, very proud of himself, as his men were also "to see their King so bravely attired".[2]

Cultural sensitivities, Lord! Today I pray for those who move away from their
own culture in order to minister in foreign lands or even different counties,
maybe not all that far from home, where important cultural norms can often be
inadvertently overlooked. What a sadness it would be, Lord, were your mission
to be hindered by inadvertent blunders, where offence is caused. Bless those who
navigate such sensitivities in the cause of Christ.

---

1   See June 12ᵗʰ.
2   From *Saints and Strangers*.

THROUGH PATIENCE A RULER CAN BE PERSUADED, AND A GENTLE
TONGUE CAN BREAK A BONE.
(Proverbs 25:15)

The coat was a small token of the Pilgrims' boundless love and esteem... and after more such persiflage circled round to the point. The Wampanoag came very often to the plantation and were always welcome, [they] assured the Big Chief, "yet we, being but strangers as yet at Patuxet alias New Plimouth, and not knowing how our corne may prosper, can no longer give them such entertainment as we have done, and as we desire still to doe. Therefore, we ask you to hinder the multitude from oppressing us with themselves" [sic]. Now, of course, if any of his people came with beaver skins to truck, that was another matter. They should come at any time – the oftener, the better. And if Massasoit were pleased to come himself, he would be most welcome, as would any of his special friends, and "to the end we may know them from others... our Government has sent you a copper chain, desiring if any messenger shall come from you to us, we may know him from his bringing it with him, and hearken and give credit to his message accordingly". [They] concluded by asking if they would trade some of their seed corn so that the planters might determine which grew best in the soil at Plimouth.[1]

The important art of diplomacy, Lord! Gracious Holy Spirit, dwell within me, so that my life and witness may be enhanced by tact and diplomatic charm. Forgive me, I pray, for those moments when I have blundered my way through delicate situations. Live your life through mine, I pray.

1   From *Saints and Strangers*.

THE EARTH IS THE LORD'S, AND EVERYTHING IN IT, THE WORLD,
AND ALL WHO LIVE IN IT...
(Psalm 24:1)

The welcome harvest approached, in the which all had some refreshment, but it arose to a little in comparison of a whole year's supply; partly by reason they were not yet well acquainted with the manner of the husbandry of the Indian corn (having no other), and also their many other employments; but chiefly their weakness for want of food, so as to appearance, famine was like to ensue, if not some way prevented. Markets there was none to go unto, but only the Indians; but they had no trading stuff. But behold now another providence of God; a ship came into the harbour, one Capt. Jones being a chief in her, set out by some merchants to discover all the harbours between Cape Cod and Virginia, and to trade along the coast. This ship had store of English beads (which were then good trade), and some knives, but would sell none but at dear rates, and also a good quantity together; yet they were glad of the occasion, and fain to buy at any rate: they were fain to give after the rate of cent per cent, if not more, and yet pay away coat beaver at three shillings per pound. By this means they were fitted again to trade for beaver and other things, and so procured what corn they could.[1]

Lord, in all my financial transactions, grant me wisdom and integrity, whether I am dealing in shillings and pounds, as it were, or larger amounts of money. Shield my heart from avarice, and bless it with honesty.
As I pray this for myself, Lord Jesus, I pray too for people engaged in corporate business, who deal in thousands and millions on a daily basis. Deliver them from any temptation of fraud and dishonesty.

---

1   From *Chronicles of the Pilgrim Fathers*.

"YOU ARE THE SALT OF THE EARTH ..."
(Matthew 5:13 *ESV*)

It was computed ... "that the four settlements of New England, viz.: Plymouth, Massachusetts, Connecticut, and New Haven, all of which were accomplished ... twenty years after the settlement of Plymouth, drained England of £400,000 or £500,000 ... a very great sum in those days; and if the persecutions of the Puritans had continued ... it is thought that a fourth part of the riches of the kingdom would have passed out of it through this channel."[1]

What a statistic, Lord! How remarkable that the exodus of the Pilgrims should have been calculated to have had such an effect on the finances of England! This loss of income – or, rather, income and revenue that was transferred to America – is significant. Help me always, I pray, to bear in mind the impact my actions might have upon the lives of others, for good or bad. Grant me that special gift of forethought and sensitivity. Let this factor be uppermost in my mind as a guiding influence. Help me to be salty today!

---

1   From *A Memorial of the Pilgrim Fathers*.

FOR IT HAS BEEN GRANTED TO YOU ON BEHALF OF CHRIST NOT
ONLY TO BELIEVE IN HIM, BUT ALSO TO SUFFER FOR HIM ...
(Philippians 1:29)

As they had eaten nothing all day, the Pilgrims looked about hopefully for supper. None was offered and they went hungry to bed, Massasoit inviting them to share the royal couch with himself and his squaw. It was hard and uncomfortable, consisting of heavy planks and a few thin mats, and two big braves came in later and lay down on top of them. The Pilgrims... spent a wretched night, being "worse wearie of our lodging than our journey" [sic]. In the morning Massasoit went fishing and about noon returned with two bass. These were thrown into a pot and boiled, but with forty famished braves to share the feast the Pilgrims felt emptier than before, hurrying to announce to their host that they must be going, saying that they wished to be back in Plymouth for the Sabbath. The sachem begged them to stay, but they could not be dissuaded, for they really feared that they might never get home, being faint and dizzy from fatigue, hunger, and want of sleep, "for what with bad lodging, the savages' barbarous singing (for they used to sing themselves to sleep), lice & fleas, indoors, with musketoes about" [sic], they had had no rest for two nights and were literally staggering on their feet.[1]

Lord, someone once said that "a missionary should have a back for any bed,
a stomach for any food, and a face for any weather"! Bless those who endure
backache, hunger, fatigue, flea bites, and all manner of discomfort for the
kingdom's sake.

---

1 From *Saints and Strangers*.

July 1st

"BLESSED ARE THE PEACEMAKERS, FOR THEY WILL BE CALLED
CHILDREN OF GOD."
(Matthew 5:9)

Captain Miles Standish went out one day hunting. As he crept through the forest he found, to his surprise, a deer lying with its antlers cut off. It had been slain by the Indian hunters. In the very next week another of the Pilgrim Colony was out hunting, and had hidden himself to wait for the passing of the deer. As he stood there he saw dusky shapes stealing silently through the trees – not deer, but men – Red Indian warriors. They were prowling in the direction of the plantation.

One day... when they had ended their work of cutting down trees in the wood, [they] left their tools. In the morning the tools had been carried off. On the opposite side of Townbrook, on the crest of the hill, two Indians suddenly appeared. [They] went forward making signs of peace and trying to signal that they wished to talk with them. The Indians raced off at once, like the flying shadows of cloudlets on a hillside.[1]

> I pray for those who today, as I read these words, are working for peace. I
> pray for those who mediate between warring people, and even nations. Bless
> their negotiations, I pray. Grant them wisdom and patience as they endeavour
> to diffuse tensions. Bless those who do so at diplomatic level, on behalf of
> governments. As they try to broker peace, help them in their efforts. Bless those
> of your children who have this special responsibility.

---

1   From *The Argonauts of Faith.*

WHOEVER REGARDS ONE DAY AS SPECIAL DOES SO TO THE LORD.
WHOEVER EATS MEAT DOES SO TO THE LORD, FOR THEY GIVE
THANKS TO GOD; AND WHOEVER ABSTAINS DOES SO TO THE LORD
AND GIVES THANKS TO GOD.

(Romans 14:6)

Were [the Pilgrims] the slaves of superstition, and miserable fanatics in religion? They held to certain superstitious notions, like that of witchcraft,[1] as all in that age did, but judged by the age in which they lived; – which is the only fair mode of estimating them aright: – they had the least superstition about them of any class in those days. They certainly did not believe in the divine right of kings, or in the divine right of bishops, as so many did; nor did they believe it necessary for ministers to wear certain vestments in order to make their services of any worth; nor did they use the sign of the cross to drive out devils and expel diseases, and keep off witches; nor would they kneel at the sacrament, as if the bread had become a god, like so many others.[2]

> God of the church, Christian denominations enjoy all kinds of diversity, ranging from clerical garments (or the absence of same) to styles of ritual and worship. Help us all, Lord, not to fall out over what are essentially secondary issues. Such divisions are regrettable and sad. Grant us that generosity of heart whereby we may, instead, altruistically value that which matters to others, even if it is of no special importance to us personally. In doing so, may we encourage and bless each other.

---

1   The meaning of this statement is unclear. The likelihood is that the Pilgrim Fathers abhorred all forms of witchcraft, probably to an overly superstitious degree. There should be no suggestion whatever that the Pilgrims were engaged in any form of witchcraft.
2   From *A Memorial of the Pilgrim Fathers*.

> "AS I WAS WITH MOSES, SO I WILL BE WITH YOU; I WILL NEVER
> LEAVE YOU NOR FORSAKE YOU."
> (Joshua 1:5)

The Pilgrims were now altogether on their own, quite cut off from the outside world, with no hope of immediate aid from any quarter. Their last tie with the homeland had been broken... with the belated departure of the *Mayflower*... Lining the shore to wave a last farewell, many had wept disconsolately as Captain Jones brought his ship round and tacked out of the harbour, never to be seen on these shores again. The accommodating skipper had delayed his departure far beyond his original intention, partly because of sickness among the crew, but also at the desperate insistence of the Pilgrims who fear to be left alone before the almost prostrate company had somewhat recovered its strength, thinking it "better to draw some more charge upon themselves & freinds than hazard all" [*sic*].[1]

"Who is alone with God, is never alone."
**Commissioner Earle Maxwell, Former Chief of the Staff of The
Salvation Army**[2]

---

1   From *Saints and Strangers*.
2   The Chief of the Staff is Second-in-Command of The Salvation Army, worldwide. Commissioner Earle Maxwell held this appointment from 1999 to 2002, and was loved and respected for his preaching and godly manner. Commissioner Maxwell once inscribed this little saying in my personal Bible.

July 4th

... I WAS SICK AND YOU LOOKED AFTER ME ...
(Matthew 25:36)

The sachem Massasoit, their friend, was sick, and near unto death, and they sent to visit him, and sent him some comfortable things, which gave him content, and was a means of his recovery.[1]

Lord, bless those who regularly take the time and trouble to visit the sick and dying: church ministers, hospital chaplains, hospice staff, and so on. Thank you for their ministry in times of need. Bless too, Lord, those who are visiting loved ones who are entering the evening of their life. Those are by no means easy visits to make, especially when those who are visiting, and those who are being visited, are aware of the fact that this could be their last time together in this life. Gracious Holy Spirit, fill such visits with your loving presence.

---

1   From *Chronicles of the Pilgrim Fathers.*

CAIN SAID TO HIS BROTHER ABEL, "LET'S GO OUT TO THE FIELD."
WHILE THEY WERE IN THE FIELD, CAIN ATTACKED HIS BROTHER
ABEL AND KILLED HIM.

(Genesis 4:8)

The summer at Plymouth passed quietly except for an Indian alarm to which the Pilgrims reacted instantly with somewhat excessive violence, the first of several such incidents reflecting the bolder and more confident spirit that now animated them. Squanto and Hobomok [one of Massasoit's men] had gone on a visit... about fifteen miles to the west... Just what happened there is not clear, but Hobomok came hurrying in a few days later "full of fear and sorrow", to report that Squanto was dead – murdered – and that his own life had been threatened by the Nemasket chief, Cauntabant, or Corbitant as the Pilgrims always wrote it. The latter had worked himself into a rage against the English and Massasoit, storming at the treaty between them and at Squanto for his part in it, suddenly seizing the latter.

"If he is killed," shouted Corbitant, whipping out his knife, "the English have lost their tongue", at which point Hobomok broke away and ran for it.

This was very disturbing news because the rumour was circulating that the powerful Narragansett had attacked and captured Massasoit, and that Corbitant was in league with them. Bradford hurriedly called a council, and the Pilgrims agreed upon the most drastic action. Captain Standish was dispatched with fourteen men, all heavily armed, "to goe & fall upon them in ye night... for if they should suffer their friends & messengers thus to be wronged, they should have none to cleave unto them, or give them any inteligence, or doe them serviss afterwards, but nexte they would fall upon themselves" [sic].[1]

How this must grieve you, Heavenly Father – to witness the people you have created arguing, fighting, warring, and murdering. This must hurt you, yet it is the way it has always been, since the dawn of human history. Holy Spirit, speak peace into the hearts of those who harbour murderous intent today: gang leaders out for revenge, military and political personnel who think nothing of bloodshed in pursuit of their aims, and individuals who regard vengeance as the way forward. Restrain them.

---

1   From *Saints and Strangers*.

"Do not spread false reports."
(Exodus 23:1)

Led by Hobomok, the party crept into the sleeping village and quietly surrounded the chief's large hut. At the arranged signal several muskets were fired and the Pilgrims burst in, shouting, "Is Corbitant here?" The Indians were speechless with terror, particularly the women and children, of whom many were in the hut. Commanding all to remain inside and not make a move, the Pilgrims explained that they were looking for Corbitant to punish him for Squanto's murder and "other matters", such as speaking disdainfully of the English, assuring the Indians that they "would not hurt their women and children". Some of the more sceptical Nemasket dashed for a side door and escaped, "but with some wounds" as the Pilgrims' blunderbusses flashed and thundered in the dark. Hobomok climbed to the roof of the hut and shouted for Squanto, who soon came ambling along with many Indians behind him, all rather fearful and carrying the choicest of their provisions as a peace offering. In the morning the Pilgrims were served breakfast in Squanto's hut, and to them came "all whose hearts were upright". Corbitant and his faction had fled, so Standish and his men came away disappointed in their plan to cut off the chief's head and carry it home in triumph as they had been instructed.

"Although Corbitant has now escaped us," was their sharp warning upon departure… "If hereafter he shall make any insurrection or offer violence to… any of Massasoit's subjects, we shall revenge it upon him to the overthrow of him and his."[1]

What a story, Lord – and what a warning as to the power of rumour and gossip.
Teach me, I pray, to hold my tongue, so that any rumours doing the rounds may
be killed outright by my refusal to pass them on. By the same token, assist me
always to think the best of people, whatever gossip may abound.

---

1   From *Saints and Strangers*.

FOR TO US A CHILD IS BORN, TO US A SON IS GIVEN, AND
THE GOVERNMENT WILL BE ON HIS SHOULDERS. AND HE
WILL BE CALLED WONDERFUL COUNSELLOR, MIGHTY GOD,
EVERLASTING FATHER, PRINCE OF PEACE.
(Isaiah 9:6)

The Pilgrim colonists could see that life or death for them might hang on the sureness of their power of defence. They, therefore, out of their small numbers, bound the able-bodied men together in a little corps of warriors to defend their women and children. The five cannon from the *Mayflower* were dragged up the hill to the fort-platform. Captain Miles Standish, who was placed in command, set the five cannon there facing in different directions, so that every line of approach from the woods or the shore to the houses was covered.[1]

Lord Jesus, I pray for those charged with the responsibility of defending my country; theirs is an unenviable responsibility and the consequences of wrong decisions can be catastrophic. Bless government officials and military leaders. Bless leaders of nations as they strive to protect their people. These officials carry great responsibility. Help them to use their power wisely in the pursuit of strong defence and peace.

---

1   From *The Argonauts of Faith*.

July 8th

[The Pilgrim Fathers] were confessedly the sturdiest theologians of their age, if not of any age, and were bravely endeavouring to harmonize reason with revelation, and systematize, and explain, and justify all the great doctrines of the Bible, in connection with the principle of human philosophy, and had so far succeeded, that their system... must be admitted to be the most intellectual, and well digested, and complete theology, that the church has known.[1]

How wonderful it is, Lord, when the teachings and truths of the Bible make that great connection with human philosophy and understanding. Grant me that privilege, I pray, in my daily readings, so that whenever I read my Bible, it resonates with my life and present circumstances; likewise, I pray, when I listen to Bible messages in church. Preserve me from dead and dusty encounters with your living Word!

---

1   From *A Memorial of the Pilgrim Fathers.*

So Abraham called that place The Lord Will Provide. And
to this day it is said, "On the mountain of the Lord it will
be provided."
(Genesis 22:14)

The planters at Plimouth ... began to think how they might raise as much corn as they could; so as they might not languish in misery... and it was thought the best way unto, that everyone should plant corn for his own particular, and in that regard provide for themselves... and so they ranged all their youths under some family, and set upon such a course, which had good success, for it made all hands very industrious, so as much corn was planted.

This course being settled, by that time all their corn was planted, all their victuals were spent, and they were only to rest on God's providence; many times at night not knowing where to have anything to sustain nature the next day, and so (as one well observed) had need to pray that God would give them their daily bread, above all people in the world; yet they bear those wants with great patience and alacrity of spirit...

In the winter season groundnuts and fowl were the principal of their refreshing, until God sent more settled and suitable supplies, by his blessing upon their industry.[1]

> *Trust and obey,*
> *For there's no other way*
> *To be happy in Jesus,*
> *But to trust and obey.*[2]

---

1   From *Chronicles of the Pilgrim Fathers*.
2   From John Henry Sammis's hymn "When We Walk With the Lord".

... THE GROUND SHALL GIVE HER INCREASE ...
(Zechariah 8:12 *KJV*)

Indian summer soon came in a blaze of glory, and it was time to bring in the crops. All in all, their first harvest was a disappointment. Their twenty acres of corn, thanks to Squanto, had done well enough. But the Pilgrims failed miserably with more familiar crops. Their six or seven acres of English wheat, barley, and peas came to nothing, and Bradford was certainly on safe ground in attributing this either to "ye badness of ye seed, or lateness of ye season, or both, or some other defecte" [*sic*]. Still, it was possible to make a substantial increase in the individual weekly food ration, which for months had consisted merely of a peck of meal from the stores brought on the *Mayflower*. This was now doubled by adding a peck of maize a week, and the company decreed a holiday, so that all might, "after a more special manner, rejoyce together" [*sic*].[1]

> Thank you for this provision, Lord, but I am mindful of those who suffer the pangs of hunger today, whose crops have failed. Lord, when the soil is but dust and the seeds die without bearing any fruit, help those who have no idea where their next meal is coming from. Give your blessing to those agencies and charities who try to help.

---

1   From *Saints and Strangers*.

JULY 11ᵀᴴ

CAN TWO WALK TOGETHER, EXCEPT THEY BE AGREED?
(Amos 3:3 *KJV*)

The Pilgrims had other things to be thankful for. They had made peace with the Indians and walked "as peaceably and safely in the woods as in the highways of England". A start had been made in the beaver trade. There had been no sickness for months. Eleven houses now lined the street – seven private dwellings and four buildings for common use. There had been no recurrence of mutiny or dissension. Faced with common dangers, Saints and Strangers had drawn closer together, sinking doctrinal differences for a time.[1]

> That tremendous blessing of harmony and unity, Lord. Thank you, Heavenly Father, for those whose company I enjoy – friends who bring great blessing. Thank you too for the unique privilege of Christian fellowship among like-minded people. I am very grateful.

---

1   From *Saints and Strangers*.

Paul gathered a pile of brushwood and, as he put it on the fire, a viper, driven out by the heat, fastened itself on his hand.

(Acts 28:3)

More than once a snake glided by, and Great Bird [an Indian brave], alert, flung his tomahawk with deadly skill, and killed it. He stopped at one point to peer down a side aisle in the forest, looking for a stream ... he went on his knees to gaze beneath a bush; something darted, and fastened on the Indian's naked back. The red man[1] twisted his head round, as if in pain. A moment more, disregarding her own danger, [one of the Pilgrim women] sprang forward, caught at the thing swiftly, and tossed it away before it had time to turn on her. It was a deadly snake, and it disappeared.

"You are hurt, Great Bird!" she exclaimed. "What will you do?"

"Nothing, for it is where I cannot suck the wound."

"What, then?" [she asked], startled, and gazing at the spot where the bite had left its blue-black mark.

"He will die," cried [another of the Pilgrims], whose face was pale with horror.

"Is it really so, Great Bird?" she asked.

The Indian nodded, and stood, stoically facing his fate.

[She] looked at him in wonder. Could she not do something for him? It was a fearful thing that a man so strong, so splendid in his savagery, should die. She braced herself for the task she resolved upon at the moment.

"Kneel down, Great Bird, and let me look at the wound."

The Indian dropped on his knees and without a word, [the Pilgrim woman], having examined the spot, put her lips to the wound.[2]

Lord, I wonder how many times you have protected me, without me even being aware of it! I thank you now, albeit belatedly, for your unseen interventions; all those occasions on which you have shielded me, both in the spiritual realm and in the physical spheres of life.

Thank you for dispatching angels to pave my way with goodness and mercy.

Thank you for your invisible, abiding, guarding presence.

---

1   This description of Great Bird is in no way meant to be offensive, even though it might be regarded as politically incorrect and even insensitive nowadays. It is included here simply to retain the historical authenticity of the period. Any other description would seem somewhat artificial.

2   From *The Maid of the Mayflower*.

THIS IS LOVE: NOT THAT WE LOVED GOD, BUT THAT HE LOVED
US AND SENT HIS SON AS AN ATONING SACRIFICE FOR OUR SINS.
(1 John 4:10)

She began to suck out the poison, only thinking of this, that she was fighting for a man's life, and, God helping her, she would not permit herself to be beaten.

"Do not!" cried [another Pilgrim]. "It may injure you."

"If I do not he will die."

"'Tis enough, I think," she said at last, when she was convinced that the poison was gone; but she swayed, threw out her hands to save herself, and would have fallen if Great Bird had not swung around and caught her in his arms.

She lay there, helpless, but had not lost her senses. The red man carried her, as gentle with her as though she had been a child, down the forest aisle to the water which was flowing at the distant end. He laved his hand in the stream to clean it; then lifted some in the hollow, and held it for her to wash her mouth. The taste of the cold water revived her, and, slipping from his arms, she knelt at the stream.[1]

Lord Jesus, you gave your life for me. You threw out your hands on the cross: "If I do not, they will die." This is love. You are my God.

---

1 From *The Maid of the Mayflower*.

I HAVE LEARNED TO BE CONTENT WHATEVER THE CIRCUMSTANCES. I
KNOW WHAT IT IS TO BE IN NEED, AND I KNOW WHAT IT IS TO HAVE
PLENTY. I HAVE LEARNED THE SECRET OF BEING CONTENT IN ANY
AND EVERY SITUATION, WHETHER WELL FED OR HUNGRY, WHETHER
LIVING IN PLENTY OR IN WANT. I CAN DO ALL THIS THROUGH HIM
WHO GIVES ME STRENGTH.

(Philippians 4:11–13)

The Pilgrim leaders… painted the country and their own accomplishments in the fairest possible colours. The climate, they said, was wonderful – or at least as good as England's, which was not hard to believe… "By the goodness of God," they wrote, "we are so far from want that we wish you partakers of our plenty… For fish and fowl, we have great abundance. Fresh cod in the summer is but coarse meat with us" [sic]. And during the winter tender clams and other shellfish all but crept in at their doors. In the spring and autumn they merely had to go out and gather in Nature's bounty. Such was the Pilgrims' "brief & true" declaration of their "joyfull building of and comfortable planting in the now well defended Town of New Plymouth" [sic].

The country… "wanteth only industrious men to employ… and if we have once but kine,[1] horses, and sheep, I make no question but men might live as contented here as in any part of the world".[2]

What a lovely account, Lord – overflowing with gratitude and contentment.
Grant me such a frame of mind, I pray; to look around me and give thanks.

Count your blessings, name them one by one,
Count your blessings, see what God has done!
Count your blessings, name them one by one,
And it will surprise you what the Lord has done.[3]

---

1   Archaic word for cows, cattle.
2   From *Saints and Strangers*.
3   From Johnson Oatman Jr's hymn "When upon Life's Billows You Are Tempest-tossed".

... GROW IN THE GRACE AND KNOWLEDGE OF OUR LORD AND
SAVIOUR JESUS CHRIST.
(2 Peter 3:18)

[The Pilgrims advised others that] in hastening to New Canaan, let them take heed of certain things. They should set aside, said the Pilgrims, profiting from their experience on the *Mayflower*, "a very good bread room" in which to store their biscuits, so that these would not become mouldy or be devoured by rats and weevils. Only iron-bound kegs should be used for beer and water. And let them bring plenty of beer, and as much fresh meat as possible, allowing the sailors to salt it for them. "Bring juice of lemons and take it fasting... For hot waters, Anniseed Water is the best, but use it sparingly. If you bring anything for comfort in the country, butter or sallet oil, or both, are very good" [*sic*]. Also, they should provide themselves with paper and linseed oil to use as windows in their houses, and cotton yarn for their lamps. Above all, they should not fail to bring plenty of clothes and bedding, and "every man a musket or fowling piece", preferably one very long in the barrel. "Fear not the weight of it, for most of our shooting is from stands... Let your shot be most for big fowls, and bring store of powder and shot."[1]

**A little bit older, and a little bit wiser! May that be true of me today, Lord. I pray
this especially in matters of faith, doctrine, and Christian living.**

---

1   From *Saints and Strangers.*

"ENLARGE THE PLACE OF YOUR TENT, STRETCH YOUR TENT
CURTAINS WIDE, DO NOT HOLD BACK; LENGTHEN YOUR CORDS,
STRENGTHEN YOUR STAKES."

(Isaiah 54:2)

They began to make some distribution of lands, having had hitherto but to every person one acre allowed him, as to propriety, besides their homesteads, or garden plots, the reason was that they might keep together, both for more safety and defence, and the better improvement of the general employments…

Notwithstanding, as aforesaid, so small a portion of land served them at the first, yet afterwards for divers reasons moving thereunto, they were necessitated to lay out some larger proportions to each persons; yet resolving to keep such a mean in distribution of lands, as should not hinder their growth by others coming to them, and therefore accordingly allotted to every one in each family, twenty acres, to be laid out five acres in breath [sic], by the water-side, and four acres in length.[1]

I realize, Lord, that numbers aren't everything, and that there is much more to church life than statistics. However, I give thanks today for those churches who are looking to plant as a result of your numerical blessing upon their fellowship. Thank you that bigger and better premises are sometimes necessary! Bless churches of all shapes and sizes, I pray, but accept my thanks today for those attracting new converts.

---

1   From *Chronicles of the Pilgrim Fathers.*

WITHOUT GOOD DIRECTION, PEOPLE LOSE THEIR WAY...
(Proverbs 11:14 *The Message*)

I may not omit the inserting of a particular... in reference unto a ship with many passengers in her, and some considerable goods, which was bound for Virginia, who had lost themselves at sea, either by the insufficiency of the master, or his illness, for he was sick and lame of the scurvy, so as he could but lie in the cabin door, and give direction, and, it should seem, was badly assisted either with mate or mariners, or else the fear of, and the unruliness of the passengers was such, as they made them steer a course between the south-west and north-west, that they might fall in with some land; whatever it was they cared not, for they had been six weeks at sea, and had no beer or water, nor wood left, but had burnt up all their empty casks, only one of the company had a hogshead of wine or two, which was also almost spent, so as they feared they should be starved at sea, or consumed with diseases, which made them run this desperate cause. But it pleased God, that although they came so near the shoals of Cape Cod, or else ran stumbling over them in the night, they knew not how, they came before a small harbour... and with a small gale of wind, and about high water, touched upon a bar of sand that lieth before it, but had no hurt, the sea being smooth; so they laid out an anchor... and were not a little glad that they had saved their lives.[1]

Heavenly Father, hear my prayers for those whose lives are adrift and all at sea.
Hear my prayers for those who have lost their way and who are desperate to find
"dry land", as it were, in order to start again. Bless them, I pray,
and send help their way.

---

1 From *Chronicles of the Pilgrim Fathers*.

I BESEECH YOU, BRETHREN, SUFFER THE WORD OF EXHORTATION:
FOR I HAVE WRITTEN A LETTER UNTO YOU IN FEW WORDS.
(Hebrews 13:22 *KJV*)

The plantation of Plimouth received messages from the Dutch plantation, sent unto them from the governor there, written in Dutch and French. The sum of the letters fore mentioned were, to congratulate the English here, taking notice of much that might engage them to a friendly correspondency [*sic*] and good neighbourhood, as the propinquity of their native country, their long continued friendship, etc., and desires to fall into a way of some commerce and trade with them[1][2]

Thank you, Heavenly Father, for those who take the time to write letters – a note of encouragement or concern, maybe, which can make all the difference to someone living on their own, or someone away from home. Thank you for their kind, thoughtful, and helpful ministry.

---

1   The Dutch engaged in trading along American shores years before the English came, but they began no plantation or settlement until after the English came and settled.
2   From *Chronicles of the Pilgrim Fathers.*

THE LORD IS MY SHEPHERD, I LACK NOTHING. HE MAKES ME LIE
DOWN IN GREEN PASTURES, HE LEADS ME BESIDE QUIET WATERS, HE
REFRESHES MY SOUL. HE GUIDES ME ALONG THE RIGHT PATHS FOR
HIS NAME'S SAKE.

(Psalm 23:1–3)

William Bradford now between the planting and the harvest determined to carry further his understanding with the Red Indian[1] tribes around the colony. He asked Edward Winslow,[2] the scholar and traveller, and Stephen Hopkins, the man whose baby Oceanus[3] was born in the *Mayflower* on the voyage, to be ambassadors...

They started out one day in the direction of the villages of Chief Massasoit... They walked through the woods and over the hills, when they came by the rapids of a river...

The Indians in this village treated them as friends and gave them food. Refreshed by this rest along the way, they started again up the river-bank and walked along by the rolling waters for a further five miles...

It was now sunset; so they slept there that night.[4]

Thank you, Good Shepherd, for green pastures along life's journey. Thank you for quiet waters. Thank you for the gift of sleep and refreshment.

---

1   See Footnote 1, July 12th.
2   See Footnote 1, January 12th.
3   See April 25th.
4   From *The Argonauts of Faith*.

IT IS OF THE LORD'S MERCIES THAT WE ARE NOT CONSUMED,
BECAUSE HIS COMPASSIONS FAIL NOT. THEY ARE NEW EVERY
MORNING...
(Lamentations 3:22–23 *KJV*)

There came over one Capt. Wollaston,[1] a man of considerable parts, and with him three or four more of some eminency, who brought with them a great many servants, with provisions and other requisites for to begin a plantation, and pitched themselves in a place within the Massachusetts Bay, which they called afterwards by their captain's name, Mount Wollaston... And amongst others that came with him, there was one Mr. Thomas Morton,[2] who should seem had some small adventure of his own or other men's amongst them, but had little respect, and was slighted by the meanest servants they kept. They having continued some time in New England, and not finding things to answer their expectation, nor profit to arise as they looked for, the said Capt. Wollaston takes a great part of the servants, and transports them to Virginia, and disposed of them there,[3] and writes back to one Mr. Rasdale, of his chief partners, and accounted their merchant, to bring another part of them to Virginia likewise, intending to put them off there, as he had done the rest.[4]

What is fascinating here, Lord, is the issue of reputation. Questions of "eminency" and, conversely, "little respect", are hard to ignore. I ask you to live your life through me today – afresh – according to your daily mercies, so that someone might notice and speak well of Christ because of my witness. Grant me this privilege, I pray.

---

1   Richard Wollaston (d. 1626), English sea captain and pirate.
2   Thomas Morton (c. 1579–1647), lawyer, writer, social reformer, and American colonist from Devon, England. He went on to found the colony of Merrymount, Massachusetts.
3   The likelihood is that they were sold (or exchanged) as slaves. If not actual slaves, then indentured servants.
4   From *Chronicles of the Pilgrim Fathers*.

WINE IS A MOCKER AND BEER A BRAWLER; WHOEVER IS LED ASTRAY
BY THEM IS NOT WISE.
(Proverbs 20:1)

The aforesaid Morton, having more craft than honesty, having been a pettifogger[1] at Furnival's Inn[2]... made them a great feast, and after they were merry, he began to tell them he would give them good counsel; you see, said he, that many of your fellows are carried to Virginia, and if you stay... you will also be carried away and sold for slaves with the rest... I, having a part in the plantation, will receive you as my partners and consociates, so you may be free from service, and we will converse, plant, trade, and live together as equals, or to the like effect. This counsel was easily followed...

After this they fell to great licentiousness of life, in all profaneness, and the said Morton became lord of misrule, and maintained, as it were, a school of Atheism, and after they had got some goods into their hands, and got much by trading with the Indians, they spent it as vainly in quaffing and drinking both wine and strong liquors in great excess, as some have reported, ten pounds' worth, in a morning, setting up a maypole, drinking and dancing about it, and frisking about it like so many fairies, or furies rather, yea, and worse practices, as if they had anew revived and celebrated the feats of the Roman goddess, Flora,[3] or the beastly practices of the mad Bacchanalians.[4]
[5][6]

Heavenly Father, this "imposition" was a source of deep unhappiness to the Pilgrims. Their fledgling way of life was under threat thanks to the unruly antics of their new neighbours. Lord, bless those whose peace has been shattered, whose peaceful and untroubled existence has been interrupted by others, and by circumstances beyond their control. Help them, I pray, as they seek to continue to serve you. Help them to manage their distress. Help them to find you there, alongside them as it seems their lives change for the worse.

---

1   A legal clerk or assistant, dealing mainly with petty or minor legal cases.
2   An Inn of Chancery (legal offices) in Holborn, London.
3   The Roman goddess of flowers and springtime.
4   From the Roman god Bacchus, the god of the grape-harvest and wine-making. "Bacchanalian" is a common byword for drunken revelry.
5   From *Chronicles of the Pilgrim Fathers*.
6   In short, this brief excerpt goes a little way towards describing the unexpected arrival of what we might generously call "noisy neighbours" – that is, the formation of a new colony of pagans whose sole interest in America was for their commercial gain. Their drunken, avaricious behaviour and general conduct was a source of deep distress to the peaceable Pilgrims. In many ways, it ruined the progress that had been made by the Pilgrim Fathers in establishing their Christian settlement. (See Footnote 2, July 20th.)

ABOVE ALL ELSE, GUARD YOUR HEART, FOR EVERYTHING YOU DO
FLOWS FROM IT.
(Proverbs 4:23)

[Thomas] Morton… composed sundry rhymes and verse, some tending to lasciviousness, and others to the detraction and scandal of some persons' names, which he affixed to his idle or idol may-pole; they changed also the name of their place, and instead of calling it Mount Wollaston, they called it the Merry Mount,[1] as if this jollity would have lasted always.[2]

Lord, how upsetting this behaviour must have been to the Pilgrims, whose reputation was one of purity and righteousness. How their hearts must have broken as they witnessed the establishment of the Mount Wollaston colony. My prayers today are for those of your people who are obliged to stand by and witness social and public behaviour that is offensive to the soul. Grant them your wisdom. Grant them your peace even in the midst of troubles. Grant them cleanliness of heart even in a polluted world.[3]

1 See Footnote 2, July 20th.
2 From *Chronicles of the Pilgrim Fathers*.
3 From *Chronicles of the Pilgrim Fathers*.

... TAKE HEED LEST BY ANY MEANS THIS LIBERTY OF YOURS BECOME
A STUMBLING BLOCK TO THEM THAT ARE WEAK.

(1 Corinthians 8:9 *KJV*)

[In order to] maintain this riotous prodigality and profuse expense, the said Morton thinking himself lawless, and hearing what gain the fishermen made of trading of pieces,[1] [gun]powder, and shot; he ... taught the Indians how to use them, to charge and discharge them, and what proportion of powder to give the piece, according to the size and bigness of the same, and what shot to use for fowl, and what for deer; and having instructed them, he employed some of them to hunt and fowl for him; so as they became somewhat more active in this employment than any of the English, by reason of their swiftness of foot, and nimbleness of body, being also quick sighted, and by continual exercise, well knowing the haunts of all sorts of game; so as when they saw the execution that a piece would do, and the benefit that might come by the same, they became very eager after them, and would not stick to give any price they could attain to for them; accounting their bows and arrows but baubles in comparison of them.

And here we may take occasion to bewail the mischief which came by this wicked man, and others like unto him; in that, notwithstanding all laws for the restraint of selling ammunition to the natives, that so far base covetousness prevailed, and doth still prevail, as that the savages became amply furnished with guns, powder, shot, rapiers, pistols, and also well skilled in repairing of defective arms; yea, some have not spared to tell them how gunpowder is made, and all the materials in it, and that they are to be had in their own land, and would, no doubt, in case they could attain to making of saltpetre, teach them how to make powder; and what mischief may fall out to the English in those parts.[2]

Oh, Lord, it's all going horribly wrong! The Indians who were gradually becoming the friends of the Pilgrims are now being educated in money-making greed and violence, and seduced by this way of life! Their attention has been transferred, as it were, from Christ to cash. Bless those of your people, I pray, whose best efforts in friendship and evangelism are (seemingly) thwarted by the cunning wiles of Satan. Help them not to be discouraged. Help them to stay on a steady course of holy living and positive influence, even in the face of what appears to be failure.

---

1   Pistols and rifles. A "piece" is any sort of portable firearm.
2   From *Chronicles of the Pilgrim Fathers*.

July 24ᵀᴴ

LOVE… KEEPS NO RECORD OF WRONGS.
(1 Corinthians 13:4–5)

Mr. Weston's people, who were now seated at ye Massachusetts,[1] and by disorder (as it seems) had made havoc of their provisions, began now to perceive that want would come upon them. And hearing that they had bought trading commodities & intended to trade for corn, they wrote to ye Governor and desired they might join with them, and they would employ their small ship in your service; and further requested either to lend or sell them so much of their trading commodities as their part might come to, and they would undertake to make payment when Mr. Weston, or their supply, should come. The Governor condescended upon equal terms of agreement, thinking to go about ye Cape to ye southward with ye ship, where some store of corn might be got.[2][3]

Gracious Father, help me, I pray, to show kindness towards those who have wronged me. Help me, by your grace, to show charity to those who come to me in need, and to do so without judgment, resentment or prejudice.

---

1 See June 24ᵗʰ.
2 From *History of Plymouth Plantation* (https://archive.org/details/historyofplymout00brad_0/page/n4).
3 This excerpt is taken from William Bradford's notes, and was therefore originally written entirely in 'Olde English'. Furthermore, a great deal of the original spelling is correspondingly archaic and at times quite difficult to follow. Therefore, in order to simplify this excerpt from *History of Plymouth Plantation* (and all subsequent excerpts from that great work), I have taken the liberty of modernizing both the phrasing and the spelling. This makes it immensely more readable, without (I hope) diluting any of Bradford's original content. This modernization also removes the need for me to continually and repeatedly employ "*sic*". (Whereas I have indeed done this elsewhere in this book, William Bradford's writings require more of this treatment than most!)

"... OPEN WIDE YOUR HAND TO YOUR BROTHER ..."
(Deuteronomy 15:11 *ESV*)

After these things, a messenger came from... Mr. Weston's men in ye bay of Massachusetts, who brought a letter showing the great wants they were fallen into; and he would have borrowed... corn of ye Indians, but they would lend him none. He desired advice whether he might not take it from them by force to succour his men till he came from ye eastward, whither he was going. The Governor & rest dissuaded him by all means from it, for it might so exasperate the Indians as might endanger their safety, and all of us might smart for it; for they had already heard how they had so wronged ye Indians by stealing their corn... as they were much incensed against them.[1]

> Lord, my thoughts and prayers are with those who will need to beg today, either literally, for food and money, or metaphorically, in terms of applying for social security benefits and the like – those reliant on "handouts". Theirs is an unenviable position, and a humiliating status, regardless of how or why their plight has occurred. Grant me wisdom, I pray, around any such matters, but help me always to be moved by compassion.

---

1   From *History of Plymouth Plantation*.

"What should we do then?" the crowd asked. John answered, "Anyone who has two shirts should share with the one who has none, and anyone who has food should do the same." (Luke 3:10–11)

In his… essay[1]… Cushman[2] quoted liberally from Scripture to prove that men need not always live where they were born. It was "lawfull" [sic] for them to live elsewhere, even among the heathen, if they brought the "true" gospel with them, for in the wilderness a "drop of the knowledge of Christ is most precious". It was their duty to go to the Indians and convert them, as the latter could not come to them…

Opportunity in the Old World[3] was so restricted, Cushman observed, that "each man is fain to pluck his means, as it were, out of his neighbour's throat. There is such pressing and oppressing in town and country about farms, trades, traffic, &c., so as a man can hardly set up a trade but he shall pull down two of his neighbours". The towns were filled with unemployed men, and the alms-houses and hospitals with the old. "The rent-taker lives on sweet morsels, but the rent-payer eats a dry crust, often with watery eyes; and it is nothing to say what one in a hundred hath, but what the bulk, body, and community hath – which, I warrant you, is short enough… Multitudes get their means by prating,[4] and so do numbers more by begging. Neither comes these straits upon men always through intemperance, ill husbandry, indiscretion, &c., as some think; but even the most wise, sober, and discreet men go often to the wall when they have done their best… Let us not thus oppress, straiten, and afflict one another, seeing that there is a spacious land, the way to which is through the sea."[5][6]

Thank you, Lord, for the beautiful charity with which this logic is presented. This speaks of Christ.

"What is the use of preaching the Gospel to men whose whole attention is concentrated upon a mad, desperate struggle to keep themselves alive?"[7]

---

1 In 1622, Robert Cushman published "Reasons and Considerations Touching the Lawfulness of Removing out of England into Parts of America".
2 See Footnote 2, January 14th.
3 England.
4 Talking nonsense.
5 From *Saints and Strangers*.
6 With social conditions in some parts of England deteriorating, especially in rural areas, the prospect of leaving for a new life in America was increasingly attractive. This option grew in popularity among the likes of farm labourers and those who relied upon the land for their livelihood. In some places, poverty was rife, hence a growing level of interest in starting afresh, overseas.
7 General William Booth, Founder of The Salvation Army.

... OUR REDEEMER, THE LORD OF HOSTS ...
(Isaiah 47:4 *KJV*)

It may be thought strange that [Weston's] people should fall to these extremities in so short a time, being left competently provided when ye ship left them, and had an addition by that moyetie[1] of corn that was got by trade, besides much they got of ye Indians where they lived, by one means & other. It must be their great disorder, for they spent excessively whilst they had, or could get it; and, it may be, wasted part away among ye Indians ... And after they began to come into wants, many sold away their clothes and bed coverings; others (so base were they) became servants to ye Indians, and would cut them wood & fetch them water, for a cap full of corn; others fell to plain stealing, both night & day, from ye Indians, of which they grievously complained. In ye end, they came to that misery, that some starved & died with cold and hunger. One in gathering shellfish was so weak as he stuck fast in ye mud, and was found dead in ye place.[2]

Oh Lord, this is fast becoming a nightmare; traders who set out for what should have been a new and better way of life, falling prey to greed and wastefulness, and ending up in a worse plight than was theirs to begin with. How sad this must have been for the Pilgrims, too, to witness this behaviour. How grieved the Pilgrims must have become as they saw the potential destruction of their hopes and dreams, thanks to those who came to share the colonies.

Lord, in your great mercy, step in when there is chaos. Lord, in your great mercy, intervene when disaster seems to hold sway. Lord, in your great mercy, lend a hand when disappointment strikes. Redeeming God, have mercy.

---

1   Old English: portion or allocation.
2   From *History of Plymouth Plantation*.

What? know ye not that your body is the temple of the Holy Ghost which is in you, which ye have of God, and ye are not your own?

(1 Corinthians 6:19 *KJV*)

The Big Chief wanted soup, some of that "good English pottage such as he had eaten at Plymouth". [They] brewed up corn, strawberry leaves, and sassafras root into something so palatable that the sachem asked for more – but with a duck or goose in it. To humour him [they] shot a mallard and tossed that into the pot. When it was ready [they wanted to] skim off the fat before serving, but Massasoit would not hear of this and in spite of every warning "made a gross meal of it", suffering a violent relapse, heaving and retching... losing his sight, bleeding profusely at the nose,[1] to the great alarm of the Wampanoag... The sachem suffered another relapse, but within a day or two was again on his feet, "lustie" as ever.[2]

> *Some hae meat and canna eat,*
> *And some wad eat that want it,*
> *But we hae meat and we can eat,*
> *And sae the Lord be thankit.*[3]

Thank you, Heavenly Father, for food and drink today. May I eat and drink well, and gratefully, giving thanks, but also sensibly, exercising restraint.

---

1   In Indian custom and superstition, bleeding from the nose was seen as a sure sign of imminent death.
2   From *Saints and Strangers*.
3   Robert Burns, Scottish poet (1759–96).

WALKING ALONG THE BEACH OF LAKE GALILEE, JESUS SAW TWO
BROTHERS: SIMON (LATER CALLED PETER) AND ANDREW. THEY
WERE FISHING, THROWING THEIR NETS INTO THE LAKE. IT WAS
THEIR REGULAR WORK. JESUS SAID TO THEM, "COME WITH ME. I'LL
MAKE A NEW KIND OF FISHERMAN OUT OF YOU. I'LL SHOW YOU HOW
TO CATCH MEN AND WOMEN INSTEAD OF PERCH AND BASS." THEY
DIDN'T ASK QUESTIONS, BUT SIMPLY DROPPED THEIR NETS AND
FOLLOWED.

(Matthew 4:19–20 *The Message*)

The men of the company organized themselves into groups of six or seven, each of which was trained as a crew for the shallop. Now rudely equipped as a fishing vessel, the boat was kept almost constantly at sea trailing schools of cod and other fish. As soon as one crew returned, another shoved off, and none came back without a catch, often staying out a week or more in the worst of weather, for... the men felt that "to goe home emptie would be a great discouragement to ye rest" [*sic*]. On their days ashore, they hunted deer and waterfowl. Men, women, and children prowled the beach for shellfish and gathered groundnuts in the woods.[1]

Must I go, and empty handed,
Thus my dear Redeemer meet?
Not one day of service give Him,
Lay no trophy at His feet?
Must I go, and empty handed?
Must I meet my Saviour so?
Not one soul which which to greet Him,
Must I empty handed go?[2]

Heavenly Father, grant me the holy privilege of helping to win someone for you, through prayer, through witness, or in whichever way you choose. Soul-winning is your work, Lord, I realize that, but perhaps you will use me to "fish" for the kingdom?

---

1   From *Saints and Strangers.*
2   From Charles Carroll Luther's hymn "Must I Go, And Empty Handed?"

… HOPE DOES NOT DISAPPOINT…
(Romans 5:5 *NASB*)

A large vessel was sighted far out in the bay. She proved to be the *Anne of London*, a ship of 140 tons, with supplies and some sixty passengers. She had set sail from England with another vessel, the *Little James*, a fine new pinnace of forty-four tons, built by the merchant adventurers "to stay in ye country". But the *Little James* had not been seen since [a] storm at sea. Hope for her was almost dead when she came limping in ten days later, the captain bitterly cursing the crew, swearing that he would never put to sea again with the green hands hired by the adventurers, for they "cared not whitch end went forwards" [sic].[1]

God of hope, draw alongside those who are feeling hopeless today, those in whose lives hope is "almost dead". Warm their hearts, I pray, especially if they are on the brink of quitting. Let hope prevail.

---

1   From *Saints and Strangers*.

BUT THE LORD SAID UNTO SAMUEL, LOOK NOT ON HIS
COUNTENANCE, OR ON THE HEIGHT OF HIS STATURE; BECAUSE I
HAVE REFUSED HIM: FOR THE LORD SEETH NOT AS MAN SEETH; FOR
MAN LOOKETH ON THE OUTWARD APPEARANCE, BUT THE LORD
LOOKETH ON THE HEART.

(1 Samuel 16:7 *KJV*)

In this… wave of immigration there were, all told, just ninety-three persons… Strangers constituted the larger part of the passengers…

The Saints on board numbered thirty-two… There was also another of the original Scrooby congregation on board – the last ever to reach Plymouth – the prosperous merchant, George Morton,[1] "a pious gracious servante of God" [*sic*]…

Hastening ashore, eager to taste the felicities of New Canaan, so rosily pictured in letters home and publicized… the newcomers were appalled by the "very low condition" of the settlers, finding them pale, haggard, and in rags, some "litle better than halfe naked". Many were so "danted and dismayed" that they openly wished themselves at home again. Others "fell a-weeping, fancying their owne miserie in what they saw in others". For their part, the planters were not altogether pleased with what they saw, frankly disliking the looks of much of the company. Some were "very usefull persons", but others were "so bad as they were faine to be at charge to send them home againe next year" [*sic*].[2]

First impressions! Lord, help me to steer clear of that human tendency of judging books by their covers! Let me avoid that pitfall today.

---

1   George Morton or George Mourt (c. 1585 – 1624), English Puritan Separatist and publisher of the first account in Great Britain of the founding of Plymouth Colony, called *Mourt's Relation*.
2   From *Saints and Strangers*.

WE ALL, LIKE SHEEP, HAVE GONE ASTRAY, EACH OF US HAS TURNED
TO OUR OWN WAY...
(Isaiah 53:6)

The cry went out that a boy was missing. The son of one of the settlers, he had wandered away from the little town and lost himself in the forest. He tried to find his way home, but all round him stood the trunks of thousands of trees. He had not learned, like the Indians, to guide himself through the woods by watching the sun for his direction. He did not know that the moss only grew on one side of the trees. So he went on and on. He cried out, but no voice answered save the call of a bird in the woods. The sun set; the darkness came down; he was tired and hungry and frightened. He took some berries from a bush and ate them; and then, in sheer weariness, he lay down on the ground and slept.[1]

Gracious God, have mercy on those who have wandered far from home. Bless them, Lord, as they navigate uncertain paths. Watch over them, I pray, and bring them safely back into the fold. I think of any known to me personally, who have ventured into unknown or precarious territory. Move in their lives, I pray.

---

1 From *The Argonauts of Faith*.

AUGUST 2ND

YOU DISCERN MY GOING OUT AND MY LYING DOWN...
(Psalm 139:3)

In the morning [the lost boy] woke and ate some more berries. All day he wandered trying to find his way home; but he did not meet any man – red or white. He began to feel that he would never see home or friends again. It seemed as though the whole world was covered with trees. Darkness fell again, and again he slept through the lonely night, with only the sough of the wind in the trees to talk to him if he walked and all around him the silence and solitude of the trackless forests.

For five days the boy wandered on; for four nights he slept under the boughs beneath the open sky. At last he saw a gleam of blue sea and yellow sand through the tree trunks. In a few moments he was out on the beach, with the sea stretching away before him in the spring sunshine.

But, even now, he did not know where he was, or how he could get back to his home; for all the beach was strange to him. He was – though he did not know it – twenty miles away from home, at the head of Buzzard's Bay. He wandered on again. Then he saw moving forms. They were men.

At last he saw that they were Red Indians. Would they scalp him; would they torture him by fire at the stake as a prisoner? In any case, it was useless to run. They surrounded him and took him to their wigwam.[1]

Lord of love, no one is ever really lost in the true sense, because you always know where each and every one of us is, at any time. You not only know where we are, but how we are. Yesterday, I prayed for those who are far from home. I do so again today, but I also thank you for your permanent awareness of our whereabouts and wellbeing. You are a God who cares.

---

1 From *The Argonauts of Faith*.

The Indians were of the Nanset tribe. They had not signed any truce with the Pilgrims as the Massasoit had. But they were kind to the boy. They took him and fed him and he slept in one of their wigwams.

The great chief of the Nansets was called Aspinet. Word passed from him along the forest tracks to Massasoit that the boy was in his tribe. Massasoit sent the news to William Bradford at Plymouth.

At once Bradford consulted with his friends, and they decided to send ten of the younger men of the Pilgrims to rescue the boy. They fitted out the shallop with provisions and armed themselves with muskets, corselets,[1] and the rest. The shallop set out for Buzzard's Bay. The little ship scudded across the water and anchored off the land near the home of Aspinet...

Landing, but leaving a guard on the boat, they plunged up the beach into the woods till the smoke and the wigwams of Aspinet came in sight through the trees. The chief had already, through his scouts, heard of their coming. He waited gravely for the white men. Around him were a full hundred warriors – his bodyguard of braves. The boy was in the midst of them.[2]

Help those who are afraid, Lord. Help those who are disorientated. Help those who are surrounded only by strangers. Help those whose hearts beat with fear.

---

1   Plate armour covering the torso.
2   From *The Argonauts of Faith.*

THEN JESUS TOLD THEM THIS PARABLE: "SUPPOSE ONE OF YOU HAS A HUNDRED SHEEP AND LOSES ONE OF THEM. DOESN'T HE LEAVE THE NINETY-NINE IN THE OPEN COUNTRY AND GO AFTER THE LOST SHEEP UNTIL HE FINDS IT? AND WHEN HE FINDS IT, HE JOYFULLY PUTS IT ON HIS SHOULDERS AND GOES HOME. THEN HE CALLS HIS FRIENDS AND NEIGHBOURS TOGETHER AND SAYS, 'REJOICE WITH ME; I HAVE FOUND MY LOST SHEEP.'"
(Luke 15:3-6)

Aspinet was friendly to [the Pilgrims]. His squaws had fed the boy. Now he hung round the boy's neck great necklaces of coloured beads. They were full of joy at having found the son who was lost. We can imagine how excited he himself was as he trudged back with them to the beach, answering their thousand questions about his adventures; and how his mother would be waiting by the shore at Plymouth for the shallop to come back. The other boys would envy him his adventures, as he told them the story of the days and nights in the woods and among the Indians. But we do not hear that any more of the boys went and lost themselves in the lonely, pathless forests.[1]

Good Shepherd, you search and search for the individual. You make it a priority. How wonderful it is to know that as I am praying today, you are searching today. Your love is relentless, and we are immensely precious in your sight. Searching God, thank you for finding me.

---

1   From *The Argonauts of Faith.*

"… YOU CAME TO VISIT ME."
(Matthew 25:36)

The ships of Plymouth, Devon [England], visited the new community of Plymouth, Massachusetts, in increasing numbers throughout the early seventeenth century – as Captain John Smith reported in 1622, "there is gone from the west of England only to fish 35 ships"… and the Plymouth Company formed in 1621 to exploit the fishing grounds and the fur trade [beaver skins] kept up a thriving relationship with New England.[1]

Lord, I know the visitors from England sailed to America for commercial reasons, but this leads me to thank you for people who make the effort to visit those who are isolated and at some distance from loved ones. Thank you for ministers who prioritize visitation as a part of their ministry, for parish visitors, and for those who simply take the time and trouble to call in on those who could really use some company. Bless them as they do this for you.

---

1   From *The Pilgrim Fathers at Plymouth*.

... LOT'S WIFE LOOKED BACK ...
(Genesis 19:26)

The Church of England was a hierarchy, as its civil government was a monarchy. It was a complicated system of ecclesiastical government, made up of bishops and all the various orders of such an establishment, at the head of which was the reigning monarch, whatever might be his character, and its authority was enforced by all the pains and penalties of the civil power. It was a state establishment which the state organized, and controlled, and corrupted necessarily by this very control. The Church of England, at this time, was only imperfectly reformed, and still retained many of the errors and superstitious practices of the Church of Rome. Indeed, some of these practices had been retained by Elizabeth on purpose to please her Roman Catholic subjects, and with the hope of uniting all in the same ecclesiastical establishment.[1]

Loving God, I pray for any today who are looking back – wondering what might have been. I pray for those who dwell on regrets and failures instead of moving towards the future by holding your hand. Bless those, Lord, whose former days are littered with problems and mistakes. Reassure them of your goodwill towards them, and help them to move gently on.[2]

---

1   From *A Memorial of the Pilgrim Fathers.*
2   I have deliberately inserted both this excerpt and this prayer into this stage of the narrative, as it is perfectly reasonable to assume that some of the Pilgrim colony were by now homesick, maybe even hankering after what, and whom, they had left behind; and likewise, the possibility of somehow forgetting just how grim their situation had been in the homeland, making the classic mistake of looking at things, maybe, with "rose tinted spectacles". This description of the Church of England serves as a deterrent to such thoughts, and an encouragement to keep moving forward with God. (I will continue with this point in tomorrow's devotion.)

Archbishop Land,[1] especially, was bent upon bringing back some of the most objectionable… practices, such as the substitution of an altar for the communion table; the wearing of all the Catholic vestments; the use of pictures and images; the sign of the cross; and kneeling before the bread in the sacrament. And these observances were to be enforced, whatever scruples one might have in regard to them.[2][3]

A reminder today, Lord, of the fact that the grass certainly isn't always greener on the other side – that is, even if the present is difficult, or trying, that doesn't necessarily mean that the past should be revisited, however tempting that might seem. Help me, Lord, in matters of faith, to always make progress, with your help. Help me always to add to my faith, and not to accidentally subtract by heading in the wrong direction.[4]

---

1   Archbishop William Laud, not Land (1573 – 1645), Archbishop of Canterbury from 1633.

2   From *A Memorial of the Pilgrim Fathers.*

3   See Footnote 2, August 6th. The situation of religious confusion and persecution in England had worsened, with a heightened political dimension affecting the very stability of the monarchy. Archbishop Laud was himself executed as one of the victims of such unrest.

4   As Footnote 3.

... I WAS A STRANGER AND YOU WELCOMED ME ...
(Matthew 25:35 *ESV*)

Tension... developed between the recent arrivals and the Old Comers... as the... groups now began to call themselves. The newcomers could not become self-supporting for a year or more, not until they had planted a crop and harvested it the next autumn; they were afraid of starving meanwhile, fearing that the hungry planters might quickly consume all the supplies brought on the ships, leaving them little or nothing. On the other hand, the Old Comers feared that the new company might prove to be an intolerable drain upon their own scanty supplies, the fruit of their conscientious labour in the meersteads[1] along the brook and the fields in the clearing. The latter went to [William] Bradford with the proposal that the newcomers be allowed to keep all the supplies on the ships if they promised to stretch them until they could gather a harvest of their own, and waived all right to share in the Old Comers' supplies. Both parties agreed with alacrity, and the compromise gave "good contente".[2]

> Thank you, Heavenly Father, for a happy outcome in this instance. My prayers today, though, are for those communities where "newcomers" have moved in – people from other countries whose assimilation into towns and cities is not always without problems or tensions. By the same token, Lord, I pray for churches in regard to the welcome they extend to guests and visitors. May such welcomes always be warm and friendly.

---

1   Plots of land staked out as belonging to someone.
2   From *Saints and Strangers*.

I APPEAL TO YOU, BROTHERS, TO WATCH OUT FOR THOSE WHO
CAUSE DIVISIONS AND CREATE OBSTACLES CONTRARY TO THE
DOCTRINE THAT YOU HAVE BEEN TAUGHT; AVOID THEM.
(Romans 16:17 *ESV*)

Under his arm [Edward Winslow][1] was carrying the manuscript of *Good Newes from New England, or a True Relation of things very remarkable at the Plantation of Plimouth in New England*[2] ... It was well titled, for it contained some truly remarkable things, especially Winslow's Preface and Epistle Dedicatory. Both were largely an attack upon Weston's men and their conduct at Wessagusset.[3] They had made "Christ and Christianity stink in the nostrils of the poor infidels," he declared, forgetting that they at least had not treacherously killed any in cold blood. Weston's men had been driven out, it now appeared, because the Pilgrims disapproved of their "lives and manners amongst the Indians", and were resolved "not to foster them in their desired courses".[4]

This is terribly sad, Lord. Such divisions, such conclusions, must always be the last resort, and only enacted when every option of reconciliation has been exhausted. This leads me to pray for church leaders who are faced with awful decisions regarding such matters as excommunication and removal from membership. Those are painful issues for all concerned. I pray for your help.

1   See Footnote 1, January 12th.
2   Published in London in 1624.
3   See June 24th, etc.
4   From *Saints and Strangers*.

But you, Lord, are … the One who lifts my head high.
(Psalm 3:3)

There came in another small ship of about forty-four tons, named the *James*, Mr. Bridges being master thereof… One of the principal passengers that came in her was Mr. John Jenny,[1] who was a godly, though otherwise a plain man, yet singular for publicness of spirit, setting himself to seek and promote the common good of the plantation of New Plimouth; who spent not only his part of this ship (being part owner thereof) in the general concernment of the plantation, but also afterwards was always a leading man in promoting the general interest of this colony. He lived many years in New England, and fell asleep in the Lord, anno 1644[2]… Many other persons [came over], who proved of good use in their places.

These passengers, seeing the low and poor conditions of those that were here before them, were much daunted and dismayed, and, according to their divers humours, were diversely affected. Some wished themselves in England again; others fell on weeping, fancying their own misery in what they saw in others; other some pitying the distress they saw their friends had been long in, and still were under. In a word, all were full of sadness; only some of their old friends rejoiced to see them, and that it was no worse with them, for they could not expect it should be better, and now hoped they should enjoy better days together. And truly it was no marvel they should be thus affected, for they were in a very low condition, both in respect of food and clothing at that time.[3]

Thank you, Lord, for the "John Jennys" you send my way – godly people who bless others with their demeanour and attitude. I pray today, though, for those whose circumstances make it difficult for them to be cheerful or optimistic. Draw alongside them and lift their spirits, as only you can.

---

1 Born in Norwich, England, in about 1589.
2 Or 1643. It is possible John Jenny died at the end of 1643, with his death being registered in 1644.
3 From *Chronicles of the Pilgrim Fathers*.

SOME WERE SAYING, "WE AND OUR SONS AND DAUGHTERS ARE NUMEROUS; IN ORDER FOR US TO EAT AND STAY ALIVE, WE MUST GET GRAIN."

(Nehemiah 5:2)

To consider seriously how sadly the Scripture speaks of the famine in Jacob's time, when he said to his sons, go buy us food, that we may live and not die; and that the famine was great and heavy in the land, and yet they had such great herds and store of cattle of sundry kinds, which, besides their flesh, must needs produce other useful benefits for food, and yet it was accounted a sore affliction. But the misery of the planters at Plimouth, at the first beginning, must needs be very great therefore, who not only wanted the staff of bread, but all the benefits of cattle, and had no Egypt to go to, but God fed them out of the sea for the most part; so wonderful is his powerful providence over his in all ages; for his mercy endureth for ever.[1]

Lord you are our Father, a loving parent who cares for us, your children. Here today we are just a few of your many million precious, loved and valued children. Help us to recognise the needs of our brothers and sisters – all made in your image. Hallowed be your name, not my name or any other. May your justice and truth reign on this planet which is stricken with poverty. When we ask for your kingdom to come, we do so laying all our resources at your feet. Help us, as part of your church, to be obedient to your call to look after people in need in your name. Give us your daily bread, and help us to share abundantly the plenty that we have been blessed with. Amen.[2]

---

1   From *Chronicles of the Pilgrim Fathers*.
2   From Peter Shaw, editor, *Tear Times* and *Prayer Diary*. http://www.tearfund.org/~/media/files/ main%20site/campaigning/if/pray/writtenprayersonhungerforyoutouseinyourchurch.pdf

LET YOUR GENTLENESS BE EVIDENT TO ALL.
(Philippians 4:5)

Capt. Robert Gorges[1] [arrived], in the bay of Massachusetts, with sundry passengers and families, intended there to begin a plantation, and pitched upon that place, which Mr. Weston forenamed had forsaken...

He, meeting with the aforesaid Mr. Weston at Plimouth, called him before him and some other of the assistants, with the governor of Plimouth... and charged him with ill carriage of his men at the Massachusetts, by which means the peace of the country was disturbed, and himself and the people which he had brought over to plant in that bay, thereby much prejudiced. To which the said Weston easily answered, that what was done in that behalf, was done in his absence, and might have befallen any man. He left them sufficiently provided, and conceived they would have been well governed; and for any error committed he had sufficiently smarted...

The said Weston excused it as well as he could, but could not wholly deny it; but after much speech about it, by the mediation of the governor of Plimouth, and some other friends, the said Capt. Gorges was inclined to gentleness... which when the said Weston perceived, he grew the more presumptuous, and gave such cutting and provoking speeches, as made the said captain rise up in great indignation and distemper, vowing, that he would either curb him, or send him home for England.[2]

"Inclined to gentleness." Lord, may that be said of me this day, even if, as was the case in this story, such gentleness is abused and exploited.

---

1   Captain Robert Gorges (1595–late 1620s), English navy. Governor-General of New England from 1623 to 1624.
2   From *Chronicles of the Pilgrim Fathers*.

BE YE NOT UNEQUALLY YOKED TOGETHER WITH UNBELIEVERS:
FOR WHAT FELLOWSHIP HATH RIGHTEOUSNESS WITH
UNRIGHTEOUSNESS? AND WHAT COMMUNION HATH LIGHT
WITH DARKNESS?

(*2 Corinthians 6:14 KJV*)

Mr. Weston will not permit letters to be sent in his ships, nor anything for your good or ours, or which there is some reason in respect of himself, &c. His brother Andrew, whom he doth send as principal in one of these ships, is a heady young man, and violent, and set against you there, and ye company here; plotting with Mr. Weston their own ends, which tend to your & our undoing in respect of our estates there, and prevention of our good ends…

The Lord, who is ye watchman of Israel & sleepeth not, preserve you & deliver you from unreasonable men. I am sorry that there is cause to admonish you of these things concerning this man; so I leave you to God, who bless and multiply you into thousands, to the advancement of ye glorious gospel of our Lord Jesus. Amen. Farewell.

Your loving friends,
Edward Pickering,[1]
William Greene.[2]

I pray conceal both ye writing and delivery of this letter, but make the best use of it.[3][4][5]

Thank you, Lord, for friends and colleagues whose counsel is wise, honest, and helpful. Give me, I pray, ears that will listen to good advice. Give me, I pray, a heart that is humble enough to accept instruction.

---

1   Thomas Weston's agent in Holland.
2   English merchant adventurer and investor.
3   Extracted from a letter to William Bradford.
4   From *History of Plymouth Plantation.*
5   See Footnote 3, July 24th.

IF IT IS POSSIBLE, AS FAR AS IT DEPENDS ON YOU, LIVE AT PEACE
WITH EVERYONE.
(Romans 12:18)

Weston was daunted, and came privately to the governor of Plimouth, to know whether they would suffer him to send him for England? It was answered him, they could not hinder it; and much blamed him, that after they had pacified things, he should thus break out by his own folly and rashness, and bring trouble upon himself and others. He confessed it was his passion, and prayed the governor aforesaid to entreat for him, and procure a pacification for him if he could; the which at last he did obtain with much difficulty. So he was called again, and the said Capt. Georges was content to take his own bond to be ready to make further answer, when either he or the lords of the council should send for him; and at last he took only his own word, and so there was a friendly parting on all hands.[1]

Lord Jesus, may I be a peacemaker today.

---

1   From *Chronicles of the Pilgrim Fathers.*

"IS NOT THIS MAN A BURNING STICK SNATCHED FROM THE FIRE?"
(Zechariah 3:2)

Capt. Gorges took his leave and went to Massachusetts by land, being very thankful for the kind entertainment. His ship stayed at Plimouth, and fitted for to go to Virginia, having some passengers to deliver there, and with her returned sundry of those from Plimouth, which came over on their particular account; some out of discontent and dislike of the country, and others by reason of fire that burnt their houses and all their provisions, so as they were necessitated thereunto.

This fire was by some of the seamen, that were roystering [*sic*] in an house where it first began, making a great fire, the weather being cold, which broke out of the chimney into the thatch, and burnt three houses, and consumed all their goods and provisions. The house in which it began, was right against the storehouse in Plimouth, which they had much ado to save; in which was the common store of the provisions of the plantation, which had it been lost, the same had been overthrown; but through God's mercy it was saved by the diligence of the people, and the care of the governor and those about him...

And soon after, when the vehemency of the fire was over, smoke was seen to rise within a shed that was joined to the aforesaid storehouse, which was wattled up with boughs, in the withered leaves whereof the fire being kindled; which some running to quench, found a long firebrand of about an ell[1] long lying on the wall on the inside, which could not come thither by casualty, but must be laid there by some hand, in the judgment of all that saw it. But God kept them from this danger, whatever might be intended.[2]

Lord, it is no doubt true that you have saved me from any number of dangers of which I am blissfully unaware. Likewise, you will have rescued me from problems that I have only avoided because of your gracious protection. Thank you, Lord, for working anonymously on my behalf!

---

1   The measurement from a man's arm to the tip of his middle finger.
2   From *Chronicles of the Pilgrim Fathers*.

... THE HAND OF THE DILIGENT MAKES RICH.
(Proverbs 10:4 *ESV*)

The Dutch sent again unto them... both kind letters, and also diverse commodities, as sugar, linen cloth, Holland finer & courser stuffs, &c. They came up with their bark to Manamete, to their house there, in which came their Secretarie Rasier;[1] who was accompanied with a noise of trumpeters, and some other attendants; and desired that they would send a boat for him, for he would not travail so far over land. So they sent a boat... and brought him to ye plantation, with ye chiefs of his company. And after some few days entertainment, he returned to his bark, and some of them went with him, and bought sundry of his goods; after which beginning thus made, they sent often times to ye same place, and had intercourse together for diverse years; and amongst other commodities, they vended much tobacco for linen cloth, stuffs, &c., which was a good benefit to ye people.[2]

Heavenly Father, I pray for Christians in business. I pray that you would bless their efforts to succeed, and that you would reward the long hours of work they invest. As they seek to work along honest lines, and with integrity, I ask you to grant them your commercial favour. I pray especially for those whose businesses compete with rivals who are much bigger.

---

1   Isaac de Rasier, Secretary of the Dutch Colony.
2   From *History of Plymouth Plantation*.

HE WILL JUDGE BETWEEN THE NATIONS AND WILL SETTLE DISPUTES
FOR MANY PEOPLES. THEY WILL BEAT THEIR SWORDS INTO
PLOWSHARES AND THEIR SPEARS INTO PRUNING HOOKS. NATION
WILL NOT TAKE UP SWORD AGAINST NATION, NOR WILL THEY TRAIN
FOR WAR ANYMORE.
(Isaiah 2:4)

Hitherto ye Indians of these parts had no pieces[1] nor other arms but their bows and arrows, nor of many years after; neither did they scarce handle a gun, so much were they afraid of them; and ye very sight of one (though out of jilter) was a terror unto them. But those Indians to ye east parts, which had commerce with ye French, got pieces from them, and they in ye end made a common trade of it; and in time our English fishermen, led with ye like covetousness, followed their example, for their own gain; but upon complaint against them, it pleased the kings majesty to prohibit ye same by a strict proclamation, commanding that no sort of arms, or munition, should by any of his subjects be traded with them.[2]

Lord, how it must grieve you when wealthy and powerful nations trade in arms, often to the brutal detriment of countries riven by war and poverty. Forgive, Lord, the gruesome dealings in bombs and instruments of death. Forgive, Lord, when such dealing is all about money, and has little to do with security and safety. How wonderful it would be to see some kind of strict legal prohibitions in place, all the while innocent people are maimed and killed. Lord, have mercy.

---

1   See Footnote 1, July 23ʳᵈ.
2   From *History of Plymouth Plantation*.

WHEN ANXIETY WAS GREAT WITHIN ME, YOUR
CONSOLATION BROUGHT ME JOY.
(Psalm 94:19)

Another ship put in to give the Pilgrims a fright. It had on board... one William Morrell, a man of "fine classical taste". But that interested the Saints far less than the fact that he was wearing Anglican vestments and came armed with "authority of superintendencie" [sic] over all churches in New England. Here was the intervention that had long been feared...

The Reverend William Morrell[1]... spent his time composing a long Latin poem on New England, being particularly impressed with its "ghusts of wind". He had made no attempt to exercise his "superintendencie" over the churches – perhaps, as Bradford said, because he "saw it was in vaine" [sic]. It was so much pleasanter to pursue tripping dactyls in Latin verse than to go poking about a hornet's nest.[2]

Lord, how often is it the case that we dread something, or fear something, which turns out to be harmless – or, at least, perfectly manageable, with your help. Thank you for your watchful love. Thank you for your knowledge of every dread and fear. Thank you, Heavenly Father, for imparting peace when once there was anxiety. Help me to trust you more. My prayers today include those who are worried about what might happen next, or who might arrive.

---

1   Anglican clergyman and American poet.
2   From *Saints and Strangers*.

THE STEADFAST LOVE OF THE LORD NEVER CEASES; HIS MERCIES
NEVER COME TO AN END; THEY ARE NEW EVERY MORNING; GREAT IS
YOUR FAITHFULNESS.
(Lamentations 3:22–23 *ESV*)

Notwithstanding any laws to ye contrary; so as ye Indians are full of pieces all over, both fouling pieces, muskets, pistols, &c. They have also their moulds to make shot, of all sorts, as musket bullets, pistol bullets, swan and goose shot, & of smaller sorts... with sundry other implements, wherewith they are ordinarily better fitted and furnished than ye English themselves. Yea, it is well known that they will have powder & shot, when the English want it, nor cannot get it; and yet in a time of war or danger, as experience hath manifested, that when lead hath been scarce, and men for their own defence would gladly have given a groat,[1] which is dear enough, yet hath it been bought up & sent to other places, and sold to such as trade it with ye Indians, at 12 pence, it is likely they give 3 or 4 ye pound, for they will have it at any rate. And these things have been done in ye same times, when some of their neighbours & friends are daily killed by ye Indians, or are in danger thereof, and live but at ye Indians mercy. Yea, some (as they have acquainted them with all other things) have told them how gunpowder is made, and all ye materials in it, and that they are to be had in their own land; and I am confident, could they attain to make saltpeter,[2] they would teach them to make powder. O the horribleness of this villainy![3]

Lord, have mercy. Forgive humankind "this villainy" and all the multitude of sins
to which we are so prone. We rely entirely on your grace as we seek your pardon.
We have no argument. We have no right to plead,
yet we call upon your steadfast love.

1 English and Irish coin worth about 4p.
2 A chemical compound used in the manufacture of explosives.
3 From *History of Plymouth Plantation*.

... YOUR HANDS ARE STAINED WITH BLOOD, YOUR FINGERS
WITH GUILT.

(Isaiah 59:3)

How many both Dutch & English have been lately slain by those Indians, thus furnished; and no remedy provided, nay, ye evil more increased, and ye blood of their brethren sold for gain, as is to be feared; and in what danger all these colonies are in is too well known. Oh! That princes and parliaments would take some timely order to prevent this mischief, and at length to suppress it, by some exemplary punishment upon some of these gain thirsty murderers (for they deserve no better title), before their colonies in these parts be overthrown by these barbarous savages, thus armed with their own weapons, by these evil instruments, and traitors to their neighbours and country... This Morton having this taught them ye use of pieces, he sold them all he could spare; and he and his consorts determined to send for many out of England.[1]

Almighty God, I pray for the "Mortons" of this world: criminals, murderers, those who deliberately choose and encourage bloodshed. Come to their hearts, Lord, as you did to the bloodthirsty Saul of Tarsus all those years ago. May grace prevail as you visit their lives.

---

1   From *History of Plymouth Plantation.*

I WILL MAKE THEM AND THE PLACES SURROUNDING MY HILL A
BLESSING. I WILL SEND DOWN SHOWERS IN SEASON; THERE WILL BE
SHOWERS OF BLESSING. THE TREES WILL YIELD THEIR FRUIT AND
THE GROUND WILL YIELD ITS CROPS; THE PEOPLE WILL BE
SECURE IN THEIR LAND. THEY WILL KNOW THAT I AM THE LORD...
(Ezekiel 34:26–27)

A drought had set in and continued for weeks, with not a drop of rain, till even the most sanguine lost hope. Their corn and beans wilted on the stalk and turned brown. In desperation the Saints appointed a "solemne day of humiliation" [sic]. They assembled in the morning and prayed eight or nine hours under a hot clear sky, and it seemed that the drought was "as like to continue as ever it was". But the meeting had no sooner adjourned... than clouds began to pile up on the horizon and during the night – and for two weeks thereafter – "distilled such soft, sweete, and moderate showers... as it was hard to say whether our withered corne or drooping affections were most quickened and revived" [sic]. [Some] Indians had noted the preparations for the meeting, and as it was not the Sabbath, had inquired the reason for it. When they saw the results, they were most impressed. It showed them... the difference between their conjurations and our invocation on the name of God for rain, theirs being mixed with such storms and tempests as sometimes, instead of doing them good, it layeth the corn flat on the ground to their prejudice, but ours in so gentle and seasonable a manner as they never observed the like. The Pilgrims promptly set aside another day to thank the Lord for "his mercies towards his Church and chosen ones".[1]

> There shall be showers of blessing:
> This is the promise of love;
> There shall be seasons refreshing,
> Sent from the Saviour above.
>
> Showers of blessing,
> Showers of blessing we need;
> Mercy-drops round us are falling,
> But for the showers we plead.[2]

---

1   From *Saints and Strangers*.
2   From Daniel Webster's hymn, written under the pseudonym of D. W. Whittle.

... ROOTED AND BUILT UP IN HIM AND ESTABLISHED IN THE
FAITH ...
(Colossians 2:7 *ESV*)

Whatever the cause [of the showers], "ye face of things was changed to ye rejoysing of ye harts of many" [*sic*]. All had raised enough to carry them through till the next harvest. Some of the more industrious had corn and other produce to sell, and Plymouth never again knew "any general wante or famine" [*sic*]. Many another colony had cracked up under far less strain and hardship. The always "answerable courage" of the Pilgrims had stood them in good stead. They were at last securely established in the wilderness, thanks to their own tireless efforts, for it is true, as Bradford declared, that the supplies brought on the *Fortune* and later ships never did more – and often did less – than provide for the needs of the additional settlers who came on these ships. It had been a terrific uphill struggle, often against apparently hopeless odds. It had been fraught with tragedy, marked by many slips and egregious blunders, but the battle had been won. The Pilgrims could now confidently "stand on their owne legs" [*sic*].[1]

Thank you, Lord, for your great faithfulness through our "many slips and egregious blunders". Thank you that you do not abandon us. On the contrary, you continue to work within us until we become more and more established in our faith, and in our circumstances. You are my God.

1   From *Saints and Strangers*.

THE ONE WHO CALLS YOU IS FAITHFUL...
(1 Thessalonians 5:24)

The planters met for their regular annual election of officers. Having nursed the infant colony through its painful teething period, Governor Bradford tried to beg off, asking to be relieved of office, saying that "if it was any honour or benefite, it was fitte others should be made pertakers of it; if it was a burthen[1] (as doubtles it was), it was but equall that others should help bear it" [sic]. The Pilgrims would not hear of this, however, and finally persuaded him to continue by agreeing to increase the number of assistant governors to five... The five assistants and the governor made up the Council which performed all functions of government, not only executive, but legislative and judicial as well, with the governor having a "duble voice" [sic] in all matters.[2]

Today, Heavenly Father, I simply pray for church leaders, including those who exercise leadership within my own fellowship. I bring them to you and ask you to meet their needs.

---

1 Archaic form of "burden".
2 From *Saints and Strangers*.

"DO NOT MISTREAT OR OPPRESS A FOREIGNER, FOR YOU WERE
FOREIGNERS IN EGYPT."
(Exodus 22:21)

There was one Mr. Ralfie Smith, & his wife and family, yet came over into ye Bay of ye Massachusetts, and sojourned at present with some straggling people that lived at Natascoe; here being a boat of this place putting in there on some occasion, he earnestly desired that they would give him & his, passage for Plimouth, and some such things as they could well carry; having before heard yet there was likelihood he might procure house-rooms for some time, till he should resolve to settle there, if he might, or elsewhere as God should dispose; for he was weary of being in ye uncouth place, & in a poor house yet would neither keep him nor his goods dry. So, seeing him to be a grave man, & understood he had been a minister, though they had no order for any such thing, yet they presumed and brought him. He was here accordingly kindly entertained & housed, & had ye rest of his goods and servants sent for, and exercised his gifts amongst them, and afterwards was chosen into ye ministries, and so remained for sundry years.[1]

> Help me always to remember, Lord, if and when a stranger comes to me in
> need, that I too was once a stranger – a stranger to grace until I was taken in
> and adopted with Christ as my Saviour. Help me, I pray, to extend that same
> hospitality of heart to those I meet, for Jesus' sake.

---

1   From *History of Plymouth Plantation.*

SOME WOMEN WERE WATCHING FROM A DISTANCE. AMONG THEM
WERE MARY MAGDALENE, MARY THE MOTHER OF JAMES THE
YOUNGER AND OF JOSEPH, AND SALOME. IN GALILEE THESE WOMEN
HAD FOLLOWED HIM AND CARED FOR HIS NEEDS. MANY OTHER
WOMEN WHO HAD COME UP WITH HIM TO JERUSALEM
WERE ALSO THERE.

(Mark 15:40–41)

This… letter shows the proceedings in their church affairs at Salem, which was ye
2nd church erected in these parts; and afterwards ye Lord established many more in
sundry places.

> Sir: I make bold to trouble you with a few lines, for to certify you
> how it hath pleased God to deal with us… . How, notwithstanding
> all opposition that hath been here, & elsewhere, it hath pleased God
> to lay a foundation, the which I hope is agreeable to his word in
> everything… It pleased ye Lord to move ye heart of our Governor
> to set… apart… a solemn day of humiliation, for ye choice of a
> pastor & teacher. The former part of ye day being spent in prayer
> and teaching, the latter part about ye election, which was after
> this manner. The persons thought on (who had been ministers in
> England) were demanded following their callings; they acknowledged
> there was a two-fold calling, when ye Lord moved ye heart of a man
> to take ye calling upon him, and fitted him with gifts for ye same;
> the second was an outward calling, which was from ye people, when
> a company of believers are joined together in covenants, to walk
> together in all ye ways of God, and every member (being men) are to
> have a free voice in ye choice of their officers, &c.[1]

"Every member (being men) are to have a free voice"! Lord of the church,
how strange it seems, in this modern day and age, to remember that women,
once upon a time, had no voice at all in church matters, but were regarded as
secondary and relatively unimportant. How wonderful it is, nowadays, to see
your Spirit releasing women into ministry. More of the same, please, Lord! Bless
female leaders, as I thank you for the progress that has been made.

---

1   From *History of Plymouth Plantation*.

FOR EVERY BEAST OF THE FOREST IS MINE, AND THE CATTLE UPON
A THOUSAND HILLS. I KNOW ALL THE FOWLS OF THE MOUNTAINS:
AND THE WILD BEASTS OF THE FIELD ARE MINE.
(Psalm 50:10–11 *KJV*)

Mr. Edward Winslow arrived at Plimouth, in New England, having been employed as an agent for that plantation, on sundry occasions, with the merchant adventurers in England,[1] who brought a considerable supply with him, the ship[2] being bound on a fishing voyage; and with him came Mr. John Lyford, a minister,[3] who was sent over by some of the adventurers.

There came over likewise in this ship, three heifers and a bull, which were the first neat cattle that came into New England.[4]

"Three heifers and a bull"! A little reminder today, Lord, within that line, of your sovereignty, and your divine right of ownership. Help me, Lord, to handle lightly that which is yours, and to remember that all that I have comes from you. Preserve my heart from the spirit of materialism!

---

1 Edward Winslow was a passenger on the *Mayflower*, but he travelled between England and New England fairly regularly, as a commercial traveller and businessman.
2 The *Charity*.
3 Reverend John Lyford (c. 1580–1634).
4 From *Chronicles of the Pilgrim Fathers*.

"No one is good – except God alone."
(Mark 10:18)

The aforesaid John Lyford, when he came first on shore, saluted them of the plantation of Plimouth with the reverence and humility, as is seldom to be seen; and indeed made them ashamed, he so bowed and cringed unto them, and would have kissed their hands, if they would have suffered him; yea, he wept and shed many tears, blessing God that he had brought him to see their faces; and admiring the things they had done in their wants, as if he had been made all of love, and the humblest person in the world.[1]

> "As if he had been made all of love". Well, Lord, John Lyford wasn't, of course, but you are! You are infinitely perfect. You are my God. I worship you today, as the One who is without fault, flaw, or blemish. As you have been, so you are, and so you will always be.

---

1   From *Chronicles of the Pilgrim Fathers.*

His victims are crushed, they collapse; they fall under his
strength. He says to himself, "God will never notice; he
covers his face and never sees."
(Psalm 10:10–11)

In the end [John Lyford] proved more like those mentioned by the Psalmist, Psalm x.10, that crouched and bowed, that heaps of the poor may fall by them; or like unto dissembling Ishmael, who when he had slain Gedaliah, went out weeping, Jer. Xli.6; and met those that were coming to offer incense in the house of the Lord, saying, come to Gedaliah, when he meant to slay them. They gave him the best entertainment they could, in all simplicity, and as their governor had used, in all weighty affairs, to consult with their elder, Mr. Brewster, together with his assistants, so now he called Mr. Lyford also on such like occasions. After some short time, he desired to join himself a member to their church, and was accordingly received; he made a large confession of his faith, and an acknowledgement of his former disorderly walking, and his being entangled with many corruptions, which had been a burden to his conscience, and blessed God for this opportunity of freedom and liberty, with many such like expressions. In some short time he fell into acquaintance with Mr. John Oldham,[1] who was a co-partner with him in his after courses; not long after, both Oldham and he grew very perverse, and showed a spirit of great malignity, drawing as many into a faction as they could; were they never so vile and profane, they did nourish and abet them in all their doings, so they would but cleave to them, and speak against the church.[2]

Heavenly Father, grant me your grace so as to live in an upright manner,
pleasing you and doing the right thing by my fellow human beings. Give me that
sensitivity of spirit whereby I shun the wrong and embrace the right, both in
public and in private. Lord, you alone know how deceitful the human heart can
be, and how easily I can be led astray. Hear my confession, and help me this day.

---

1   John Oldham (1592–1636), Puritan settler, ship's captain, merchant trader.
2   From *Chronicles of the Pilgrim Fathers*.

... A LAND OF WHEAT AND BARLEY...
(Deuteronomy 8:8 *ESV*)

The *Charity* reappeared in the harbour, again under the command of Captain William Peirce,[1] renowned as the "ferryman of the North Atlantic" because he had brought across so many of New England's early settlers, later settling down himself at Boston. On board was Edward Winslow, returning from his visit to London with a few provisions, articles for the Indian trade, a quantity of hooks and nets and other fishing gear, a ship's carpenter, a salt-maker,[2] the Reverend John Lyford, and "3 heifers & a bull, the first beginning of any cattle of that kind in ye land". In a letter to his brethren, Cushman[3] apologized for not sending such "comfortable things as butter, sugar, &c.". There was no money for that. Rather, all available funds had been spent to provide Plymouth with the means of establishing itself in the fishing, salt-making, and boat-building trades. Once that were done, the planters could take care of themselves and be freed from dependence upon irregular and uncertain shipments of supply. Let them give the ship's carpenter "absolute command over his servants & such as are put to him", Cushman advised, suggesting the immediate construction of two ketches,[4] a lighter,[5] and six or seven shallops. Let others be assigned to work with the salt-maker, "a skillfull and industrious man" [*sic*], so that they might quickly learn the "misterie" [*sic*] of it.[6]

> **Some days, Lord, are spent without "comfortable things as butter, sugar" –**
> **ordinary days, mundane moments, which appear to hold nothing particularly**
> **special or attractive. On those days, Lord, help me to appreciate "the everyday",**
> **which has blessings of its own. Help me, though, to give thanks for the "butter**
> **and sugar" days too, whenever they appear!**

---

1   Died between 1645 and 1647. Ship's captain, tobacco merchant, slave trader.
2   Someone skilled at harvesting salt from sea water, for commercial purposes.
3   See Footnote 2, January 14th.
4   A two-masted sailboat.
5   A shallow barge.
6   From *Saints and Strangers*.

... THE LIGHT HAS COME INTO THE WORLD, AND PEOPLE LOVED THE
DARKNESS RATHER THAN THE LIGHT BECAUSE THEIR WORKS WERE
EVIL. FOR EVERYONE WHO DOES WICKED THINGS HATES THE LIGHT
AND DOES NOT COME TO THE LIGHT, LEST HIS WORKS SHOULD BE
EXPOSED.

(John 3:19–20 *ESV*)

When the ship he came in was ready to return to England, and it was observed that Lyford was long in writing, and sent many letters, and could not forbear to communicate to his intimates such things as made them laugh in their sleeves, and thought he had done their errand sufficiently. The governor and some of his friends, knowing how things stood in reference to some known adversaries in England, and what hurt these things might do, took a boat, and went out with the ship a league or two, and called for all Lyford's and Oldham's letters. Mr. William Pierce being master of the ship, and knew well their evil dealings (both in England and here), afforded them all the assistance he could; he found about twenty of Lyford's letters, many of them large and full of slanders and false accusations, tending not only to prejudice, but ruin and utter subversion. Most of them they let pass, only took copies of them, but some of the most material they sent true copies of them and kept the originals, lest he should deny them, and that they might produce his own hand against him. Amongst these letters they found the copies of two letters which were sent in a letter of his to Mr. John Pemberton, a minister, and a great opposite to the plantation; these two letters, of which he took copies, were one of them written by a gentleman in England, to Mr. Brewster here, the other by Mr. Winslow to Mr. Robinson in Holland; at his coming away, as the ship lay at Gravesend, they lying sealed in the great cabin, while Mr. Winslow was busy about the affairs of the ship, the sly merchant opens them, takes copies of them, and seals them up again, and not only seals the copies of them thus, To his friend and their adversary, but adds thereto in the margin many scurrilous and flouting annotations.[1]

What a complicated problem, Lord! What a complexity of sin and skulduggery! Grant me, I pray, from this moment on, a transparent life. Forgive that which has not been so, and which has hindered my witness for Christ. Reign in me today as I come to you for cleansing, pardon, and renewal.

---

1   From *The Chronicles of the Pilgrim Fathers.*

... BE SURE YOUR SIN WILL FIND YOU OUT.

(Numbers 32:23 *KJV*)

They found a letter... in which it was written that Mr. Oldham and Mr. Lyford intended a reformation in church and commonwealth, and as soon as the ship was gone they intended to join together and have the sacrament; a few of Oldham's letters were found in the aforesaid search, being so bad a scribe as his hand was scarce legible, yet he was as deep in the mischief as the other; and thinking they were now strong enough, they began to pick quarrels at everything...

It was now thought high time, to prevent further mischief, to call them to account; so the governor called a court, and summoned the whole company together, and they charged Lyford and Oldham with such things as they were guilty of... but they were stiff, and stood resolutely upon the denial of most things, and required proof...

Lyford denied, and made strange of sundry things laid to his charge. Then his letters were produced, at which he was struck mute. Oldham began to be furious, and to rage...

After their trial and conviction, the court sentenced them to be expelled the plantation; John Oldham presently to depart, though his wife and family had liberty to stay all the winter, or longer, until he could make provision to remove them comfortably. Lyford had liberty to stay six months; it was with some eye to his release, if he carried himself well in the meantime, and that his repentance proved sound. Lyford acknowledged that his censure was far less than he deserved, and afterwards he confessed his sin publicly in the church, with tears.[1] [2]

Heavenly Father, you are gracious and compassionate. When I confess my sins to you in prayer, you do not gloat, neither do you exploit. Rather, you cry with me, alongside me, and you point me to the cross. Thank you. I pray today for any who fear you, for those who are frightened of approaching you in case they are punished and treated harshly. Whisper words of love and reassurance to them. You are indeed a pardoning God who delights in mercy.

---

1 From *Chronicles of the Pilgrim Fathers*.
2 Space does not permit me to include much more about this episode, but I would refer you to https://en.wikipedia.org/wiki/John_Lyford if you would like to read about Reverend Lyford in greater detail.

THE MEN STEPPED FORWARD, SEIZED JESUS AND ARRESTED HIM. WITH
THAT, ONE OF JESUS' COMPANIONS REACHED FOR HIS SWORD, DREW IT OUT
AND STRUCK THE SERVANT OF THE HIGH PRIEST, CUTTING OFF HIS EAR.
"PUT YOUR SWORD BACK IN ITS PLACE," JESUS SAID TO HIM, "FOR ALL WHO
DRAW THE SWORD WILL DIE BY THE SWORD."

(Matthew 26:50–52)

Sir Christopher Gardener,[1] being... descended of ye house [of] the Bishop of Winchester... (who was so great a persecutor of God's saints in Queen Maries [sic] days),[2] and being a great traveller, received his first honour of knighthood at Jerusalem, being made Knight of ye Sepulchre[3] there. He came into these parts under pretence of forsaking ye world, and to live a private life, in a godly course, not unwilling to put himself upon any mean employments, and take any pains for his living; and sometime offered himself to join to ye churches in sundry places. He brought over with him a servant or 2 and a comely young woman, whom he called his cousin, but it was suspected... was his concubine. Living at ye Massachusetts, for some miscarriages which he should have answered, he fled away from authority, and got among ye Indians of these parts; they sent after him, but could not get him, and promised some reward to those [who] should find him. The Indians came to ye Governor here, and told where he was, and asked if they might kill him; he told them no, by any means, but if they could take him and bring him thither, they should be paid for their pains. They said he had a gun and a rapier, & he would kill them if they went about it; and ye Massachusetts Indians said they might kill him. But ye Governor told them no, they should not kill him, but watch their opportunity, & take him.[4]

Gracious God, teach us the ways of peace.

And there's another country, I've heard of long ago,
Most dear to them that love her, most great to them that know;
We may not count her armies, we may not see her King;
Her fortress is a faithful heart, her pride is suffering;
And soul by soul and silently her shining bounds increase,
And her ways are ways of gentleness, and all her paths are peace.[5]

---

1   Or Gardiner (1596–1662).
2   Bishop Stephen Gardiner, who persecuted Protestants at the behest of Queen Mary.
3   The Roman Catholic Equestrian Order of the Holy Sepulchre of Jerusalem, also called Order of the Holy Sepulchre or Knights of the Holy Sepulchre. The Order enjoys the protection of the Holy See.
4   From *History of Plymouth Plantation*.
5   From Sir Cecil Spring Rice's poem, "I Vow to Thee, My Country", set to music by Gustav Holst.

… THE LORD ADDED TO THEIR NUMBER DAILY THOSE WHO WERE
BEING SAVED.
(Acts 2:47)

Having oxen grown [the Pilgrims] must have land for ploughing and tillage. And no man thought he could now live, except he had cattle and a great deal of ground to keep them; all striving to increase their stocks. By which means they were scattered all over ye bay, quickly, and ye town, in which they lived compactly till now, was left very thin, and in a short time almost desolate. And if this had been all, it had been less, though too much; but ye church must also be divided, and those [that] had lived so long together in Christian & comfortable fellowship must now part and suffer many divisions.[1]

This excerpt leads me to think of issues surrounding church growth, Lord, when mother/daughter churches grow and then divide into fresh expressions of worship and witness. I thank you for growth, and for converts, but I pray regarding the sensitivities surrounding such issues. Blessings and hurts can sometimes arrive side-by-side! Help those churches, Lord, who grapple with these matters.

---

1   From *History of Plymouth Plantation.*

... THE PEOPLE THAT DO KNOW THEIR GOD SHALL BE STRONG, AND
DO EXPLOITS.
(Daniel 11:32 *KJV*)

Through all our history, it is easy enough to trace the influence of the Pilgrims, and their ideas and characteristics and work, and to see where their influence has been the strongest, what kind of churches it builds up, and what legislation it secures, and what state of society it produces. And now it seems no longer difficult, in view of such results, to form a just estimate of these men, and of their work in settling this country. Need one doubt any longer whether the Puritans were essentially right in the protest against the absolute power of kings, and the spiritual despotism of a hierarchy? Need one doubt any longer whether men are capable of governing themselves in both Church and State, or suppose that freedom necessarily leads to heresy and impiety in the one, any more than to license and revolution in the other? Or need one doubt any longer what sort of a population, and what state of society, such civil and religious institutions will produce, and whether, on the whole, any other form of government, or religious faith, have shown themselves to be preferable to these?[1]

Heavenly Father, here and now, today, I offer you all that I am, and all that I can be. If you feel you can use me in some way, then please do so. To that end, please guide me and instruct me. May my days be pleasing in your sight. I pray that, when the influence of my life is traced, it may be seen to have carried some of the hallmarks of your Lordship.

---

1   From *A Memorial of the Pilgrim Fathers*.

BUT WHEN THEY MEASURE THEMSELVES BY ONE ANOTHER AND COMPARE THEMSELVES WITH ONE ANOTHER, THEY ARE WITHOUT UNDERSTANDING.

(2 Corinthians 10:12 *ESV*)

Foreigners[1] are accustomed to regard our experiment[2] as not yet complete, and to think that time enough has not yet elapsed to enable us to judge well of results. True we cannot boast, like Russia, or England, of a thousand years of national existence, nor point, with the Jews, to institutions that remained essentially unchanged for fifteen hundred years. But if we reckon existence, not so much by years, as by intellectual activity and experience, and events, and achievements, it may be a question whether our national life of two hundred and fifty years will not compare with some of the longest of them. In the dull and changeless East, and in patriarchal times, when nothing ever happened more important than the death of a camel; or the birth of a child[3] ... was a century in reality any longer than some of the decades of years? And why may we not speak of results as well as they?[4]

> What an interesting human trait this is, Lord – the tendency to compare! And what a dangerous habit it can become, if comparison emerges as the thief of joy! Grant me, I pray, freedom from the pattern of comparing my life – and my achievements – to those of other people. May my entire satisfaction come from knowing that I have done your will today.

---

1   That is, non-Americans.
2   In essence, that of establishing an entire nation based upon the original primitive colony established by the Pilgrim Fathers.
3   I am assuming these sentiments were written with tongue-in-cheek – exaggerating to make a point!
4   From *A Memorial of the Pilgrim Fathers*.

THE ONE WHO HAS KNOWLEDGE USES WORDS WITH RESTRAINT,
AND WHOEVER HAS UNDERSTANDING IS EVEN-TEMPERED. EVEN
FOOLS ARE THOUGHT WISE IF THEY KEEP SILENT, AND DISCERNING
IF THEY HOLD THEIR TONGUES.
(Proverbs 17:27–28)

In heaven's name, Cushman added, let some discretion be used in writing letters home.[1] Some pictured New Plimouth as a virtual paradise. On the other hand, "some say you are starved in body & soule; others, that you eate pigs and dogs that dye alone; others that ye things here spoken of, ye goodness of ye country, &c., are gross and palpable lyes... It is a miserie when ye whole state of a plantation shall be thus exposed to ye passionate humours of some discontented men" [sic].[2]

That underrated quality of discretion, Lord! Grant me, today, that presence of mind whereby I might think before I speak, or write. Should I feel any influence of your Holy Spirit to keep quiet, or not to put something in writing, then help me to trust and obey, rather than run the risk of fuelling unhealthy debate.

---

1 The settlers were able to send letters home to England, via trading ships visiting their coastline from time to time.

2 From *Saints and Strangers*.

... HUMAN ANGER DOES NOT PRODUCE THE RIGHTEOUSNESS
THAT GOD DESIRES.
(James 1:20)

At the time of their election court, John Oldham came again amongst them; and though it was a part of his censure, for his former mutiny, not to return without leave first obtained, yet he presumed, without leave at all, to come, being set on and hardened by the ill counsel of others; and not only so, but suffered his unruly passion to run beyond the bounds and limits of all reason and modesty, insomuch that some strangers that were with him were ashamed of his outrages, and rebuked him, but all reproofs were but oil to the fire, and made the flame of his choler the greater. He called them all to naught in his fury, an hundred rebels and traitors; but in conclusion, they committed him until he was tamer, and then appointed a guard of musketeers, which he was to pass through, and everyone was ordered to give him a blow on his hinder parts, with the butt end of his musket, and then he was conveyed to the waterside, where a boat was ready to carry him away, with this farewell, Go and mend your manners.[1]

This day, Heavenly Father, help me to discern between righteous anger and hot temper! Teach me the difference, I pray.

---

1   From *Chronicles of the Pilgrim Fathers.*

JONAH RAN AWAY FROM THE LORD AND HEADED FOR TARSHISH.
HE WENT DOWN TO JOPPA, WHERE HE FOUND A SHIP BOUND FOR
THAT PORT. AFTER PAYING THE FARE, HE WENT ABOARD AND SAILED
FOR TARSHISH TO FLEE FROM THE LORD. THEN THE LORD SENT
A GREAT WIND ON THE SEA, AND SUCH A VIOLENT STORM AROSE
THAT THE SHIP THREATENED TO BREAK UP… THEN THE SAILORS
SAID TO EACH OTHER, "COME, LET US CAST LOTS TO FIND OUT WHO
IS RESPONSIBLE FOR THIS CALAMITY." THEY CAST LOTS AND THE
LOT FELL ON JONAH … SO THEY ASKED HIM, "WHAT SHOULD WE
DO TO YOU TO MAKE THE SEA CALM DOWN FOR US?" "PICK ME UP
AND THROW ME INTO THE SEA," HE REPLIED, "AND IT WILL BECOME
CALM. I KNOW THAT IT IS MY FAULT THAT THIS GREAT STORM HAS
COME UPON YOU."

(Jonah 1:3–12)

After the removal of his family [John Oldham] fell into some straits, and about a year after intended a voyage to Virginia; and so it pleased God that himself and sundry passengers being in the bark, they were in great danger, so as they despaired of life, and fell to prayer, and to examination of their hearts and consciences, and confessed such sins as most burdened them, and the said John Oldham did make a free and large confession of the wrong he had done to the church and the people at Plimouth in many particulars; and that as he had sought their ruin, so God had now met with him, and might destroy him; yea, he feared that they all fared the worse for his sake; he prayed God to forgive him, and made vows, that if the Lord spared his life he would become otherwise. This was reported by some of good credit, not long since living in the Massachusetts Bay, that were themselves partners in the same danger, which was on the shoals of Cape Cod.

It pleased God to spare their lives, but they lost their voyage; and some time afterwards, the said Mr. John Oldham carried himself fairly towards them, and acknowledged the hand of God to be with them, and seemed to have an honourable respect for them; and so far made his peace with them.[1][2]

> Is it me, Lord? Am I the problem? Is my sin to blame? If so, hear my confession, I pray, and in your mercy, don't allow anyone else to suffer the consequences of my wrong choices. Convict me, Lord, if I am at fault.

---

1   From *Chronicles of the Pilgrim Fathers*.
2   John Oldham worked subsequently as an independent trader, operating a small sailing vessel among the Indians. Sadly, he fell into a quarrel with a group of Indians, and "they slew him with a hatchet".

PRECIOUS IN THE SIGHT OF THE LORD IS THE DEATH OF HIS SAINTS.
(Psalm 116:15 *KJV*)

They heard of Capt. Standish's arrival, and sent a boat to fetch him home; welcome he was, but the news he brought was sad in many regards... Mr. John Robinson, their pastor,[1] was dead, which struck them with much sorrow and sadness, as they had great cause; his and their adversaries had been long and continually plotting how they might hinder his coming into New England, but now the Lord had appointed him to a greater journey, at less charge, to a better place.

He was prevented by disappointments from those in England who undertook to provide for the passage of him and his congregation. It appeared that... others were at this time determined that New England should be settled under Episcopacy; and though they would encourage and allow the people to settle here, they were unwilling that any Puritan ministers should accompany them... They took care to obstruct the coming over of so important a man as Mr. Robinson, a great man, and father of the Independents.[2]

Help me, Lord, to keep the faith.

And our eyes at last shall see Him,
Through His own redeeming love;
For that Child so dear and gentle
Is our Lord in heaven above,
And He leads His children on
To the place where He is gone.[3]

---

1   See Footnote 2, January 4ᵗʰ.
2   From *Chronicles of the Pilgrim Fathers*.
3   From Cecil Frances Alexander's carol "Once in Royal David's City".

... THE LEVITES (WHO HAVE NO ALLOTMENT OR INHERITANCE OF
THEIR OWN) AND THE FOREIGNERS, THE FATHERLESS AND THE
WIDOWS WHO LIVE IN YOUR TOWNS MAY COME AND EAT AND BE
SATISFIED, AND SO THAT THE LORD YOUR GOD MAY BLESS YOU IN
ALL THE WORK OF YOUR HANDS.
(Deuteronomy 14:29)

It is but the truth to say that many tens of thousands of Christian men hold [John Robinson's] name in honourable remembrance. He yet lives, by his example, and by the influences of his sacrifices and toils; and in the third century after his death, he enjoys the singular distinction of being equally honoured in the east and the west – in two countries separated by a mighty ocean.

It was four or five years after the death of Mr. Robinson, before provision could be made for the removal of his wife and children to Plymouth... Thirty-five families were transported from Leyden to New England, at the heavy expense of £500, paid by the brethren in the colony. Another company came over the next year, at a still greater expense. In one of these companies were the wife and children of Mr. Robinson.

We have the names of but two of his children, John and Isaac. John settled at, or near Cape Ann, Isaac settled near Plymouth, at Scituate, where he was a freeman... The descendants of Robinson are numerous, scattered over New England and other States of the Union, and in various respectable and useful stations in life.[1]

Father, my prayers today are extended towards those who are "left behind": widows, widowers, and children, especially any known to me personally. Stay close to them, Lord Jesus.

---

1   From *Chronicles of the Pilgrim Fathers.*

September 10th

Some of the Strangers were filling the adventurers' ears with loud complaints that they were denied the sacraments at Plymouth, religious disputes were incessant, family duties were neglected on the Lord's Day, children were not taught their catechism, and not taught how to read, many in the colony were thieves and many more were incurably lazy, the water was unwholesome and the country barren, and the plantation was much annoyed by foxes, wolves, and mosquitoes. "These are the cheefe objections... made against you and countrie," [*sic*] wrote Sherley,[1] always friendly to the Pilgrim leaders. "I pray you consider them and answer then by the first conveniencie" [*sic*].[2]

**Help me, Lord, not to be discouraged by unreasonable and invalid complaints
and criticisms, but to recognize what is, often, their true source, and to brush
them off. Teach me not to be intimidated by the devil's lies, tricks, and wiles, but
to see them for what they are.**

---

1   James Sherley (christened 1587), London goldsmith, financier, merchant adventurer.
2   From *Saints and Strangers*.

ALL YOUR CHILDREN WILL BE TAUGHT BY THE LORD...
(Isaiah 54:13)

[In response to the complaints made by the Strangers] Bradford was furious, and drafted a spirited but somewhat disingenuous reply. There had never been any controversy or opposition about religion "either publicke or private (to our knowledge)" [sic], he declared – and he might have added that it was a good thing no opposition had presumed to show its face, for the Saints demanded as strict uniformity of belief and observance as ever the Anglican bishops had under James or Elizabeth. The settlers did not enjoy the sacraments, Bradford acknowledged, but "the more is our greefe", he said, "that our pastor is kept from us, by whom we might injoye them, for we used to have the Lord's Supper every Saboth, and baptisme as often as there was occasion" [sic]. Plymouth had "no commone schoole for want of a fit person, or hitherto means to maintaine one, though we desire now to begine" – the first was not established till more than half a century later [sic].[1]

> What a privilege it is, Lord, to receive a formal education. Thank you for this news of the first school established in the colony. I think of countries where schooling is expensive, and out of the reach of many families. Bless those people, Lord, who are denied an education because they can't afford it, and whose futures might be crippled by that deprivation. Bless those charities and churches who are working to rectify this injustice; strengthen their efforts.

---

1   From *Saints and Strangers*.

You strain out a gnat but swallow a camel.
(Matthew 23:24)

[Amongst the Pilgrims] most parents were at pains to teach their children what they could. To say that many of the settlers were lazy and shirked their work was "not wholly true, for though some doe it not willingly, & others not honestly, yet all doe it" [sic]. There were thieves among them, of course, but if "London had been free from that crime, then we should not have been trobled with these here; it is well known sundrie have smarted well for it, and so are ye rest like to doe, if they be taken" [sic]. But it was false to say that the country was barren and without grass. As for the quality of the water, "if they mean not so wholesome as ye good beere and wine in London (which they do dearly love), we will not dispute with them, but els, for water, it is as good as any in ye world (for ought we knowe)" [sic]. And who were those that complained about the mosquitoes! "They are too delicate and unfitted to begine new plantations and collonies that cannot enduer the biting of a muskeeto," he concluded scornfully, and it would be well for "such to keepe at home till at least they be muskeeto-proofe" [sic].[1]

> Oh Lord! I sigh as I pray, today! Teach me what matters, and, by the same token, teach me what doesn't. Help me to pick my battles well, and wisely, and to quickly consign trivia to the bin before it gathers an importance that is disproportionate and even potentially destructive.

---

1 From *Saints and Strangers.*

So Abram said to Lot, "Let's not have any quarrelling
between you and me, or between your herders and mine,
for we are close relatives. Is not the whole land before
you? Let's part company. If you go to the left, I'll go to
the right; if you go to the right, I'll go to the left." Lot
looked around and saw that the whole plain of the
Jordan toward Zoar was well watered, like the garden of
the Lord, like the land of Egypt.

(Genesis 13:8–10)

Ye people of ye plantation began to grow in their outward estates, by reason of ye flowing of many people into ye country, especially into ye Bay of Massachusetts: by which means corn and cattle rose to a great price, by which many were much enriched, and commodities grew plentiful; and yet in other regards this benefit turned to their hurt, and this accession of strength to their weakness. For now as their stocks increased, and ye increase vendible, there was no longer any holding them together, but now they must of necessity go to their great lots; they could not otherwise keep their cattle…

To prevent any further scattering from this place, and weakening of ye same, it was thought best to give out some good farms to special persons, yet would promise to live at Plimouth, and likely to be helpful to ye church or commonwealth, and so to tie ye lands to Plimouth as farmes for the same; and there they might keep their cattle and tillage by some servants, and retain their dwellings there. And so some special lands were granted at a place general, called Green's Harbour, where no allotments had been in the former division, a place very well meadowed, and fit to rear and keep cattle, good store.[1]

I thank you today, Lord, for farmers and those who work hard to look after
farms and crops, ensuring food on my plate! How easy it is for me, when I look
forward to my dinner, to overlook the fact that a great deal of effort has gone into
providing that meal. Accept my overdue thanks, I pray, and give your blessing to
those workers.

---

1   From *History of the Plymouth Plantation*.

... I HAVE SEEN VIOLENCE AND STRIFE IN THE CITY.
(Psalm 55:9 *KJV*)

Alas! This remedy proved worse than ye disease; for within a few years those who had thus got footing there rent themselves away, partly by force, and partly wearying ye rest with importunity and pleas of necessity, so as they must either suffer them to go, or live in continual opposition and contention. And others still, as yet conceived themselves straitened, or to want accommodation, break away under one pretence or another, thinking their own conceived necessity, and the example of others, a warrant sufficient for them. And this, I fear, will be ye ruin of New England, at least of ye churches of God there, and will provoke ye Lord's displeasure against them.[1]

Forgive us, Lord, when we act selfishly.

---

1   From *History of Plymouth Plantation.*

*... SPEAKING TO ONE ANOTHER WITH PSALMS, HYMNS, AND SONGS
FROM THE SPIRIT. SING AND MAKE MUSIC FROM YOUR HEART TO
THE LORD...*

(Ephesians 5:19)

The swelling seas thou doest asswage,
And make their streams full still:
Thou doest refrayne the peoples' rage,
And rule them at thy will.
Thou deckst the earth of thy good gace,
With fayre and pleasaunt crop:
Thy cloudes distill their dew apace,
Great planty do they drop.
Whereby the desert shall begyn,
Full great increase to bring:
The little hilles shall joy therein;
Much fruits in them shall spryng.
In places playne the flocke shall feede,
And cover all the earth;
The vallyes with corn shall so exceede;
That men shall sing for myrth [sic].[1] [2] [3]

**Thank you, Lord, for hymn books, those underrated channels of grace. Thank
you, Lord, for hymn-writers. Thank you for words and verses that helpfully frame
and articulate great expressions of praise. Thank you for so many options of sung
worship, all of which are to your glory.**

---

1   This hymn, a paraphrase of Psalm 65, is taken from *The Booke of Psalmes; collected into English meeter*
    [*sic*], which is the hymnal many of the Pilgrim Fathers treasured, and carried with them from their days
    in Holland.
2   I have reproduced this hymn with all of its original spelling because I feel that lends a certain
    authenticity to its inclusion here. Although I have modernized quite a lot of narrative elsewhere – that
    which is taken from diaries and journals, etc. – I felt a hymn should be left intact, as it does not represent
    the "spoken" word.
3   From *The Argonauts of Faith*.

WE ARE HARD PRESSED ON EVERY SIDE, BUT NOT CRUSHED;
PERPLEXED, BUT NOT IN DESPAIR ...
(2 Corinthians 4:8)

[The settlers] received divers letters from their friends at Leyden, in Holland ... Although their wills were good to come over to their brethren in New England, yet they saw no probability of means how it might be affected, but concluded, as it were, that all their hopes were cut off, and many, being aged, began to drop away by death. All which things before related, being well weighted and laid together, it could not but strike them with great perplexity, and to look humanly on the state of things, as they presented themselves at this time, but they gathered up their spirits, and the Lord so helped them, whose work they had in hand, as now, when they were very low, they began to rise again; and being stripped in a manner, of all human helps and hopes, he brought things about otherwise in his divine providence, so as they were not only upheld and sustained, but their proceedings both honoured and imitated by others.[1]

What a great example, Lord! Faith in the midst of adversity. Perseverance in the midst of problems. My prayers today, Heavenly Father, are with those who feel as though life is pressing in all around them. I pray for sustaining grace to permeate their circumstances.

---

1   From *Chronicles of the Pilgrim Fathers.*

... THE HAND OF GOD WAS ON THE PEOPLE TO GIVE THEM UNITY OF
MIND...

(2 Chronicles 30:12)

The plantation of Plimouth received messages from the Dutch plantation, sent unto them from the governor there, written both in Dutch and French. The sum of the letters forementioned were, to congratulate the English here, taking notice of much that might engage them to a friendly correspondency and good neighbourhood, as the propinquity of their native country, their long continued friendship, etc., and desires to fall into a way of some commerce and trade with them.

The Dutch had trading in those southern parts divers years before the English came, but they began no plantation until after the English came and were here seated.

To which the governor and council of Plimouth returned answerable courteous acceptance of their loving propositions, respecting their good neighbourhood in general, and particularly for commerce. And accordingly the Dutch, not long after, sent their secretary... with letters and goods, who laid the foundation of a trade that continued between them many years after, to their mutual benefit.[1]

Unity! "Long continued friendship... courteous acceptance... mutual benefit"–
how it must please you, Lord, when you see good and harmonious
relationships in place!

In Christ there is no east or west,
In him no south or north,
But one great fellowship of love
Throughout the whole wide earth.[2]

---

1   From *Chronicles of the Pilgrim Fathers.*
2   From John Oxenham's hymn (written under the pseudonym of William A. Dunkerley).

BUT THE LORD GOD CALLED TO THE MAN AND SAID TO HIM,
"WHERE ARE YOU?"
(Genesis 3:9 ESV)

In the three ships that came over to Salem... besides many godly Christians, there came over three ministers, two of them, Mr. Skelton[1] and Mr. Higginson,[2] were non-conformists, who, having suffered much in their native land upon that account, they came over with a professed intention of practising church reformation; the third minister, Mr. Bright,[3] was a conformist, who, not agreeing in judgment with the other two, removed to Charlestown, where also, not agreeing with those godly Christians there, that were for reformation, after one year's stay in the country, he returned to England.[4]

Gracious God, draw close to those who don't quite fit in; those who aren't entirely sure where they should be. Come to them in their sense of displacement, and guide their steps to the right place, and the most suitable setting. Be with the "outsiders" and the "misfits" as they struggle to find their niche in life.

---

1 Samuel Skelton (c. 1592 [dubious]–1634), who went on to become pastor of the First Church of Salem, Massachusetts.
2 Francis Higginson (1588–1630), who went on to become a Puritan minister in New England.
3 Reverend Francis Bright.
4 From *Chronicles of the Pilgrim Fathers.*

... YOU YOURSELVES LIKE LIVING STONES ARE BEING BUILT UP AS A
SPIRITUAL HOUSE, TO BE A HOLY PRIESTHOOD, TO OFFER SPIRITUAL
SACRIFICES ACCEPTABLE TO GOD THROUGH JESUS CHRIST.
(1 Peter 2:5 *ESV*)

The passengers that came over with [Mr. Skelton and Mr. Higginson]... consulted with them about settling a reformed congregation; from whom they found a general and hearty concurrence, so that, after some conference together about this matter, they [entered upon] a solemn covenant with God and one another, and also for the ordaining of their ministers; of which they gave notice to the church of Plimouth, that being the only church that was in the country before them. The people made their choice of Mr. Skelton for their pastor, and Mr. Higginson for their teacher. Mr. Higginson, having eight children, is to have ten pounds a year more than [Mr. Skelton]. And accordingly, it was desired of Mr. Higginson to draw up a confession of faith and covenant in scripture language; which being done, was agreed upon... Thirty copies of the aforesaid confession of faith and covenant being written out for the use of thirty persons, who were to begin the work.[1]

> Great news, Lord – a new church! Thirty workers, a teacher, and a pastor! May we
> see the same again, Lord? New fellowships? Mission teams reaching out? Bless all
> such endeavours, I pray, especially those known to me personally.
> **Build your church, Lord!**

---

1   From *Chronicles of the Pilgrim Fathers.*

... HE TOOK THE BOOK OF THE COVENANT, AND READ IN THE
AUDIENCE OF THE PEOPLE: AND THEY SAID, ALL THAT THE LORD
HATH SAID WILL WE DO, AND BE OBEDIENT.

(Exodus 24:7 *KJV*)

[When the time came, for the formation of the new church in Salem], it was kept as a day of fasting and prayer, in which, after the sermons and prayers of the two ministers, in the end of the day, the aforesaid confession of faith and covenant being solemnly read, the forenamed persons did solemnly confess their consent thereunto; and then proceeded to the ordaining of Mr. Skelton pastor, and Mr. Higginson teacher of the church there. Mr. Bradford, the governor of Plimouth, and some others with him, coming by sea, were hindered by cross winds, that they could not be there at the beginning of the day, but they came into the assembly afterward, and gave them the right hand of fellowship, wishing all prosperity, and a blessed success unto such good beginnings. After which, at several times, many others joined to the church in the same way. The confession of faith and covenant, forementioned, was acknowledged only as a direction, pointing unto that faith and covenant contained in the Holy Scripture.[1]

Lord God, thank you for Holy Scripture. What a miracle the Bible is! I praise you for it, and for its worth to me. Teach me to value the time I spend reading these sacred and beloved pages.

---

1   From *Chronicles of the Pilgrim Fathers.*

September 21ˢᵀ

... HE WHO BEGAN A GOOD WORK IN YOU WILL CARRY IT ON TO
COMPLETION UNTIL THE DAY OF CHRIST JESUS.
(Philippians 1:6)

Mr. Roger Williams[1] (a man godly and zealous, having many precious parts, but very unsettled in judgment) came over first to ye Massachusetts, but upon some discontent left ye place, and came thither [to Plymouth] (where he was friendly entertained, according to their poor ability), and exercised his gifts amongst them, & after some time was admitted a member of ye church; and his teaching well approved, for ye benefit whereof I still bless God, and am thankful to him, even for his sharpest admonitions and reproofs, so far as they agreed with truth. He... began to fall into some strange opinions, and from opinion to practise; which caused some controversy between ye church and him, and in ye end some discontent on his part, by occasion whereof he left them something abruptly. Yet afterwards sued for his dismissing to ye church of Salem, which was granted, with some caution to them concerning him and what care they ought to have of him. But he soon fell into more things there, both to their and ye government's trouble & disturbance.[2]

Teach me, I pray, the importance of not only starting well, but finishing well too.
Help me to do so in all that I undertake. Thank you, Lord, for your steadfast love.

---

1 Roger Williams (1603–83), Puritan minister, theologian, and author.
2 From *History of Plymouth Plantation*.

EVERY HIGH PRIEST IS SELECTED FROM AMONG THE PEOPLE AND
IS APPOINTED TO REPRESENT THE PEOPLE IN MATTERS RELATED
TO GOD, TO OFFER GIFTS AND SACRIFICES FOR SINS. HE IS ABLE TO
DEAL GENTLY WITH THOSE WHO ARE IGNORANT AND ARE GOING
ASTRAY, SINCE HE HIMSELF IS SUBJECT TO WEAKNESS.

(Hebrews 5:1–2)

[Roger Williams] is to be pitied, and prayed for, and so I shall leave ye matter, and desire ye Lord to show him his errors, and reduce him into ye way of truth, and give him a settled judgment and constancy in ye same; for I hope he belongs to ye Lord, and he will show him mercy.[1]

What a lovely, gentle, compassionate attitude, Lord. With pity, not with blame.
Help me to learn from this.

---

1   From *History of Plymouth Plantation*.

SO HE ORDERED THAT THEY BE BAPTIZED IN THE NAME
OF JESUS CHRIST.

(Acts 10:48)

The two ministers there [Skelton and Higginson] being seriously studious of reformation, they considered of the state of their children, together with their parents; concerning which, letters did pass between Mr. Higginson and Mr. Brewster, the reverend elder of the church at Plimouth, and they did agree in their judgments, namely, concerning the church membership of the children with their parents; and that baptism was a seal of their membership; only when they were adult, they being not scandalous, they were to be examined by the church officers, and upon their approbation of their fitness, and upon the children's public and personally owning of the covenant, they were to be received into the Lord's supper. Accordingly, Mr. Higginson's eldest son, being about fifteen years of age, was owned to have been received a member together with his parents, and being privately examined by the pastor, Mr. Skelton, about his knowledge in the principles of religion, he did present him before the church when the Lord's supper was to be administered, and the child then publicly and personally owning the covenant of the God of his father, he was admitted unto the Lord's supper; it being then professedly owned, according to 1 Cor. Vii. 14.[1]

> Heavenly Father, I pray for ministers and church leaders whose responsibility it is, to prepare candidates for baptism. Grant them wisdom. I pray too for those who are considering church membership at any level. May they find help and encouragement along their way, as they explore options.

---

1   From *Chronicles of the Pilgrim Fathers*.

NOW YOU ARE THE BODY OF CHRIST, AND EACH ONE OF YOU IS A
PART OF IT.

(1 Corinthians 12:27)

It pleased God, of his rich grace, to transport over into the bay of the Massachusetts divers honourable personages, and many worthy Christians, whereby the Lord began in a manifest manner and way to make known the great thoughts which he had of planting the gospel in this remote and barbarous wilderness, and honouring his own way of instituted worship, causing such and so many to adhere thereunto, and fall upon the practice thereof; among the rest, a chief one amongst them was that famous pattern of piety and justice.[1]

What is interesting, Lord, is how different Christian denominations will invariably emphasize certain points of doctrine or style. "Piety and justice" were mainstays of the Puritan movement, whereas even today, similar emphases are evident. Bless us all, I pray, as we each work together as the body of Christ. Assist us, by your grace, as we each play our part.

---

1   From *Chronicles of the Pilgrim Fathers*.

Let us not become weary in doing good, for at the proper time we will reap a harvest if we do not give up.
(Galatians 6:9)

It was a marvel, said the Pilgrims, that all their woes and troubles did not entirely "sinck them" [sic]. But they gathered up their spirits and were so helped by the Lord, "whose worke they had in hand, as now when they were at their lowest, they began to rise againe" [sic]. As corn was the staple of their diet and the common medium of exchange, they diligently cultivated their fields and in off seasons extended their operations in the fur trade, pushing ever farther afield, usually by sea. The ship's carpenter... had completed two shallops and a lighter... and he was working on two large ketches when he died of a fever. Recalling that they had an "ingenious man that was a house carpenter", the Pilgrims faced him with the problem of providing them with a sizeable vessel. The latter took a shallop, cut it in two, lengthened it to six or seven feet, put in a new waist, laid on a deck, and fitted it up into a "comfortable" vessel, though the master and his crew had to stand out at all times no matter how rough and bitter the weather.

The vessel was badly needed, for competition in the corn and beaver trade was increasing. Scattered settlements were now beginning to appear along the coast.[1]

Encouraging God, draw close to those whose spirits are flagging. Honour their intention to keep going. Keep them afloat!

---

1   From *Saints and Strangers*.

... THINE IS THE KINGDOM, AND THE POWER, AND THE GLORY,

FOR EVER ...

(Matthew 6:13 *KJV*)

Out of small beginnings, greater things have been produced by [God's] hand that made all things of nothing; and, as one small candle may light a thousand, so the light here kindled hath shone into many, yea, in some sort, to our whole nation. Let the glorious name of Jehovah have all the praise in all ages.[1]

Almighty God, let me always be quick to deflect the glory and the praise to you.

---

1   From *History of Plymouth Plantation.*

... I Daniel fainted, and was sick certain days...
(Daniel 8:27 *KJV*)

It pleased God to visit Plimouth with an infectious fever, of which many fell very sick, and upwards of twenty died, men, women, and children, and sundry of them were of their ancient friends; amongst the rest, Mr. Samuel Fuller[1] then died, after he had much helped others, and was a comfort to them; he was their surgeon and physician, and did much good in his place, as he was a godly man, and served Christ in the office of a deacon in the church for many years, and... was much missed after God removed him out of this world.

One of these ancient friends who died at this time, was Mr. Thomas Blossom[2]... On his arrival at Plimouth, he was elected a deacon of the church.[3]

Today, Lord, I pray for your healing touch upon any known to me who are sick this day.

Jesus, in sickness and in pain,
Be near to succour me;
My sinking spirit still sustain;
To thee I turn, to thee.[4]

---

1   See April 23ʳᵈ.
2   Born c. 1580. One of the first Puritan settlers in New England, having previously emigrated from England to Leiden in Holland. Of special note is that Thomas Blossom's American descendants include former US Presidents Barack Obama and George W. Bush.
3   From *Chronicles of the Pilgrim Fathers*.
4   From Thomas Gallaudet's hymn.

For Scripture says, "Do not muzzle an ox while it is
treading out the grain," and "The worker
deserves his wages."

(1 Timothy 5:18)

At last the planter "owned" Plymouth... And now what was to be done? How were
the "stocks, shares, lands, merchandise, and chatles" [sic] to be distributed? For a time
Bradford and his council toyed with the idea of excluding the "untowarde persons
mixed amongst them from the first" [sic] – in other words, many of the Strangers
who had come on the *Mayflower* and later ships. This would have touched off a terrific
explosion, but wiser counsel finally prevailed. As all had borne the hardships and toil
of building Plymouth, all should share equally in the division – at least all "of abillity,
and fee, and able to govern themselves with meete discretion" [sic]. Indentured
servants were to receive nothing but what their masters were disposed to give them
or what "their deservings should ontaine from ye company afterwards" [sic].[1]

God of justice, I pray for all those who campaign for workers' rights and a fair
day's pay for a fair day's work: campaigning charities, political groups, churches,
and individuals who raise their voices on behalf of the marginalized. Bless them,
Lord, as they seek to promote equality in the workplace.

---

1   From *Saints and Strangers*.

"YOU SHALL APPOINT JUDGES AND OFFICERS IN ALL YOUR TOWNS THAT THE LORD YOUR GOD IS GIVING YOU, ACCORDING TO YOUR TRIBES, AND THEY SHALL JUDGE THE PEOPLE WITH RIGHTEOUS JUDGMENT."

(Deuteronomy 16:18 *ESV*)

Each family was to receive as many shares [in the joint income] as it had members, including men, women, children, and servants. Each man retained the house and garden allotted to him along the street, but those who obtained the better houses were to compensate those who fell heir to the worse. An exception was made for Governor Bradford and for or five "spetiall men" [*sic*] who were presented with their houses and gardens in recognition of the many services they had performed without salary. The livestock was rounded up, appraised "for age & goodnes" [*sic*], divided into equal units and assigned by lot. A unit consisted of several swine, a cow, and two goats for every thirteen persons. Next, the clearings on both sides of Town Brook were divided into farms or "great lots" of twenty acres each, and these were assigned by lot. As some lay relatively far from town, those with farms close by agreed to allow others to share their fields for four years. Considerable farm land was reserved to provide for future settlers. No meadows were assigned at this time, for Plymouth had few good pastures and hay fields.[1]

Heavenly Father, my prayers today are for those in authority who are faced with the difficult and complex task of allocating land and housing. Theirs is an unenviable responsibility, as they try to do their best to treat people equally and fairly, often working with limited resources and finite budgets. I pray for local government officials who sometimes have to bear the brunt of unpopular decisions. Help them, I pray, as they weigh up planning applications, housing appeals, and so on. I pray for my own local councillors and officials, asking you to guide them.

---

1   From *Saints and Strangers*.

AND I WILL RESTORE TO YOU THE YEARS THAT THE LOCUST HATH
EATEN, THE CANKERWORM, AND THE CATERPILLAR, AND THE
PALMERWORM, MY GREAT ARMY WHICH I SENT AMONG YOU.
(Joel 2:25 *KJV*)

Sickness caused much sadness amongst [the Pilgrims] and, according to their duty, they besought the Lord by fasting and prayer, and he was entreated of them, and towards winter the sickness ceased. This sickness, being a kind of pestilent fever, swept away also many of the Indians from places near adjoining to Plimouth.

It is to be observed, that the spring before this sickness, there was a numerous company of flies, which were like for bigness unto wasps or bumblebees; they came out of little holes in the ground, and did eat up the green things, and made such a constant yelling noise as made the woods ring of them, and ready to deafen the hearers; they were not any of them heard or seen by the English in the country before this time; but the Indians told them sickness would follow, and it did…

They are known by the name of locusts. The prevailing opinion is, that they make their appearance *Septem decennially*, and this seems to be confirmed by long observation. Their chrysalis state seems not to be known, and probably they have several transmutations during the long interval of their appearance. By what means they make "such a yelling noise" seems not to be well agreed. But as to their "eating up the green thing," this is a mistake. They pitch upon the young branches of oak trees generally, and with a kind of chisel in their posterior, they penetrate and split the limb and deposit their *ova* in the pith, and in a short time the limb breaks, and the leaves die, and give the appearance of being eaten.[1]

Gracious God, I pray for any whose lives have been laid waste by "locusts", as it were – addictions, calamities, awful choices, mistakes, sins, wrong pathways, and all that can wreck happiness. Have mercy, Lord, and strengthen those who seek to rebuild their lot. Turn not away from them, I pray, even if their misfortune and misery is self-inflicted. Lift up the fallen. May your church reach out with a message of grace, hope, and restoration.

---

1   From *Chronicles of the Pilgrim Fathers*.

> "... GOD SAID TO HIM, 'YOU FOOL! THIS VERY NIGHT YOUR LIFE
> WILL BE DEMANDED FROM YOU.'"
> (Luke 12:20)

One Capt. Stone,[1] who had sometimes lived... in the West Indies, came into these parts; of whom I have nothing to speak in the way of commendation, but rather the contrary. After he had been to and fro in the country, he returned towards Virginia, with one Capt. Norton;[2] and so it was, that, as they returned, they went into Connecticut River, where the Indians killed the said Stone as he lay in his cabin, and threw a covering over him. They likewise killed all the rest of his company, but the said Capt. Norton, he defending himself a long time in the cook-room of the bark, until, by accident, the gunpowder took fire, which for readiness he had set in an open thing before him, which did so burn and scald him, and blind his eyes, as he could make no longer resistance, but was slain also by them, and they made a prey of his goods.[3]

Gracious God, help me, I pray, to be ready to die. I know not when my death may come about, or how, but help me not to shirk the subject just because it might be something I would rather not think about. The end of my days will surely come, Lord, sooner or later! Help me to live in that light.

---

1   Known as "the notorious Captain John Stone" (c. 1580–c. 1634), ship's captain, dealer, slave trader.
2   Captain Walter Norton (c. 1576–1633 or 1634), professional soldier.
3   From *Chronicles of the Pilgrim Fathers*.

"I WILL SAVE YOU FROM THE HANDS OF THE WICKED AND DELIVER
YOU FROM THE GRASP OF THE CRUEL."
(Jeremiah 15:21)

It is to be observed, that the said Stone, being at the Dutch plantation… a certain bark of Plimouth being there likewise on trading, he kept company with the Dutch governor, and made him drunk, and got leave of him, in his drunkenness, to take the said bark, without any occasion or cause given him; and so, taking his time when the merchant and some of the chief of the men were on shore, with some of his own men, made the rest of them weigh anchor, and set sail to carry her away to Virginia; but some of the Dutch seamen, who had been at Plimouth, and received kindness, seeing this horrible abuse, got a vessel or two and pursued them, and brought them back. After this he came into the Massachusetts Bay, where they commenced suit against him; but by the mediation of some it was taken up, and afterwards, in the company of some gentlemen, he came to Plimouth, and was kindly entertained; but revenge boiling in his breast, as some conceived, he watched a season to have stabbed the governor, and put his hand to his dagger for that end, but by God's providence, ordering the vigilance of some that were about him, he was prevented.[1][2]

Jehovah Nissi – "our deliverer". You are my God.

---

1 From *Chronicles of the Pilgrim Fathers*.
2 A charge of piracy against Captain Stone was considered, in the hope of forcing him to answer before the Admiralty in England. This was withdrawn, though, as the Pilgrims felt this might "turn to their reproach".

... SET ASIDE FOR YOURSELVES THREE CITIES... IF THE LORD YOUR
GOD ENLARGES YOUR TERRITORY...
(Deuteronomy 19:7–8)

The Pilgrims pushed their trade to the south and west by means of another trading post built twenty miles to the south on the outer shore of Cape Cod, at Aptuxcet, now the village of Bourne... Here the Cape was almost cut from the mainland by the Scusset River on the near side and the Manomet River flowing westerly into Buzzards Bay. Both were navigable by small craft, and as there was short easy portage between, the Pilgrims used this route – now that of the Cape Cod Canal – to avoid the long dangerous voyage around the Cape. Here on the banks of the Manomet, just above Buzzards Bay, they built a stout trading post of hewn oak timbers and kept two agents there winter and summer. They also built a pinnace and kept it at the post, using it to push their trade and explorations along the southern New England coast into Long Island Sound. It was by way of Aptuxcet that relations were established with the Dutch at New Amsterdam.[1]

Enlarge my spiritual vision, Lord, regarding that which you might want to do in and through me. Challenge me to believe, in faith, for new and larger possibilities within my church. Widen my horizons, so that I might not limit potential or inadvertently hinder kingdom opportunities. Greater things!

---

1   From *Saints and Strangers*.

... HE THAT WAVERETH IS LIKE A WAVE OF THE SEA DRIVEN WITH
THE WIND AND TOSSED. FOR LET NOT THAT MAN THINK THAT
HE SHALL RECEIVE ANY THING OF THE LORD. A DOUBLE MINDED
MAN IS UNSTABLE IN ALL HIS WAYS.

(James 1:6–8 *KJV*)

Scurvy and infectious fever had broken out at sea ... Carried ashore, disease soon cut the Puritan vanguard in half ... The Pilgrims sent Deacon Samuel Fuller[1] [to seafarers who arrived in a poor state of health]. It was a momentous visit, for Deacon-Doctor Fuller tended not only the ailing bodies, but the troubled souls of his patients. Though more and more critical of the Anglican Church and its ways, these hesitant Puritans had never dared separate and go their way. They continued a nominal conformity, partly because they had ideological objections to "schism", but chiefly because they were trimmers without the courage of their convictions. They were deterred by fear of the heavy hand of the bishops and the magistrates ... Fuller had no difficulty in converting them ... They quickly joined the Separation and embraced the Holy Discipline, though for politic reasons they still protested – a feeble rationalization – that they had separated not from the Church of England, but its "corruptions".[2]

**Help those, Lord, who are "double minded" and can't decide what to do next.
Help those who procrastinate! Bless them with an improved sense of decision
making, especially when it comes to spiritual matters. Deliver us from dithering!**

1   See April 23rd.
2   From *Saints and Strangers*.

... IS THERE NO PHYSICIAN THERE?

(Jeremiah 8:22 *KJV*)

[Deacon-Doctor Samuel Fuller] wore a "longe beard and a garment like the Greeke" [*sic*] ... Fuller had been "bred a butcher" and was always ready to practise his trade upon the unsuspecting. Nor was his physic any good. "He takes a patient and the urinall, eyes the state there, finds the crasis symmptomes and attomi natantes, and tells the patient that his disease was winde, which he had taken by gapeing feasting overboard at sea" [*sic*]. In short, he was seasick. Still, Fuller had worked a marvellous cure for Endecott,[1] that "great swelling fellowe... the cow-keeper of Salem" [*sic*]. He had "cured him of a disease called a wife"[2] ... The "Quacksalver" then treated other ailing Saints, some forty in all, who had no complaints to make, for all went promptly to heaven.[3]

Oh, Lord! Today, I can but give grateful thanks for competent doctors and surgeons! I pray specifically for anyone known to me who is due to have surgery soon. Calm any nervousness within them, I ask, and guide the minds and hands of all those involved in the operation.

---

1   John Endecott, or Endicott (before 1600–1664 or 1655), one of the Fathers of New England and the longest-serving governor of the Massachusetts Bay Colony.

2   John Endecott's first wife, Anne Gourer, died in New England, and this tongue-in-cheek reference leads us to believe that her death may have been attributed to Fuller's incompetence as a doctor and surgeon.

3   From *Saints and Strangers*.

... GOD SENT ME BEFORE YOU TO PRESERVE YOU... AND TO SAVE
YOUR LIVES BY A GREAT DELIVERANCE.
(Genesis 45:7 *KJV*)

There was a company of people lived in ye country, up above in ye river of Conigtecut, a great way from their trading house there, and were enemies to those Indians which lived about them, and of whom they stood in some fear... About a thousand of them had enclosed themselves in a fort, which they had strongly palissadoed[1] about. Three or four Dutch men went up in ye beginning of winter to live with them, to get their trade, and prevent them from bringing it to ye English, or to fall into enmity with them; but at spring to bring all down to their place. But their enterprise failed, for it pleased God to visit these Indians with great sickness, and such a mortality that of a 1000 above 900 and a half of them died, and many of them did rot above ground for want of burial, and ye Dutch men almost starved before they could get away, for ice and snow... They got with much difficulty to their trading house; whom they kindly relieved, being almost spent with hunger. Being thus refreshed by them... they got to their own place, and ye Dutch were very thankful for this kindness.[2]

When other helpers fail and comforts flee
Help of the helpless, oh, abide with me.[3]

---

1   Palisade.
2   From *History of Plymouth Plantation*.
3   From Henry Francis Lyte's hymn "Abide With Me".

GREATER LOVE HAS NO ONE THAN THIS: TO LAY DOWN ONE'S LIFE
FOR ONE'S FRIENDS.
(John 15:13)

Those Indians that lived about their trading house there fell sick of ye smallpox, and died most miserably; for a sorer disease cannot befall them; they fear it more than ye plague; for usually they that have this disease have them in abundance, and for want of bedding... and other helps, they fall into a lamentable condition, as they lie on their hard mats, ye pox breaking... and running one into another, their skin cleaving (by reason thereof) to the mats they lie on; when they turn them, a whole side will flee off at once... and they will be all of a gore blood, most fearful to behold; and then being very sore, what with cold and other distempers, they die like rotten sheep. The condition of this people was so lamentable, and they fell down generally of this disease, as they were (in ye end) not able to help another; no, not to make a fire, nor to fetch a little water to drink, nor any to bury ye dead; but would strive as long as they could, and when they could procure no other means to make fire, they would burn ye wooden trays and dishes they ate their meat in, and their very bows and arrows; and some would crawl out on all fours to get a little water, and sometimes die by ye way & not be able to get home again. But those of ye English house (though at first they were afraid of ye infection), yet seeing their woeful and sad condition, and hearing their pitiful cries and lamentations, they had compassion on them, and daily fetched them wood & water, and made them fires, got them victuals while they lived, and buried them when they died. For very few of them escaped, notwithstanding they did what they could for them, to ye hazard of themselves.[1]

Lord, draw alongside those who put their own lives at risk for the sake of others – doctors and nurses, missionaries who minister in isolated areas around the globe, and those who sacrifice their own home comforts in order to reach out to deprived communities. Honour their altruism, I pray, and bless their efforts to serve humankind. Thank you for such people.

---

1   From *History of Plymouth Plantation.*

LET YOUR FOOT BE SELDOM IN YOUR NEIGHBOU'S HOUSE, LEST HE
HAVE HIS FILL OF YOU AND HATE YOU.
(Proverbs 25:17 *ESV*)

Some of their neighbours in ye Bay, hearing of ye fame of Conightecute River, had a hankering mind after it... and now understanding that ye Indians were swept away with ye late great mortality, the fear of whom was an obstacle unto them before, which being now taken away, they began now to prosecute it with great energies. The greatest differences fell between [them] for they set their minds on that place... whose doings and proceedings were conceived to be very injurious, to attempt not only to intrude themselves upon ye rights and possessions of others, but in effect to thrust them out of all.[1]

This day, Lord, help me to be a good neighbour.

---

1 From *History of Plymouth Plantation.*

LET NOTHING BE DONE THROUGH STRIFE...
(Philippians 2:3 *KJV*)

While the novice Saints on the Bay were a comfort to the Pilgrims, they were also a problem. It was obvious from the start that they would be serious rivals in trade. Thanks to a storm that drove their ship into the harbour, Plymouth discovered that some of them were already trespassing, carrying on a surreptitious trade with Cape Cod. Bradford sent the ship back to Boston with the warning that such attempts would be resisted, "even to the spending of our lives"... Plymouth's boundaries had never been sharply defined. The powers of government were derived from no higher authority than the *Mayflower* Contract and might be seriously challenged at any time.[1]

> Lord, matters such as this can be difficult and even worrying – uncertain boundaries, vague or non-existent contracts, decisions regarding who is in charge of certain issues, legal documents, financial arrangements, and so on. Help me, I pray, when it comes to issues like this, to make sure my affairs are properly organized. Give me that presence of mind, I pray, and send along the right people who can offer sound advice. Protect me from being misled or tricked in any way.

---

1   From *Saints and Strangers*.

The French in Canada had always regarded the Pilgrims' trading post on the Penobscot[1] as an encroachment on their territory. One day… a small French ship put into the harbour on the pretence that she had lost her way was leaking badly, needing to be hauled ashore for repair. The officers were very polite, "and many French compliments they used" in asking permission of the post, which was granted by three of four… servants left in charge by the resident agent… who happened to be in Plymouth getting supplies. Learning this, the visitors began praising the muskets in racks along the walls of the post, taking them down and examining them. Suddenly they turned on their hosts, robbing them of everything at hand – rugs, blankets, coats, biscuit, and beaver worth £500. They even compelled the servants to carry the loot on board and stow it down before they leisurely sailed away.

"When your master comes," was the final taunt, "tell him that some gentlemen from the Ile de Rey [2] have been here."[3]

What a dreadful story, Lord. My prayers today are with those who have fallen victim to burglars or thieves, and those who have been mugged. Help them, I pray, to manage such a trauma – the loss of possessions and the ensuing emotional ordeal. I pray your blessing, too, on law enforcement agencies and those who try to bring offenders to justice. Help their efforts.

---

1   An indigenous peoples in North America with members in the United States and Canada.
2   An island off the west coast of France.
3   From *Saints and Strangers*.

... MY GOD WILL MEET ALL YOUR NEEDS ACCORDING TO THE
RICHES OF HIS GLORY IN CHRIST JESUS.
(Philippians 4:19)

It pleased God, in these times, to bless ye country with such access & confluence of people into it, as it was thereby much enriched, and cattle of all kinds stood at a high rate for diverse years together. Kine[1] were sold at 20,[2] and some at 25 apiece, yes sometimes at 26. A cow-calf usually at 10. A milk-goat at 3 & some at 4. And female kids at 30 and often at 40 apiece. By which means ye ancient planters which had any stock began to grow in their estate. Corn also went at a sound rate, 6 a bushel.[3]

Today, Heavenly Father, I simply want to say thank you.

Praise to the Lord,
Who doth prosper thy work and defend thee.[4]

1　Cows collectively.
2　The exact financial denomination and coinage referred to here, and throughout, is uncertain, but an excellent explanation of likely options can be found at https://www.philadelphiafed.org/education/teachers/resources/money-in-colonial-times
3　From *History of Plymouth Plantation.*
4　From Joachim Neander's hymn "Praise to the Lord, the Almighty".

… THIS WATER SYMBOLIZES BAPTISM THAT NOW SAVES YOU ALSO –
NOT THE REMOVAL OF DIRT FROM THE BODY BUT THE PLEDGE OF A
CLEAR CONSCIENCE TOWARD GOD.
(1 Peter 3:21)

Ye church here had invited and sent for Mr. Charles Chansey,[1] a reverend, godly, and very learned man, intending upon trial to choose him as pastor of ye church here, for ye more comfortable performance of ye ministry with Mr. John Reinor,[2] the teacher of ye same. But there fell out some difference about baptising, he holding it ought to only be by dipping, and putting ye whole body under water, and that sprinkling was unlawful. The church yielded that immersion, or dipping, was lawful, but in this cold country not so convenient. But they could not, nor dare not yield to him in this, that sprinkling (which all ye churches of Christ do for ye most part this day) was unlawful, & an human invention… but they were willing to yield to him as far as they could, and to do ye utmost; and were content to suffer him to practise as he was persuaded; and when he came to minister that ordinance, he might so do it to any that did desire it in any way, provided he could peaceably suffer Mr. Reinor, and such as desired to have theirs otherwise baptised by him, by sprinkling… of water upon them; so as there might be no disturbance in ye church hereabouts.[3]

Gracious God, I pray that you would move, by your Holy Spirit, to lead many into a new life in Christ. Whatever the finer points of baptism, what matters is that people turn to Jesus as their Lord and Saviour. I pray for those known to me personally who have yet to respond to your love. Touch their hearts.

---

1   Or Chauncy (baptized 5 November 1592–1672), Anglo-American clergyman, educator, and physician.
2   Or Reynor or Reyner or Rayner (1605–69).
3   From *History of Plymouth Plantation*.

... THE LORD ORDAINED THAT THEY WHICH PREACH THE GOSPEL
SHOULD LIVE OF THE GOSPEL.
(1 Corinthians 9:14 *KJV*)

The church procured some other ministers to dispute ye point with [Charles Chansey] publicly; as Mr. Ralfe Patrich[1] ... who did it sundry times, very ably and sufficiently, as also some other ministers within this government. But he was not satisfied, so ye church sent to many other churches to crave their help and advice in this matter and, with his will and consent, sent them his arguments written under his own hand ... and received very able & sufficient answers, as they conceived, from them and their learned ministers, who all concluded against him. But himself was not satisfied there ... They conceived ye church had done what was meet in ye thing, so Mr. Chansey, having been ye most part of 3 years here, removed himself to Sityate.[2] [3]

My prayers today, Heavenly Father, are for ministers who are moving from one church to another, perhaps especially if they are doing so under something of a cloud, like Mr. Chansey. Transition is never easy, and the "spotlight" placed upon church leaders as they take up a new position sometimes tends to accentuate that unease. Bless them, Lord, and be with their families too.

---

1 Or Ralph or Rodolphus Partridge (before April 1579–between September 1655 and April 1658), Church of England minister driven out by the severity of Bishop Laud (see Footnote 1, August 7th), hence his arrival in New England.
2 Or Scituate, Massachusetts.
3 From *History of Plymouth Plantation*.

Marvellous[1] it may be to see and consider how some kind of wickedness did grow and break forth here, in a land where the same was so much witnessed against, and so narrowly looked unto, & severely punished when it was known; as in no place more, or so much, that I have known or heard of; insomuch as they have been somewhat censured, even by moderate and good men, for their severity in punishments. And yet all this could not suppress ye breaking out of sundry notorious sins… One reason may be, that ye devil may carry a greater spite against the churches of Christ and ye gospel here, by how much ye more they endeavour to preserve holiness and purity amongst them, and strictly punish the contrary when it arises either in church or commonwealth; that he might cast a blemish & stain upon them in ye eyes of ye world, who are rash in judgment. I would rather think thus, than that Satan has more power in these heathen lands, as some have thought, than in more Christian nations, especially over God's servants in them.[2]

This day, Almighty God, strengthen me against the wiles of my enemy. Keep me alert to the dangers of various temptations. Grant me sustaining grace that will enable me to live victoriously.

Leave no unguarded place,
No weakness of the soul,
Take every virtue, every grace,
And fortify the whole.
To keep your armour bright
Attend with constant care,
Still walking in your Captain's sight
And watching unto prayer.[3]

---

1   As in incredulous, not as in impressive.
2   From *History of Plymouth Plantation*.
3   From Charles Wesley's hymn "Soldiers of Christ, Arise". (This hymn features in my book *Through the Year with Charles Wesley*.)

TAKE NO PART IN THE UNFRUITFUL WORKS OF DARKNESS, BUT
INSTEAD EXPOSE THEM.
(Ephesians 5:11 *ESV*)

As it is with waters when their streams are stopped or dammed up, when they get passage again they flow with more violence, and make more noise and disturbance, than when they are suffered to run quietly in their own channels. So wickedness being here more stopped by strict laws… so as it cannot run in a common road of liberty as it would, and is inclined, it searches everywhere, and at last breaks out when it gets vent.

[There is] not more evil here… as in other places, but they are here more discovered and seen, and made public by due search, inquisition, and due punishment, for ye churches look narrowly to their members, and ye magistrates over all, more strictly than in other places. Besides, here the people are but few in comparison of other places, which are full and populous, and lie hid, as it were, in a wood or a thicket, and many horrible evils by that means are never seen or known; whereas here, they are, as it were, brought into ye light, and set in ye plain field, or rather on a hill, made conspicuous to ye view of all.[1]

Cleanse my heart, Lord, so that I may not dread the light of your love shining into my life. Cleanse me afresh today, I pray.

---

1 From *History of Plymouth Plantation.*

See, I am doing a new thing!
(Isaiah 43:19)

Though the Pilgrims reached out into distant parts of new England, and established trading posts far and wide, from upper Main to the Connecticut River, they made no attempt... to establish any permanent settlements... Within two years [though], the Bay had attracted several thousand settlers... which caused a sudden shift of weight in all New England affairs. The centre of gravity was no longer at Plymouth, but at Boston, and the effects of this were immediately felt along Town Brook. The presence of the larger population to the north profoundly and permanently altered the Pilgrims' primitive economy. With economic change came fundamental shifts in the general social pattern, which in turn affected the frame of government and all institutions, even the church.[1]

Ah, Lord – a shift in the balance of power! How quickly it can seem at times, that our established patterns and preferences are changed – and how uncomfortable that can be! Grant me that special grace, I pray, whereby change is not seen as threatening and alarming, but something to be embraced, in terms of new opportunities. Deliver us from staleness, Lord, when it comes to church behaviour, however much we may sometimes wish things could always be the same. Help us when our comfort zones begin to disappear!

---

1   From *Saints and Strangers*.

THE HEAVENS DECLARE THE GLORY OF GOD; AND THE FIRMAMENT
SHEWETH HIS HANDYWORK.
(Psalm 19:1 *KJV*)

There appeared a sign in the heavens, in the form of a spear, something thicker in the midst than at either end, of a whitish, bright colour; it was seen, several nights together, in the west, about an hour within the night; it stood stooping, and the one end pointing to the setting of the sun, and so settled downward, by little and little, until it quite vanished, and descended beneath our horizon. God awaken us that we be not heedless spectators of his wonderful works.

(This appearance is supposed to have been the zodiacal light, though some thought it the tail of a comet which was below the horizon. It was seen in several other places. All such unusual appearances were supposed to forebode evil. No doubt imagination assisted in giving it the spear-pointing form.)[1]

Creator God, Lord of heaven and earth, I worship you today.

---

1   From *Chronicles of the Pilgrim Fathers.*

MAY THE LORD ANSWER YOU WHEN YOU ARE IN DISTRESS; MAY THE
NAME OF THE GOD OF JACOB PROTECT YOU.
(Psalm 20:1)

[The Pilgrim Fathers] went from England to Holland, where they found both worse air and diet than that they came from; from thence (enduring a long imprisonment, as it were, in ye ships at sea) into New England; and how it has been with them has already been shown; and what crosses, troubles, fears, wants, and sorrows they have been liable to, it is easy to conjecture; so as in some sort they may say with ye Apostle, 2 Cor:11. 26, 27 they were in journeyings often, in perils of waters, in perils of robbers, in perils of their own nation, in perils among ye heathen, in perils in ye wilderness, in perils in ye sea, in perils among false brethren; in weariness and painfulness, in watching often, in hunger and thirst, in fainting often, in cold and nakedness. What was it then that upheld them? It was God's visitation that preserved their spirits. Job 10.12 Thou hast given me life and grace, and thy visitation hath preserved my spirit. He that upheld ye Apostle upheld them.[1]

> Lord God, in your mercy, uphold those who need your special touch today. Lend them your strength as the hours pass. I pray especially for any known to me personally, who require a new and loving touch upon their souls. Be with those whose circumstances are trying and difficult, even in this very hour.

---

1 From *History of Plymouth Plantation*.

... THEY THAT WILL BE RICH FALL INTO TEMPTATION AND A SNARE,
AND INTO MANY FOOLISH AND HURTFUL LUSTS, WHICH DROWN
MEN IN DESTRUCTION AND PERDITION.

(1 Timothy 6:9 *KJV*)

A staple of their diet from the first, often the famished Pilgrims' only food, corn had acquired a new value... it became a principal medium of exchange in the beaver trade. As the Indians were always hungry for corn and eager to barter for it, the Pilgrims planted as much as possible. But its value as a trading commodity began to decline and production fell off with the introduction of wampum[1]... For several years the planters followed agriculture only for their home needs, having no market for surplus grain, cattle, hay, and other produce. Now all this was suddenly changed... Corn was shelling at [the equivalent of] 8 shillings a bushel... The Pilgrims went eagerly to increase their crops and livestock, "by which many were much inriched" [*sic*] – a quite unfamiliar state of affairs for most of them.

"No man now thought he could live except he had catle and a great deale of ground to keep them... and having oxen growne, they must have land for plowing and tillage" [*sic*]. Again there was a clamour for division of the common lands. It became so loud and insistent that the authorities gave way... distributing thousands of acres among the fifty-eight Purchasers in proportion to the number of shares each held in the colony. As the better farm lands and meadows lay in that direction, most of the assignments were made to the north of town.[2]

How times changed for the Pilgrims, Lord! One minute, their only desire was for religious freedom, and they were so grateful just to have escaped England and landed safely. Now their hearts are turning towards the new desire of prosperity! Forgive me, I pray, if ever my heart has followed a similar trajectory. Teach me to look around me today, to count my blessings, and to be thankful!

---

1 Indian necklaces and jewellery made from shells and beads, used either directly as currency, or sold as trinkets.
2 From *Saints and Strangers*.

PUT YOUR OUTDOOR WORK IN ORDER AND GET YOUR FIELDS READY;
AFTER THAT, BUILD YOUR HOUSE.
(Proverbs 24:27)

Anxious to develop their new farms and profit from soaring prices, people began moving out of Plymouth at an alarming rate.

"And if this had been all," said Bradford, "it had been less, though too much," for now "ye church must also be divided, and those that lived so long together in Christian and comfortable fellowship must now part and suffer many divisions."

The pull of larger and more fertile fields was so strong that many of the old comers, including some eminent Saints, were drawn across the harbour to Duxbury, the first of Mother Plymouth's daughters. The venerable Brewster... went to live there with his two younger sons, Love and Wrestling...

According to an old and generally accepted tradition, the town was named after Duxbury Hall, later discovered to be one of the properties of the powerful Standish family, from which Captain [Standish] claimed descent. Unfortunately for the tradition, Duxbury Hall was not so named until many years after the town was founded. Indeed, for half a century the town was not known as Duxbury at all, but as Buxbarrow (often written as "Ducksburrow"), which would suggest that it was named for the large flocks of waterfowl that nested in the extensive salt marshes along its shores.[1]

> **Lord of our lives, I pray your blessing upon those who are in the process of moving house, with all that it entails: financial concerns, new neighbours, a sense of upheaval, and so on. Bless them, I pray, especially if they are new families starting out in life and perhaps buying their first home. Help them to stay calm with all that needs to be done. Likewise, be with those who are looking for somewhere else to live; guide their footsteps according to your will.**

---

1 From *Saints and Strangers*.

THE STEPS OF A GOOD MAN ARE ORDERED BY THE LORD: AND HE
DELIGHTETH IN HIS WAY.
(Psalm 37:23 *KJV*)

Capt. Miles[1] Standish expired his mortal life. He was a gentleman, born in Lancashire, and was heir apparent unto a great estate of lands and livings, surreptitiously detained from him; his great-grandfather being a second or younger brother from the house of Standish. In his younger time he went over into the low countries, and was a soldier there, and came acquainted with the church at Leyden, and came over into New England, with such of them as at the first set out into the planting of the plantation at New Plimouth, and bare a deep share of their first difficulties, and was always very faithful to their interests. He growing ancient, became sick of the stone,[2] or stranguary,[3] whereof, after his suffering of much dolorous pain, he fell asleep in the Lord, and was honourably buried at Duxbury.[4]

How wonderfully you led Captain Standish to Leyden, Lord, where he met up with the Pilgrims. Quite possibly, as he set out for Holland, he had little idea of the direction his life would take. Yet, your good hand was upon him. I pray for anyone seeking your direction, that you may similarly guide their footsteps.

---

1 Sometimes, Myles.
2 Possibly, kidney stone.
3 Or strangury. An infection or blockage at the base of the bladder.
4 From *Chronicles of the Pilgrim Fathers*.

THE LORD WILL PERFECT THAT WHICH CONCERNETH ME...
(Psalm 138:8 *KJV*)

There is little recorded of [Captain] Standish after his prowess had brought the Indians to submission. Often when military action was expected and soldiers called for, he was appointed generalissimo, and he was active in military life until within three years of his death. He was also one of the assistants or council during most of his life. There is a traditionary [*sic*] anecdote relative to Capt. Standish and his friend John Alden.[1] The lady who had gained the affections of the captain is said to have been Priscilla Mullins.[2] John Alden was sent to make proposals on behalf of Standish. The messenger, though a pilgrim, was then young and comely, and the lady expressed her preference by the question, "Prithee [*sic*], John, why do you not speak for yourself?" The captain's hope was blasted, and the brief overture soon ended in the marriage of John Alden and Priscilla Mullins, from whom, it is said, are descended all of the name of Alden in the United States.[3]

Lord, preserve me from missed opportunities! If I feel a course of action is right, give me the courage to pursue it.

---

1 Captain John Alden Sr (d. 1687), crew member on the *Mayflower*. Rather than return to England with the ship, he stayed at what became Plymouth Colony.

2 1602–80.

3 From *Chronicles of the Pilgrim Fathers*.

O DEATH, WHERE IS THY STING? O GRAVE, WHERE IS THY VICTORY?
THE STING OF DEATH IS SIN; AND THE STRENGTH OF SIN IS THE
LAW. BUT THANKS BE TO GOD, WHICH GIVETH US THE VICTORY
THROUGH OUR LORD JESUS CHRIST.
(1 Corinthians 15:55–57 *KJV*)

Brave Captain Standish, while he grew less fierce as he got older, was still head of the defence of the settlement in face of enemies.

At last the call came for Captain Miles Standish, the Pilgrims' Mr. Valiant-for-Truth.

And we can say of him what John Bunyan wrote in *The Pilgrim's Progress*:

"Then Mr. Valiant-for-Truth said, I am going to my Father's; and though with great difficulty I have got hither, yet now I do not repent me of all the troubles I have been at to arrive where I am. My sword I give to him that shall succeed me in my pilgrimage, and my courage and skill to him that can get it. My marks and scars I carry with me to be a witness for me that I have fought His battles who now will be my rewarder.

"When the day that he must go hence was come, many accompanied him to the riverside, into which as he went he said, 'Death, where is thy sting?' And as he went down deeper, he said, 'Grave, where is they victory?'

"So he passed over, and all the trumpets sounded for him on the other side."[1]

Lord of life! Lord of death! Lord of eternity! Thanks be to God indeed!

---

1   From *The Argonauts of Faith*.

THEN THE LORD SAID UNTO MOSES, NOW SHALT THOU SEE WHAT
I WILL DO TO PHARAOH: FOR WITH A STRONG HAND SHALL HE LET
THEM GO, AND WITH A STRONG HAND SHALL HE DRIVE THEM OUT
OF HIS LAND. AND GOD SPAKE UNTO MOSES, AND SAID UNTO HIM,
I AM THE LORD: AND I APPEARED UNTO ABRAHAM, UNTO ISAAC,
AND UNTO JACOB, BY THE NAME OF GOD ALMIGHTY, BUT BY MY
NAME JEHOVAH WAS I NOT KNOWN TO THEM. AND I HAVE ALSO
ESTABLISHED MY COVENANT WITH THEM, TO GIVE THEM THE LAND
OF CANAAN, THE LAND OF THEIR PILGRIMAGE, WHEREIN THEY
WERE STRANGERS.

(Exodus 6:1–4 *KJV*)

Many strange and stirring happening came upon the Pilgrims...

For there came sailing to the harbour at the Plymouth Settlement, away there in the west, other men and women from England as colonists. The *Little James*, a pinnace of forty-four tons, the ship *Anne*, and then the ship *Charity* brought new faces to the colony. Gradually the Pilgrims of the *Mayflower* grew older and some died, while more and more new settlers came to the little town.[1]

> *Guide me, O Thou great Jehovah,*
> *Pilgrim through this barren land;*
> *I am weak, but Thou art mighty,*
> *Hold me with Thy pow'rful hand.*[2]

---

1 From *The Argonauts of Faith*.
2 From William Williams' hymn.

... TO ME, TO LIVE IS CHRIST AND TO DIE IS GAIN. IF I AM TO GO ON
LIVING IN THE BODY, THIS WILL MEAN FRUITFUL LABOUR FOR ME.
YET WHAT SHALL I CHOOSE? I DO NOT KNOW! I AM TORN BETWEEN
THE TWO: I DESIRE TO DEPART AND BE WITH CHRIST, WHICH IS
BETTER BY FAR ...
(Philippians 1:21–23)

Certain verses left by the honoured William Bradford, Esq., governor of the jurisdiction of Plimouth, penned by his own hand, declaring the gracious dispensations of God's providence towards him in the time of his life, and his preparation and fittedness [*sic*] for death.

"From my years young in days of youth, God did make known to me his truth,
And call'd me from my native place for to enjoy the means of grace.
In wilderness he did me guide, and in strange lands for me provide.
In fears and wants, through weal and woe, a pilgrim, passed I to and fro:
Oft left of them whom I did trust; how vain it is to rest on dust!
A man of sorrows I have been, and many changes I have seen.
Wars, wants, peace, plenty, have I known; and some advanc'd,
and some thrown down.
The humble poor, cheerful and glad; rich, discontent, sower and sad:
When fears and sorrows have been mixt, consolations came betwixt.
Faint not, poor soul, in God still trust, fear not the things thou suffer must;
For, whom he loves he does chastise, and then all tears wipes from their eyes.
Farewell, dear children, whom I love, your better Father is above;
When I am gone, he can supply; to him I leave you when I die.
Fear him in truth, walk in his ways, and he will bless you all your days.
My days are spent, old age is come, my strength it fails, my glass near run.
Now I will wait, when work is done, until my happy change shall come,
When from my labours I shall rest, with Christ above for to be blest."[1]

The best is yet to come! Thank you, Lord Jesus, for this great hope.

---

1   From *Chronicles of the Pilgrim Fathers*.

"... 'WELL DONE, GOOD AND FAITHFUL SERVANT!'"
(Matthew 25:23)

It pleased God to put a period to the life of his precious servant, Mr. William Bradford, who was the second governor of the jurisdiction of New Plimouth, and continued in the same place for the most part of his time, with little intermission ...

> *Why mourns the people thus for me, since I*
> *In heavens dwell, shall to eternity?*
> *Let not so many tears fall from my friends;*
> *Live holy, happy, God will recompense*
> *Into your bosoms all your love again,*
> *And your affections whilst I did remain*
> *'Mongst you, but now you must refrain.*
> *Bear up your hearts, dear hearts, when thoughts of me*
> *Run in your minds, with this the time will be,*
> *And every hour brings it on apace,*
> *Dear friends, when we for ever shall embrace.*
> *Farewell but for a season then, farewell;*
> *Our next embraces shall the rest excel,*
> *Rest happy, children, friends, and tender wife,*
> *Death but begins the godly's happy life.*[1] [2] [3]

Lord, I thank you for those officers of the church who have served you faithfully for decades; those who have stayed at their post, as it were, through thick and thin. Bless them for their faithfulness, and their sense of duty. I thank you for such people in my own church. I pray for them as they carry out their responsibilities.

---

1   A memorial poem written by Major Josias (or Josiah) Winslow (1628–80). Winslow was born in the Plymouth Colony.
2   This poem reads as an acrostic, and sharp-eyed readers will notice the name "William Bradford" running down the left-hand spine of this poetic tribute.
3   From *Chronicles of the Pilgrim Fathers*.

NOT FORSAKING THE ASSEMBLING OF OURSELVES TOGETHER, AS
THE MANNER OF SOME IS; BUT EXHORTING ONE ANOTHER: AND SO
MUCH THE MORE, AS YE SEE THE DAY APPROACHING.
(Hebrews 10:25 *KJV*)

For several years the Duxburrow people journeyed to Plymouth every Sabbath to attend the meeting there, probably crossing the harbour in the shallop whenever the weather was good, for it was an exhausting ten miles' journey by land. And it had to be made on foot or on the back of plodding oxen, for there were as yet no roads and no horses in the colony. Stephen Hopkins[1] appears to have owned the first horse in the Old Colony, a mare … Trails were rough and often muddy, and there was constant complaint about "dangerous and hazzerous" [*sic*] bridges, which were usually just a few trees felled across the stream, and difficult to manage, even on foot. Soon the distant brethren were complaining that it was a "great burthen" [*sic*] to bring their wives, children, and servants to the meeting at Plymouth every Sabbath and asked to be allowed to "become a body to themselves". They sued for their dismission [*sic*], which was finally granted … "though very unwillingly", for Plymouth had recently lost many of its abler men and more experienced Saints.[2]

Lord, as I read these words, I realize that for some people, even the act of actually getting to church can be a real struggle. I pray for those believers whose access to their church buildings is hindered by poor roads, inadequate transport, and difficult journeys. Bless them as they make every valiant effort to meet and worship together.

---

1   Stephen Hopkins (1581–1644) a passenger on the *Mayflower*.
2   From *Saints and Strangers*.

EVERY GOOD GIFT AND EVERY PERFECT GIFT IS FROM ABOVE, AND
COMETH DOWN FROM THE FATHER OF LIGHTS, WITH WHOM IS NO
VARIABLENESS, NEITHER SHADOW OF TURNING.
(James 1:17 *KJV*)

To check the diaspora of the Saints, it was decided to give out some good farms to spetiall persons… lickly to be helpful to ye church or commonewelth [*sic*], if they would promise to live in town and arrange matters so that their servants might cultivate their fields and tend their livestock. Accordingly, large tracts of fine meadowland were staked out beyond Duxbury, at a place called Green's Harbour, soon named Marshfield, and were bestowed upon some of the "Old Standards"…

But alass! This rememdy proved worse than ye disease [*sic*]. As soon as their farms were developed, these also broke away "partly by force, and partly by wearying ye rest with importunitie and pleas of necessitie", for those at Plymouth were getting tired of living "incontinuall opposition and contention" [*sic*]. This encouraged still others to please "their owne conceived necessitie" and depart, which will be ye ruine of New England, or at least of ye churches of God there … & will provock ye Lord's displeasure against them [*sic*].[1]

Heavenly Father, today's reading reminds me that you are a faithful God. You are not capricious. Your love remains the same, even when we, your people, make mistakes and do things our way. Your steadfast love covers a multitude of our faults and failings.

Great is Thy faithfulness, O God my Father,
There is no shadow of turning with Thee;
Thou changest not, Thy compassions, they fail not
As Thou hast been, Thou forever wilt be.[2]

---

1   From *Saints and Strangers*.
2   From Thomas Obadiah Chisholm's hymn.

LET ANOTHER PRAISE YOU, AND NOT YOUR OWN MOUTH; A
STRANGER, AND NOT YOUR OWN LIPS.
(Proverbs 27:2 *ESV*)

Beyond Marshfield, almost halfway to Boston, there was another Old Colony town, Scituate... It was an offshoot of Plymouth, but was populated by Saints of a closely related school. The merchant adventurer Timothy Hatherly[1] had settled there about 1633, and... a large company arrived from England under the Reverend John Lothrop,[2] a man "indowed with a Competent measure of Gifts", according to the Pilgrims, "and eminently Indowed with a Great Measure of brokenness of hart and humilittie of sperrit" [*sic*]. Lothrop was a disciple of Henry Jacob,[3] founder of English Congregationalism,[4] once an exile in Holland... With Jacob's departure for Virginia... Lothrop succeeded to [Jacob's] pulpit at Southwark and occupied it for ten years. At length, despairing of England under Archbishop Laud, he and most of his congregation decided to migrate to New England. Scituate evidently did not please them, for they soon packed up and moved down to Cape Cod, settling at Barnstable.[5]

Great gifting coupled with a great measure of brokenness and humility – what a challenging recipe for spiritual strength! So help me, God.

1   1588–1666. Felt maker, merchant, and gentleman.
2   Reverend John Lothrop (1584–1653) — or Lothropp or Lathrop, Anglican clergyman.
3   1563–1624, English clergyman.
4   See https://en.wikipedia.org/wiki/Congregational_church
5   From *Saints and Strangers*.

THEN THEIR NUMBERS DECREASED ...
(Psalm 107:39)

Many having left this place ... and their finding of better accommodations elsewhere, more suitable to their own ends & minds; and sundry others still upon every occasion desiring their dismissions [sic], the church began seriously to think whether it were better jointly to remove to some other place, than to be thus weakened, and as it were insensibly dissolved. Many meetings and much consultation was held hereabouts, and diverse were men's minds and opinions. Some were still for staying together in this same place, alleging men might live, if they would be content with their conditions; and yet it was not for want or necessity so much they removed, as for ye enriching of themselves. Others were resolute upon removal, and so signified they could not stay; but if ye church did not remove, they must ... So ... ye greater part consented to a removal to a place called Nawsett, which had been superficially viewed and ye goodwill of ye purchasers (to whom it belonged) obtained.[1]

My prayers today, Lord, are for those church officials who decide upon the closure of churches, if and when such recommendations are deemed necessary. Those are not popular decisions, Lord, even though, to be honest, some dead churches really should have been given a decent burial long ago! Give those officials the courage to think bravely and clearly about what needs to be done, the wisdom to consider all options, and the sensitivity to bear in mind the feelings of all concerned.

---

1   From *History of Plymouth Plantation.*

PAY CAREFUL ATTENTION TO YOURSELVES AND TO ALL THE FLOCK,
IN WHICH THE HOLY SPIRIT HAS MADE YOU OVERSEERS, TO CARE
FOR THE CHURCH OF GOD,
WHICH HE OBTAINED WITH HIS OWN BLOOD.
(Acts 20:28 *ESV*)

[Those who were keen to move away] began to see their error, that they had given away already the best and most commodious places to others, and now wanted themselves; for this place was about 50 miles hence, and at an outside of ye country, remote from all society; also, that it would prove so straight, as it would not be competent to receive ye whole body, much less be capable of any addition or increase; so as (at least in the short term) they should be worse there than they are now here. The which, with sundry other like considerations and inconveniences, made them change their resolutions; but such as were before resolved upon removal took advantage of this agreement, & went on notwithstanding, neither could ye rest hinder them, they having made some beginning. And thus was this poor church left, like an ancient mother, grown old, and forsaken of her children (though not in their affections), yet in regard of their bodily presence and personal helpfulness. Her ancient members being most of them worn away by death; and these of later time being like children translated into other families, and she like a widow left only to trust in God. Thus she that had made many rich became herself poor.[1]

Faithful God, draw alongside those who have made mistakes! Reassure them that a mistake – even a serious one – does not constitute the end of the road. Help them not to succumb to feelings of failure and despair, but to trust in you to navigate them through to a new start. You are the God of endless possibilities.

---

1   From *History of Plymouth Plantation.*

I HAVE HIDDEN YOUR WORD IN MY HEART...
(Psalm 119:11)

[William Bradford] was interred with the greatest solemnities that the jurisdiction to which he belonged was in a capacity to perform, many deep sighs, as well as loud volleys of shot declaring that the people were no less sensible of their own loss, who were surviving, than mindful of the worth and honour of him that was deceased.

Governor Bradford died... lamented by all colonies of New England, as a common father to them all. His talents, well-tempered spirit, and acquirements, are celebrated... The Dutch tongue... was almost as vernacular to him as the English. The French tongue he could also manage; the Latin and the Greek he had mastered, but the Hebrew he most of all studied, because, he said, he would see, with his own eyes, the ancient oracles of God, in their native beauty.[1]

What a lovely ambition, Lord – to study Hebrew in order to better understand the Scriptures! Place such a hunger and desire within my heart – a new and refreshed love of the Bible.

Holy Bible, book Divine,
Precious treasure, thou art mine.[2]

---

1   From *Chronicles of the Pilgrim Fathers.*
2   From John Burton's hymn.

... LET THE WEAK SAY, I AM STRONG.
(Joel 3:10 *KJV*)

You might now easily discern a heavy heart in the mournful countenance of every sober-minded and considerate man; for as you have heard ... God was pleased greatly to weaken this poor tottering colony of Plimouth, by taking away several of the most useful props thereof, both in church and civil state; some others, who had been of singular use, now stooping under the infirmities of old age, could not be so serviceable as in times past; and others removed so far from the centre of the government, that they could not, without great difficulties, attend their public concerns, nor could possibly so constantly as our necessities required, which did greatly aggravate our troubles; we were become weak when we had need of the greatest strength; had lost many of our chieftains, when we stood in need of the best conduct and guidance.[1]

> Heavenly Father, my prayers today are for those who feel weak and perhaps even somewhat helpless: the frail elderly, those whose physical strength has failed, and those who cannot help themselves. Be close to them, I pray. May they feel your loving presence, even in the midst of their weakness. Be with, too, carers, family members, and any who try to help.

---

1   From *Chronicles of the Pilgrim Fathers.*

AFTER THE DEATH OF MOSES THE SERVANT OF
THE LORD, THE LORD SAID TO JOSHUA SON OF NUN, MOSES'
AIDE: "MOSES MY SERVANT IS DEAD. NOW THEN, YOU AND ALL
THESE PEOPLE, GET READY TO CROSS THE JORDAN RIVER INTO THE
LAND I AM ABOUT TO GIVE TO THEM – TO THE ISRAELITES."
(Joshua 1:1–2)

The Lord many times delighteth to appear in the mount of his people's miseries, distresses, and troubles, that his power and wisdom may appear when they are weakest, and that they may know that their salvation is from him. At such a time, and when the condition of this colony was such as hath been declared, God was pleased to mind it, even in its low estate, and when he had taken to himself not only our Moses, but many of the elders and worthies of our Israel, he hath not hitherto left us without a Joshua, to lead us in the remaining part of our pilgrimage.[1]

Gracious God, you do not abandon your people. When Moses dies, you send Joshua! Even at our lowest ebb, we are safe within the boundaries of your love. Help me, in the darkness, to remember the truths you have taught me in the light.

---

1 From *Chronicles of the Pilgrim Fathers.*

Cast all your anxiety on him because he cares for you.
(1 Peter 5:7)

Through the goodness of God, those storms that seemed to threaten the subversion of our all, and did at first prevail, to the disturbing and shaking of many towns and churches, and to the great discouragement of the ministers in diverse places, do seem to be pretty well blown over; such uncomfortable jars, as have sometimes thought incurable, seem to be thoroughly reconciled and healed; our towns, for the most part, supplied with godly and able ministers, and we sit under our vines and fig trees in peace, enjoying both civil and religious liberties; for which goodness of the Lord, let his holy name be praised; and may he grant us to improve our present opportunities, as he may have some suitable returns, and we may have cause to hope in his grace for the continuance of such favours.[1]

> *Let nothing disturb you,*
> *Let nothing frighten you,*
> *All things are passing away:*
> *God never changes.*
> *Patience obtains all things*
> *Whoever has God lacks nothing;*
> *God alone suffices.*[2]

---

1   From *Chronicles of the Pilgrim Fathers.*
2   Attributed to St Teresa of Ávila.

"Today I fulfilled my vows…"
(Proverbs 7:14)

Another company had settled [at Barnstable]… led from Weymouth (Wessagusset) by the Reverend Joseph Hull,[1] who dealt in real estate and cattle when not saving souls. As the raw hamlet of Barnstable obviously could not afford two pastors, Hull was soon forced out and moved a few miles down the Cape to where another Pilgrim town, Yarmouth, was being hacked out of the wilderness. Stephen Hopkins[2] built a house here, but soon turned it over to his son Giles and returned to Plymouth. In the other direction, at the shoulder of the Cape, the town of Sandwich had been settled by a group led by Edmund Freeman[3]… This group frankly avowed the purpose of its enterprise, which was "to worship God and make money".[4]

What an interesting vow! What personal vows have I made to you? Remind me of them today, so that I might refresh them.

1   Reverend Joseph Hull (1595–1665) led a company of 106 from England to Massachusetts. This became the Hull Colony.
2   See Footnote 1, October 27th.
3   Edmund (or Edmond) Freeman (c. 1596–1682), Assistant Governor of the Plymouth Colony under Governor William Bradford.
4   From *Saints and Strangers*.

RIGHTEOUSNESS EXALTETH A NATION…
(Proverbs 14:34 *KJV*)

The growth of [the] towns raised many puzzling new problems. Technically, all of Plimouth Plantation belonged to Bradford… He now agreed to surrender it, signing over his rights to "ye freemen of this corporation of New Plimouth," having first set aside several huge tracts of land… The rank and file of the Pilgrims… were allowed to share "in some weightie matters, when we thinke good" [*sic*]… It was evident that the old frame of government was inadequate and would have to be expanded to provide proper administration of the new towns… A committee was appointed – four representatives from Plymouth, two each from Duxbury and Scituate – to consider this problem, and the matter of drawing up a general code of laws. Previously, law had been improvised as occasion demanded. A few scattered enactments had been placed on the books, but for the most part the Pilgrims used the Scriptures, the Mosaic code in particular, as legal writ.[1]

> What a concept, Lord – Scripture as the law of the land! A complex matter, that's for sure, but an interesting one. I pray for lawmakers, judges, and legislators as they manage difficult issues. Grant them wisdom as they seek to implement justice and ease the passage of laws which are fair and reasonable.

---

1   From *Saints and Strangers.*

By me kings reign and rulers issue decrees ...
(Proverbs 8:15)

Mother Plymouth clashed with her daughters now and again, but they were generally inclined to be dutiful. They, too, had an aversion to "strangers" and were quick to "warn them out". For years the towns were not civil communities at all, but private corporations run for the benefit of the principal stockholders – the local Proprietors ... Under the eagle eye of Plymouth they sold or donated lots to desirable settlers, scrutinized the credentials of all newcomers, set aside common fields and pastures, and were responsible for putting in roads, bridges, and other public improvements. Except at Plymouth, there was no representative local government until ... Sandwich won the right to govern itself by an annually elected board of selectmen, an institution soon established in all the Pilgrim towns.[1]

The advent of American democracy! Lord, in this significant moment in human history, we see your hand at work, whereby structures of government are gradually established. Democracy is by no means a perfect system, Lord, but so much better and fairer than political structures whereby people are denied a vote. I pray for those living under the thumb of totalitarian regimes, who have little say in decision making, and are denied many liberties.

---

1 From *Saints and Strangers*.

... HE WILL COMMAND HIS ANGELS CONCERNING YOU TO GUARD
YOU IN ALL YOUR WAYS ...
(Psalm 91:11)

An Indian came presumptuously and with guile, in ye day time, and murderously assaulted an English woman in her house ... and by 3 wounds, supposed mortal, left her for dead, after which he robbed ye house. By which ... ye English ... called to a due consideration of their own safety; and ye Indians generally in those parts arose in an hostile manner [and] refused to come to ye English to carry on treaties of peace, departed from their wigwams, left their corn unweeded, and showed themselves tumultuously about some of ye English plantations, and shot their pieces within hearing of ye town; and some Indians came to ye English and told them ye Indians would fall upon them. So most of ye English thought it unsafe to travel in those parts by land, and some of ye plantations were put upon strong watches and ward, night & day, & could not attend their private occasions, and yet distrusted their own strength for their defence.[1]

Lord God, we are not so naïve as to think that Christians are always protected from every danger. History tells us that simply isn't the case, much as we would like it to be. We don't understand why events like this take place. Nevertheless, in the midst of that mystery, I pray for any who are scared – those who tremble behind locked doors and can't sleep for anxiety. In your mercy, Lord, impart peace and courage. May they know the truth of today's Bible text.

---

1   From *History of Plymouth Plantation.*

DEARLY BELOVED, AVENGE NOT YOURSELVES, BUT RATHER GIVE
PLACE UNTO WRATH: FOR IT IS WRITTEN, VENGEANCE IS MINE; I
WILL REPAY, SAITH THE LORD.

(Romans 12:19 *KJV*)

Another broyle [*sic*][1] was begun by ye Narigansets; though they unjustly had made war upon Uncass[2]... and had... earnestly pressed ye Governor of Massachusetts that they might still make war upon them to revenge ye death of their sagamore, who, being taken prisoner, was by them put to death... pretending that they had first received and accepted his ransom, and then put him to death. But ye Governor refused their presents, and told them it was themselves had done ye wrongs... and he nor ye English could nor would allow them to make any war upon him... But notwithstanding... they gathered a great power, and fell upon Uncass, and also sundry of his men, and wounded more, and also had some losses themselves.[3]

Lord, forgive me if and when I harbour ill-will, or even thoughts of revenge, towards those who have wronged me. Teach me the grace of praying for my enemies, and leaving them in your hands – even if I think I am in the right!

---

1   Brawl?
2   Or Uncas (c. 1588–c. 1683), a Mehegan (Native American tribe) sachem.
3   From *History of Plymouth Plantation*.

They must turn from evil and do good; they must seek peace and pursue it.

(1 Peter 3:11)

The commissioners this year were called to meet together at Boston ... partly in regard of some differences fallen between ye french and ye government of Massachusetts ... partly about ye Indians, who had broken ye former agreements about the peace concluded ...

Besides some underhand assaults made on both sides, the Narigansets gathered a great power, and fell upon Uncass, and slew many of his men, and wounded more, by reason they far exceeded him in number, and had got store of pieces, with which him they did most hurt. And as they did this without ye knowledge and consent of ye English (contrary to former agreements), so they were resolved to prosecute ye same ... So, being encouraged by their late victory, and promise of assistance ye Mowaks (being a strong, warlike, and desperate people), they had already devoured Uncass and his, in their hope; and surely they would have done it in deed too, if ye English had not timely set in for his aid, for the English sent him 40, and were a garrison to him, until ye commissioners could meet and take further order.[1]

Lord, I ask your blessing and guidance upon all those whose work (ministry) necessitates them treading carefully in matters of diplomacy. Equip them for their tasks.

---

1   From *History of Plymouth Plantation.*

As they continued to ask him, he stood up and said to
them, "Let him who is without sin among you be the first to
throw a stone at her."
(John 8:7 *ESV*)

The criminal code adopted at this time was quite simple and, for its day, remarkably humane in the matter of capital offences. England inflicted the death penalty for hundreds of offences, down to thefts of 5 shillings or more. Plymouth limited the number to seven – treason, murder, witchcraft, adultery, rape, sodomy, and arson – and actually life for only two, murder and sodomy. Contrary to popular belief, the Pilgrims never hanged a witch.[1]

Have mercy.

---

1   From *Saints and Strangers*.

... WHEN HE, THE SPIRIT OF TRUTH, COMES, HE WILL GUIDE YOU
INTO ALL THE TRUTH.

(John 16:13)

There arrived in the... colony many of that pernicious sect called Quakers,[1] whose opinions are a composition of many errors, and whose practices tend greatly to the disturbance both of church and state; many unstable people amongst us were leavened with their errors, and proved very troublesome to this as well as other colonies in New England...

The proceedings against the Quakers[2] were far less severe in Plymouth colony than in Massachusetts. In regard to their persecution, Cotton Mather[3] says, "If any man will appear in the vindication of it, let him do as he pleases, for my part I will not."[4]

"Live and let live." "Love and let love." Heavenly Father, grant me your wisdom when it comes to disagreements over points of principle and Christian teaching. Help me to know which battles to fight, and which to ignore. Teach me the worth of tolerance, while at the same time having the courage to highlight error.

---

1   So-called "Foxian Quakerism" after George Fox. See https://en.wikipedia.org/wiki/George_Fox
2   Quakers were treated with suspicion and some hostility because of their proclaimed belief in an individual's "inner light". Puritans and Pilgrims maintained that the "inner light" teaching whereby each individual was at liberty to follow the leadings of their conscience, was at odds with established scriptural truth. Some Quakers were imprisoned or banished.
3   Reverend Cotton Mather (1663–1728), New England Puritan minister, author, and pamphleteer.
4   From *Chronicles of the Pilgrim Fathers.*

... I SAW ANOTHER ANGEL FLY IN THE MIDST OF HEAVEN, HAVING
THE EVERLASTING GOSPEL TO PREACH UNTO THEM THAT DWELL ON
THE EARTH, AND TO EVERY NATION, AND KINDRED, AND TONGUE,
AND PEOPLE...
(Revelation 14:6 *KJV*)

Mr. Garret[1] set sail on a voyage to England, from Boston; in whose ship, amongst many considerable passengers, there went Mr. Thomas Mayhew, jun.,[2]... who was a very precious man. He was well skilled, and had attained to a great proficiency in the Indian language, and had a great propensity upon his spirit to promote God's glory in their conversion, whose labours God blessed for the doing of so much good amongst them; in which respect he was very much missed amongst them, and bewailed by them, as also in reference unto the preaching of God's word amongst the English there. The loss of him was very great.[3]

> Thank you, Heavenly Father, for linguists, and those who use that particular
> gift for the extension of your kingdom. Bless them, I pray, as they work hard to
> translate the Scriptures into many languages. They may never know the results of
> their special ministry, but I ask you to encourage them in their
> "missionary" endeavours.

---

1   Identity uncertain.
2   1618–57. Reverend Thomas Mayhew, Junior, died at sea aged 38 or 39. He was renowned as a "famous Indian missionary".
3   From *Chronicles of the Pilgrim Fathers*.

[GOD] HAS ... SET ETERNITY IN THE HUMAN HEART.
(Ecclesiastes 3:11)

Mr. Ralph Partridge[1] died in a good old age, having, for the space of forty years, dispensed the word of God with a very little impediment by sickness. His pious and blameless life became very advantageous to his doctrine; he was much honoured and loved by all that conversed with him. He was of a sound and solid judgment in the main truths of Jesus Christ, and very able in dispensation to defend them; he was very singular in this, that, notwithstanding the paucity and poverty of his flock, he continued in his work amongst them to the end of time. He went to his grave in peace, as a shock of corn fully ripe, and was honourably buried at Duxbury.[2]

Thank you, Lord, for the gift of "a good old age". That is of course something denied to many, but I give thanks today for those who have used their years well, and set a good example. Help me, I pray, to do just that, with whatever time I may have left on earth.

---

1 See Footnote 1, October 13th.
2 From *Chronicles of the Pilgrim Fathers*.

"LORD, HAVE MERCY ON MY SON," HE SAID. "HE HAS SEIZURES AND IS
SUFFERING GREATLY. HE OFTEN FALLS INTO THE FIRE OR INTO THE
WATER."
(Matthew 17:15)

The only town touched by... witch hysteria was Scituate, and there it was quickly scotched. Mary Ingham[1] was tried and acquitted when charged with causing one Mehitable Woodworth[2] to "fall into violente fits, and causing great paine unto severall parts of her body att severall times, soe as shee, the said Mehitable Woodworth, hath bin almost bereaved of her sencis" [sic].[3]

Thank you, Heavenly Father, for the huge strides made in both medical and
social understanding, whereby those once declared to be evil witches are now
treated with considerably more sympathy as victims of mental illnesses and
psychological trauma. In your mercy, draw close to those who suffer
in such ways.

1   Wife of Thomas Ingham of Scituate. She was known as an elderly matron/nurse.
2   1662–85. She would have been about thirteen when this incident took place, having suffered all her life from "witchcraft", which would nowadays be diagnosed as mental illness or something like epilepsy.
3   From *Saints and Strangers*.

THE SPIRIT CLEARLY SAYS THAT IN LATER TIMES SOME WILL
ABANDON THE FAITH AND FOLLOW DECEIVING SPIRITS AND THINGS
TAUGHT BY DEMONS.
(1 Timothy 4:1)

Mary Ingham, wife of Thomas Ingham of Scituate cleared of charge of witchcraft in relation to 13 year old Mehitable Woodworth. Mary an elderly matron was charged with bewitching Mehitable, causing her to fall into violent fits until almost bereaved of her senses…

"Mary Ingham, thou art indicted by the name of Mary Ingham, the wife of Thomas Ingham of Scituate, for thou, not having the feare of God before thine eyes, hast, by the helpe of the Devil, in a way of witchcraft or sorcery, maliciously procured much hurt, mischieff and paine, unto the body of Mehitable Woodworth, daughter of Walter Woodworth of Scituate, and to some others, particularly causing her to falle into violent fits, and causing her great paine unto several partes of her body at several tymes, so that the said Mehitable hath been almost bereaved of her senses; and hath greatly languished to her much suffering thereby, and procuring of greate grieffe sorrow and charge to her parents: all which thou hast procured and done, against the law of God, and to his greate dishonor, and contrary to our Sovereign Lord the King, his crown and dignity" [sic].

She was tried by a jury of twelve men – "Verdict, not guilty." It was natural at that superstitious day, that a person affected with nervous insanity, should look round for someone on whom to charge those sufferings. Ingham's wife was aged, and probably lived in retirement, conversing little with this world, and hence was suspected to hold converse with invisible beings. Thus, however, ended indictments for witchcraft in this Colony, happy would it have been, had good sense elsewhere as soon triumphed over superstition.[1]

Gracious Spirit, grant me wisdom and discernment to know what is mere superstition, and what is a manifestation of spiritual evil. Help me not to ignore or dismiss the realities of demons and their business but, by the same token, help me not to imagine them lurking behind every tree.

[1] From *The Pilgrim Republic*, said copy from newspaper article March 1676 (https://www.geni.com/people/Mehitable-Woodworth/6000000006440672875).

He grants a treasure of common sense...
(Proverbs 2:7 *NLT*)

The wife of William Holmes, Standish's lieutenant, was likewise tried on complaint of one Dinah Sylvester.

"What evidence have you of the fact?" the Sylvester woman was asked by the presiding magistrate...

"She appeared to me as a witch."

"In what shape?"

"In the shape of a bear, your honour."

"How far off was the bear?"

"About a stone's throw from the highway."

"What manner of tail did the bear have?"

"I could not tell, your honour, as his head was towards me."

To discourage such nonsense, Dinah was fined [the equivalent of] £5 and whipped. And that was the end of witchcraft in the Old Colony, though the law against it long remained on the books. The Pilgrims' common sense here is the more remarkable in light of the gross superstitions of the day and the almost universal belief in the supernatural powers of those "possessed by Sathan" [*sic*]. The nineteen "witches" hanged or crushed to death at Salem Village... were few, compared with the 40,000, so it has been estimated, who were put to death in England during John Alden's lifetime.[1] [2]

Thank you, Lord, for common sense!

---

1   From *Saints and Strangers*.
2   Witchcraft mania assumed terrible proportions after Pope Innocent VIII (1432–92) issued a papal bull on the subject in 1484. The infamous Salem witch trials were an extension of this superstitious craze.

THE DAUGHTERS OF ZELOPHEHAD... BELONGED TO THE CLANS OF MANASSEH SON OF JOSEPH... THEY CAME FORWARD AND STOOD BEFORE MOSES, ELEAZAR THE PRIEST, THE LEADERS AND THE WHOLE ASSEMBLY AT THE ENTRANCE TO THE TENT OF MEETING AND SAID, "OUR FATHER DIED IN THE WILDERNESS. HE ... DIED FOR HIS OWN SIN AND LEFT NO SONS. WHY SHOULD OUR FATHER'S NAME DISAPPEAR FROM HIS CLAN BECAUSE HE HAD NO SON? GIVE US PROPERTY AMONG OUR FATHER'S RELATIVES." SO MOSES BROUGHT THEIR CASE BEFORE THE LORD, AND THE LORD SAID TO HIM, "WHAT ZELOPHEHAD'S DAUGHTERS ARE SAYING IS RIGHT... SAY TO THE ISRAELITES, 'IF A MAN DIES AND LEAVES NO SON, GIVE HIS INHERITANCE TO HIS DAUGHTER. IF HE HAS NO DAUGHTER, GIVE HIS INHERITANCE TO HIS BROTHERS. IF HE HAS NO BROTHERS, GIVE HIS INHERITANCE TO HIS FATHER'S BROTHERS. IF HIS FATHER HAD NO BROTHERS, GIVE HIS INHERITANCE TO THE NEAREST RELATIVE IN HIS CLAN, THAT HE MAY POSSESS IT. THIS IS TO HAVE THE FORCE OF LAW FOR THE ISRAELITES, AS THE LORD COMMANDED MOSES.'"

(Numbers 27:1–11)

The Puritans who settled New England adopted the idea of the equal distribution of property, in case there was no will – giving to the eldest son, however, in some colonies a double portion, according to the Old Testament injunction – and thence it has spread over the whole United States. Some writers have attributed this equal division of property to a custom handed down from the Anglo-Saxons in the county of Kent. But this custom gave the real estate of intestates to the males alone. The American law, borrowed from Holland, includes females as well. We have not yet advanced far enough to prohibit the capricious disinherison [sic] of a faithful wife or dutiful children. That too, however, will come in time, when we have shaken off a little more of our barbaric traditions.[1]

> That which I do today, Lord, might well have a bearing on tomorrow. Just as the laws and customs decided upon in New England have evolved into American statute, so it is possible that some of my actions may have lasting consequences, both for good and bad. Help me, I pray, to bear this in mind as I make my way through this day.

---

1   From *The Puritan in Holland, England, and America.*

A GOOD PERSON LEAVES AN INHERITANCE FOR THEIR CHILDREN'S CHILDREN...
(Proverbs 13:22)

There was one custom in connection with the law of inheritance which was picturesque in Holland, and no less so in New York, where it was established by the early settlers, and prevailed until the English rule began. All the property of a debtor, including his land – something unknown in England – was subject to the claims of his creditors, before and after death. But the law went further. A widow was entitled to her dower in all her husband's estate, but, on the other hand, she was bound for her share of his debts. If the debts exceeded the estate, the obligations might sweep away all her personal property, for which the law made careful provision, and so a mode was provided for renouncing her dower, which also released her from her creditors. In England, until a very recent day, the husband took not only all the wife's property, but also all her earnings.[1]

> Thank you, God of justice, for the evolution of these laws, whereby the bereaved are not left without provision. My prayers today are for those left destitute in countries where there is no such recourse to legal support. Help them, Lord, as they not only carry the burden of grief, but also seek our practical assistance from churches and charities.

---

1   From *The Puritan in Holland, England, and America.*

He that believeth on the Son of God hath the witness in
himself...

(1 John 5:10 *KJV*)

The Pilgrims of Plymouth, coming also from Holland, passed a law requiring that for the prevention of frauds, all conveyances, including mortgages and leases, should be recorded. Connecticut followed... the Puritans of Massachusetts... Subsequently every State of the Union established the same system...

Much of the prosperity of New England is attributable to her laws relating to the transmission of land... These laws not only mark the spirit of the people, but were probably the cause of more lasting consequences.[1]

Today, Heavenly Father, I give thanks for that "contract" whereby my salvation is recorded – not only in the Bible, but in my heart too. Thank you that this is a contract that can't be broken – a covenant penned in blood.

---

1   From *The Puritan in Holland, England, and America.*

THE LORD IS GOOD... HE CARES FOR THOSE WHO TRUST IN HIM...
(Nahum 1:7)

Old William Brewster... had been the first to call the Pilgrims together to worship in the Manor at Scrooby. He took the brunt of the persecution in England. He led them across to Amsterdam and Leyden. He was their chief at the sailing of the *Mayflower*. For more than thirty-six years he faced with them exile and tempest, the arrows of the Indian and famine and pestilence on the soil of America. He led the Pilgrims, old and young, sinner and saint, into the presence of God.[1]

What a challenge, Lord! Will my life count in terms of leading others into the presence of God? I hope so! I pray so! Guide my steps aright, I ask, so that mine is a kingdom influence. Hear my prayers as I pray for those I love and care for. May my words and deeds represent an influence of holiness.

---

1   From *The Argonauts of Faith*.

... THE HAND OF GOD WAS ON THE PEOPLE TO GIVE THEM UNITY OF
MIND...

(2 Chronicles 30:12)

The cheerful, strong face of William Brewster was with the Pilgrims for over twenty years till... with his white hairs and mellow face, honoured and loved by all the people, he died...

When William Brewster had come to be a white-haired old man four colonies of Englishmen had grown up on the coast of America; they were Massachusetts, New Plymouth, Connecticut, and New Haven. Within ten days of William Brewster's death, these four colonies joined themselves together in one body.

They declared in their Articles of Confederation that all four colonies were founded with the same end, "to advance the Kingdom of our Lord Jesus Christ, and to enjoy the liberties of the Gospel in purity and peace," the confederacy to be called the United Colonies of New England – "a league of friendship."[1]

The pursuit of unity, Lord – what a marvellous objective. Unity in the home, unity in the church, and unity in national affairs. Thank you for the blessing of unity. I pray for homes known to me personally where unity is absent. Likewise, I pray for my own church, regarding any areas of disunity that exist.
I pray for my country too.

---

1   From *The Argonauts of Faith*.

**For you have been my hope, Sovereign Lord, my
confidence since my youth.**
(Psalm 71:5)

[The declaration of the Articles of Confederation] saw the beginning of the union of states which was to become, in the dim distance of the years that were still hidden behind the mists of the future, the great Republic, the United States of America...

They laid, I say, in that hour, the keel of a... more glorious ship of adventure for freedom into all the world.

The Pilgrims... had dared the rage of the gales of the Atlantic in their little ship, the *Mayflower*... To them the quest was for liberty to worship in the way that seemed most fitting the God whose they were and whom they served.

For that sacred prize they faced the fury of tempests, the bitter cold of freezing gales on a shelter-less coast, the tomahawks and arrows of Red Indians, the dreadful scythe of plague, and exile for life from the home of their fathers.[1]

When I look back, Lord, when I review the years, help me to know it has all been worth it – every battle, every adventure, every risk, every parting. Grant me that knowledge that my pilgrimage with you has been worthwhile.

I know that my Saviour will never forsake,
I know that my faith in Him never will shake;
My journey a pathway of gladness He'll make,
He'll walk with me all the way.[2]

---

1   From *The Argonauts of Faith*.
2   From L. J. Williams' hymn.

Now the works of the flesh are evident… enmity, strife,
jealousy, fits of anger, rivalries, dissensions… But the
fruit of the Spirit is love, joy, peace, patience, kindness,
goodness, faithfulness, gentleness, self-control; against
such things there is no law.
(Galatians 5:19–23 *ESV*)

About ye middle of… [the] year, came in 3 ships into the harbour, in war-like order; they were found to be men of war. The captain's name was Crumwell,[1] who had taken sundry prizes from ye Spaniard in ye West Indies. He had a commission from ye Earl of Warwick. He had about his vessels about 80 lusty men (but very unruly), who, after they came ashore, did so distemper themselves with drink as they became like madmen, and though some of them were punished & imprisoned, yet could they hardly be restrained; yet in ye end they became more moderate & orderly. They continued… about a month or 6 weeks, and then went to ye Massachusetts; in which time they spent and scattered a great deal of money, notwithstanding all ye care and watchfulness that was used toward them, to prevent what might be.

In which time one sad accident fell out. A desperate fellow of ye company fell a quarrelling with some of his company. His captain commanded him to be quiet & cease his quarrelling; but he would not, but reviled his captain with base language, & in ye end half drew his rapier & intended to ruin his captain; but he closed with him and wrested his rapier from him, and gave him a box on ye ear; but he would not give over, but still assaulted his captain.[2]

Lord Jesus, fill me afresh with your Spirit today. Come, gracious Spirit, and abide with me.

---

1   Or Cromwell. Captain Thomas, sea captain, merchant, and pirate.
2   From *History of Plymouth Plantation*.

... WHAT THE LAW WAS POWERLESS TO DO BECAUSE IT WAS
WEAKENED BY THE FLESH, GOD DID BY SENDING HIS OWN SON IN
THE LIKENESS OF SINFUL FLESH TO BE A SIN OFFERING.

(Romans 8:3)

[The Saints did not] execute Quakers and "other Notoriouse heretiques" [*sic*], or pass laws against "gay apparel", as was done at Boston... Still, the Pilgrims were never ones to spare the rod and spoil the child, and now that they had a statute book, they rapidly filled it up with enactments of all kinds. They were imbued with a naïve confidence, part of their legacy to us, that if anything went wrong, the sure cure was to pass a law against it. For firing a gun "at night, save at a wolfe or for a man lost" [*sic*] – later amended to read, "except at an Indean or a wolfe" [*sic*] – the fine was 20s. Swearing cost the profane 12d.[1] for each offence, or three hours in the stocks, or three days in jail, "according to the nature and qualitie of the person" [*sic*]. In this as in all discretionary sentences, the higher the station of the culprit, the less the punishment, for the Pilgrims were not equal before the law.[2]

> Gracious God, you know full well that we are inherently unable to keep the law. We are flawed; we are fallen. Nevertheless, you do not leave us with that predicament. You sent your Son as the remedy, the answer to our impossible dilemma. Thank you for Jesus, who fulfilled the demands of the law when we were helpless to do so.

---

1 It appears there came about, at some point, the application of the English currency of pounds and shillings. There were 12 pence in a shilling and 20 shillings in a pound. The British system used the abbreviations £ for pound, "s" for shilling and "d" for pence, from the Latin *libra*, *solidus* and *denarius*.

2 From *Saints and Strangers*.

... IF THE SON SETS YOU FREE, YOU WILL BE FREE INDEED.

(John 8:36)

It was forbidden to make "motion of marriage to any man's daughter or maid-servant, not having first obtained leave and consent of the parent or master to do so". The penalty was a fine, or corporal punishment, or both... Wages were strictly controlled. No worker was to be paid more than 12d. a day with board, or 18d. without. The General Court kept a sharp lookout for "idlers", and anyone not able to give a satisfactory account of himself was subject to forced labour "according to the wisdome of the government" [sic].

Young Francis Billington was one of the first to pay 10s. for violating the ordinance against smoking – or, as the phrase went, for "drinking tobacco... in a very uncivill manner openlie in the towne streets, and as men pass upon the highways, as also in the fields, and as men are at work in the woods and fields, to the neglecte of their labour and to the great reproach of the Government" [sic]. No liquor was to be sold "either within doors or without, excepte in inns or victualling-houses allowed" [sic]. Only the most respectable could keep a tavern, for "mine host" was personally responsible for the sobriety of his guests, and care was taken that no licence was issued to a man who drinks druncke himself" [sic].[1]

> Father God, my prayers today turn towards those who are imprisoned by addictions of one kind or another: smokers who can barely breathe, yet won't abandon their cigarettes; alcoholics whose next drink might well be their last. Have mercy, I pray, and set them free by your grace and power. I remember their loved ones and friends, whose hearts are broken as they stand by and watch them suffer. I pray too for those who work with addicts, to offer help and support. Give them hearts of compassion and bless their efforts.

---

1   From *Saints and Strangers*.

"... ADVANCED YEARS SHOULD TEACH WISDOM."
(Job 32:7)

Viewing the United States from the standpoint of England and her writers, one would conclude that its people – certainly those who have given character to the nation – were of almost pure English descent. But such a conclusion has no more basis in fact than has the theory which deduces the institutions of America from those of England. New England, with her Puritan population, has played a great part in American history – a part which no fair-minded student would desire to underestimate; but even in Revolutionary days her four colonies were not America. Their... associates which made up the Union have also played their part in history, with results which no one caring for the truth can afford to overlook. They stood up with their Puritan brethren in New England to establish American independence, and, in time, they all adopted the un-English institutions which have given to America its distinctive character.[1]

> Thank you, Heavenly Father, for all those influences and factors that have contributed to making me "me". Just as the United States of America evolved and developed with many contributors over many years, so the "jigsaw" of my life owes much to other people and other experiences. Help me, I pray, as I reflect upon the different elements of my character, to sift through what is good, and to leave to one side that which is not good.

---

1   From *The Puritan in Holland, England, and America.*

Love does no harm to a neighbour.
(Romans 13:10)

That New York, New Jersey, Delaware, and Pennsylvania had a large Dutch population is known to every reader. So is the fact that French Huguenots were found scattered through all the American colonies... Added to these men of un-English birth were the Germans, who... found a home mainly in Pennsylvania and in central New York... All these foreign elements of our population have been noted by historians, although due credit has not always been accorded to their influence. But taken all together, the Hollanders, French, and Germans in the American colonies were less in number and very much less in influence than the men of another race, who were found mainly in Pennsylvania and the South.

These were the Scotch-Irish. Driven from their adopted home in the North of Ireland by English persecution... they were un-English in their origin, and they came to America – which they have always looked upon as their only country – hating England, her Church, and her form of government with the intensest [sic] hatred... They contributed elements to American thought and life without which the United States of today would be impossible.[1]

What do I contribute to my community, Lord? What is there that I may offer to my neighbours today?

Jesus bids us shine with a clear, pure light,
Like a little candle burning in the night;
In this world of darkness, we must shine,
You in your small corner, and I in mine.[2]

---

1   From *The Puritan in Holland, England, and America.*
2   From Susan B. Warner's hymn.

... LOVE COVERS OVER A MULTITUDE OF SINS.

(1 Peter 4:8)

Nothing was too large or too small to escape the attention of the General Court. For telling a lie, "though not a pernicious lie, only inadvisedly" [sic], Goodwife Crispin escaped the usual fine of 10s. But a fine and also the lash upon John Till "for lying & alluring John Bryan to drinking and slandering his dame Emerson, saying he would goe whome and lye with her" [sic]. Up for "dealing fraudulentlie about a flitch of bacon" [sic], Edward Dotey paid an extra 50s. for calling the complainant "a rogue".[1] The General Court, it must be said, did not spare its own members. Granted leave to build a girst mill on the banks of Town Brook, near Billington Sea, Assistant Governor John Jenney[2] was called on the carpet ... "for not grinding well and seasonable". After his death a few years later his wife was cited for not keeping the mill clean ... Assistant Governor Stephen Hopkins was fined £7 for assault – £2 for "suffering servants and others to sitt drinking in his house [sic] ... and to play at shovel board & such like misdemeanours", and as if that were not enough, "upon the Lord's day, before the meeting be ended" – £1 on each of five counts for selling beer, wine, and "strong waters" above established ceiling prices, and for talking back to his colleagues.[3]

Thank you, Lord, that there is grace sufficient, my every debt to pay.

---

1   These names are those of Pilgrims and residents of the colony.

2   Or Jenne (1596–1643).

3   From *Saints and Strangers*.

"With the merciful you show yourself merciful …"

(2 Samuel 22:26 *ESV*)

The General Court decreed that "in every Constablerick there be a paire of stocks erected and a whipping post" [*sic*]. To judge from the first three entries in the records… the Saints evidently recognised a great and growing need of these:

John Holmes [Messenger to the General Court] was censured for drunkenness, to sitt in the stocks, and amerced in twenty shillings fine [*sic*].

John Hews & Jone, his wife, adjudged to sitt in the stocks because the said Jone conceived with childe by him before they were publickly married, though in the time of contract [*sic*].

John Thorp & Alice, his wife, likewise adjudged to sitt in the stocks, & amerced in forty shillings fine, because his wife conceived with childe before marriage [*sic*].

The Thorps were so poor that they were granted a year's grace in which to pay their $100[1] fine – altogether, a remarkably lenient sentence, for at this time it was usual for the husband also to be well whipped in sight of his red-faced and anguished wife.[2]

Father, forgive your church for such barbaric practices. Forgive your church for such brutal punishments, often, over the centuries, carried out in the name of Christ. Forgive so-called justice which is cruel and horribly lacking in mercy. Thank you, Lord, for the steady evolution of compassion within matters of church government. Guide your people in such ways, so that governance is increasingly couched in empathy and grace.

---

1   I am uncertain why this amount is stated in dollars, and not British currency.

2   From *Saints and Strangers*.

DECEMBER 1ST

IN MY FATHER'S HOUSE ARE MANY MANSIONS: IF IT WERE NOT SO, I
WOULD HAVE TOLD YOU. I GO TO PREPARE A PLACE FOR YOU.
(John 14:2 *KJV*)

It pleased God to take away, by death, Mr. William Paddy,[1] who was a precious
servant of Christ, endued with a meek and quiet spirit, of a courteous behaviour
to all men, and was very careful to nourish an intimate communion with God. He
was instrumental in his place for common good, both in church (being sometimes
by office a deacon of the church of Plimouth), and in other respects very officious,
as occasion did require. He having a great temporal estate, was occasioned thereby
to have abundance of business upon him, but when he was to put off his earthly
tabernacle, he laid aside all his earthly incumbrances [*sic*] and occasions, even as one
would have taken off a garment, and laid it down; and without any trouble of spirit,
on that behalf, prepared himself for his journey to the everlasting mansions, prepared
for him by his Lord and Master in the highest heavens, whereof he was well assured;
as to the like effect he spake … near unto the period of his life; and so falling asleep in
the Lord, he was buried at Boston, with honour and great lamentation.[2]

What a beautiful story, Lord, of dying well in your grace. I pray for anyone known
to me who has reached the evening of their life. May they too, like William Paddy,
make confident preparations, taking you at your Word. I ask you to draw close to
them, by your Spirit, as the sun begins to set. Blessed assurance!

---

1   Deacon and Deputy of the General Court (1600–58).
2   From *Chronicles of the Pilgrim Fathers.*

"WHAT NO EYE HAS SEEN, WHAT NO EAR HAS HEARD, AND WHAT NO HUMAN MIND HAS CONCEIVED" – THE THINGS GOD HAS PREPARED FOR THOSE WHO LOVE HIM ...

(1 Corinthians 2:9)

One, who was well acquainted with [William Paddy's] worth and gracious endowments, presented this following, as a testimonial of his good respects for him.

Weep not dear wife, children, nor dear friends,
I live a life of joys that never ends.
Love God, and fear him to end of your days;
Live unto him, but die to sin always.
In heavenly place of bliss my soul doth rest,
Among the saints and angels I am blest;
Much better here, than in the world at best.
Praising my God is now my great employ,
Above such troubles as did me annoy.
Did but my friends know what I here possess,
Doubtless it would cause them to mourn the less;
Your souls with mine e'er long shall meet in bliss.[1] [2]

Keep me faithful, Lord. What a day of rejoicing that will be!

---

1   Readers will notice the clever use of the first letters of each line, spelling out William Paddy.
2   From *Chronicles of the Pilgrim Fathers*.

> ... God is not a God of disorder but of peace – as in all the
> congregations of the Lord's people.
> (1 Corinthians 14:33)

What then have been the results of this emigration of the pilgrims?

They settled this country.

This was not the first, or the only settlement made here. But most of them were failures, and such as were permanent had never had any such influence in securing this result, or ever left so much of its impress upon the nation, as this colony.

More than a century before the pilgrims came, the Spaniards had taken possession of Florida, and attempted to found a colony there, but they were driven off... Eighty years before, the Spaniard, De Soto,[1] with several hundred followers, had fought his way to Mississippi and penetrated two hundred miles beyond, but only to return to the river and die there, and his discouraged followers to abandon the expedition. The French Huguenots, who first settled at Port Royal, in South Carolina, and afterwards in Florida, in 1565, were massacred by the Spaniards; while of Sir Walter Raleigh's[2] settlement on Roanoke Island, in North Carolina, in 1585, in a few years not a trace remained. The English settlement at the mouth of the Kennebee in Maine, and the French settlement at Mount Desert, both of which preceded the one at Plymouth, were soon abandoned, or broken up.[3]

> Thank you, Heavenly Father, for those things in my life which are settled, and governed by your settling hand. There is of course no telling what tomorrow might bring, but today I give thanks for those areas of my daily routine that are calm, and ordered, and sorted. These are precious gifts. Lord, be with those today whose lives are in disarray and blighted by chaos. Visit them with your peace. Bring them stability.

---

1   Hernando de Soto (c. 1500–42), Spanish explorer and conquistador who led the Spanish and European expedition into the modern-day United States.
2   1552 or 1554–1618.
3   From A *Memorial of the Pilgrim Fathers*.

... BEING STRENGTHENED WITH ALL POWER ACCORDING TO HIS
GLORIOUS MIGHT SO THAT YOU MAY HAVE GREAT ENDURANCE
AND PATIENCE ...
(Colossians 1:11)

The successful settlement at Plymouth, led in eight years to the planting of the Massachusetts colony, and within ten years more, to the planting successively of the colonies of Connecticut, Rhode Island and New Haven. So that within twenty years after the landing of the pilgrims, twenty-one thousand persons, almost exclusively English, and mostly of the Puritan faith, had come over and found a home in this new country. After that came on the troubles and civil wars in England, and such emigration almost entirely ceased... But that first emigration was sufficient to demonstrate the practicability of the enterprise, and to ensure the settlement of the whole country, and to determine the character of its population, and the nature of its institutions.

At that time the subject of colonization was less understood, and attended with more difficulties, than at present. The ocean was more formidable, and a voyage across it more uncomfortable and dangerous, than it is now. The popular dread of the sea, such small and frail ships, and a passage of nine or ten weeks, instead of about as many days, were great hindrances to the founding and successful establishment of a distant colony. Besides, governments did less then, than they do now, to foster such enterprises. They were quite apt to hamper them with restrictions upon their legislation and trade, and when they began to prosper, and especially to show any independence, instead of tolerating it, and regarding it as a part of their own prosperity, they too often became jealous of them, and reduced their privileges, and took away their charters.[1]

Lord, I pray for those whose dreams and ambitions are thwarted and suffocated
by fears and uncertainties. I pray for those who would love to cross oceans, as
it were, but hesitate to do so because they dare not face obstacles. Grant them
enabling courage, I pray. Likewise, those whose plans come up against brick walls
of red tape and discouragement – help them to persevere!

---

1   From *A Memorial of the Pilgrim Fathers.*

HAVE NOTHING TO DO WITH GODLESS MYTHS
AND OLD WIVES' TALES ...
(1 Timothy 4:7)

With the entire community watching eagle-eyed for evidences of sin, many a hapless young couple went to the stocks "for having a childe before the natural time of women after marriage" [sic], which the Pilgrims assumed to be exactly nine months. Occasionally they made an allowance of a few days, but never more than a week or two. The [wedding] ring was not given either in the Pre-contract or the marriage ceremony. To the Saints it was "anti-Christian", a relic of popery, "a diabolicall circle for the Devill to daunce in" [sic]. The phenomenon of premature birth was not recognized in their book, and the advent of a child in the seventh or eighth month of marriage was always a disaster – conclusive proof of illicit relations before marriage and always promptly punished as such, for "fornication" [sic] was a legal as well as a moral offence. After a time, learning something of the facts of life, the Pilgrims liberalized their attitude, adopting the "seven months' rule", but only after hundreds of innocent couples... had suffered public shame and disgrace for natural causes quite beyond their control.[1]

> Superstition, Lord! Guesswork! "Godless myths"! I pray for Christians who are working in countries and communities that are dominated by those particular influences. I pray especially for those who minister among believers who hold tight to vestiges of superstitious tradition and belief. Help those ministers, Lord.

---

1   From *Saints and Strangers.*

[JESUS] SAID TO THEM, "PRAY THAT YOU WILL NOT FALL
INTO TEMPTATION."
(Luke 22:40)

From the records it is also evident that many of the younger generations were as curious as Adam and Eve to taste forbidden fruit. And with the many opportunities afforded them under a curious institution long in favour among the Saints, the wonder is that more did not indulge – or, at least, did not get caught.

The institution was known as pre-contract, and under it an enamoured pair could assure themselves of an unusual degree of privacy by appearing before two witnesses and formally announcing their intention to marry in due course. This was more than an engagement. Essentially, it was a semi-marriage, entitling the betrothed to almost all of the intimacies of wedlock – all but the last and most intimate. But this exception, as might have been expected, was often more than aroused desire could brook, a fact recognized even by the Saints, who drew a distinction between a lapse "in time of contract" and plain fornication, so to speak. The latter was far more severely punished, ordinarily with the stocks, the lash, three days in jail, and a £10 ($500)[1] fine.[2]

> Oh, Lord! Help me, I pray, with whatever temptations are mine, not to rely upon man-made rules and systems, but upon your grace in times of need. Help me, I pray, to resist temptation because of my love for you, rather than my fear of punishment. Let my desire to please you, and to live according to your will, be my greatest motivation.

---

1   As previously, I do not understand the system of currency as stated here.
2   From *Saints and Strangers*.

THE LORD SENDS POVERTY AND WEALTH; HE HUMBLES
AND HE EXALTS.
(1 Samuel 2:7)

The Pilgrims passed a number of measures to stimulate economic activities. Towns were urged to improve and extend their roads, to build bridges and keep them in good repair. Steps were taken to promote the fishing industry by encouraging boatbuilding, salt making, and the manufacture of barrel staves. Other measures were designed to stimulate agriculture and the breeding of livestock. For several years, with many circumstances favouring, the Old Colony enjoyed unusual prosperity.[1]

Lord, the Pilgrims had known hard times. They had come through any number
of struggles and challenges. Thank you for this evidence of your faithfulness and
blessing. Thank you that your love remains the same, through every circumstance
of life. Help those who are struggling, I pray, and bring them through
to better times.

---

1   From *Saints and Strangers.*

... EAT YOUR FOOD WITH GLADNESS ...
(Ecclesiastes 9:7)

"Some Observations of God's Mercifull Dealings with us in this Wildernesse, and His Gracious Protection over us These Many Years, Blessed be His Name" [sic] ... goes on in this wise:

All sorts of roots and herbs in gardens grow,
Parsnips, carrots, turnips, or what you'll sow,
Onions, melons, cucumbers, radishes,
Skirrets,[1] beets, coleworts,[2] and fair cabbages ...
Nuts and grapes of several sorts here are,
If you will take the pains them to seek for.[3]

Thank you, Heavenly Father, for my food and drink today.

---

1   *Sium sisarum*, commonly known as "skirret", is a perennial plant of the family *Apiaceae* sometimes grown as a root vegetable. The English name skirret is derived from the Middle English "skirwhit" or "skirwort", meaning "white root". In Scotland it is known as *crummock*. Its Danish name *sukkerrod*, Dutch name *suikerwortel*, and German name *Zuckerwurzel* translate as "sugar root" (from https://en.wikipedia.org/wiki/Sium_sisarum).
2   A type of cabbage.
3   From *Saints and Strangers*.

BUT THERE WERE ALSO FALSE PROPHETS AMONG THE PEOPLE,
JUST AS THERE WILL BE FALSE TEACHERS AMONG YOU. THEY WILL
SECRETLY INTRODUCE DESTRUCTIVE HERESIES, EVEN DENYING THE
SOVEREIGN LORD WHO BOUGHT THEM...

(2 Peter 2:1)

Having noted before, that... there arrived in the colony of New Plimouth, many of the pernicious sect, called Quakers; the reader may take notice that... for some years after, New England, in divers parts of it, abounded with them, and they sowed their corrupt and damnable doctrines, both by word and writings, almost in every town of each jurisdiction, some whereof were, "that all men ought to attend the light within them, to be the rule of their lives and actions;" and, "that the Holy Scriptures were not for the enlightening of man, nor a settled and permanent rule of life." They denied the manhood of the Lord Jesus Christ, and affirmed, "that, as man, he is not in heaven." They denied the resurrection from the dead. They affirmed, "that an absolute perfection in holiness or grace, is attainable in this life." They placed their justification upon their patience and suffering for their opinions, and on their righteous life and retired demurity, [sic] and affected singularity both in word and gesture.

As to civil account, they allowed not nor practised any civil respect to man, though superiors, either in magistratical [sic] consideration, or as masters or parents, or the ancient, neither by word nor gesture. They deny also the use of oaths for the deciding of civil controversies, with other abominable opinions, dreams, and conceits, which some of them have expressed, tending to gross blasphemy and atheism.[1]

God of truth, I pray for any who are seeking after truth. Bless them in their search, and honour their sincere intentions. Thank you for your grace and guidance in such ways.

---

1   From *Chronicles of the Pilgrim Fathers.*

HAVE WE NOT ALL ONE FATHER? HATH NOT ONE GOD CREATED US?
(Malachi 2:10 *KJV*)

The settlers of New England, although mostly Englishmen, had, as we have seen, been living for many years... under the direct influence of the Netherland Republic. Coming to America, they brought with them a system for republican institutions, borrowed from the Netherlands... In the Middle and Southern colonies, these institutions were largely unknown, but in this quarter an un-English influence was exerted by the settlers from Holland, France, and Germany, and, to a much larger extent, by the multitude of immigrants from the North of Ireland, to whom the English were an alien race... [1]

Different faces, different races, different backgrounds, different political systems, different influences. Lord, in your mercy, help us all to get along!

---

1   From *The Puritan in Holland, England, and America.*

JESUS REPLIED, "NO ONE WHO PUTS A HAND TO THE PLOUGH AND
LOOKS BACK IS FIT FOR SERVICE IN THE KINGDOM OF GOD."
(Luke 9:62)

After the death of the first settlers there was a marked decline, not only in education, but in all manifestations of a liberal spirit in every direction... we see "Puritanism gone to seed, grown narrow and harsh and petty, and rapidly becoming mundane and Philistine". But such a general decline is hardly comprehensible under the commonly accepted theory relating to these settlers... In their new home they were not excluded from public office, liberalizing pursuits, and all opportunities of higher education, as were there brethren of the middle class in England... They ruled the State, and the first college of the colonies was the work of their hands, and under their control. In addition, they were many thousands in number... in what were for the time rather populous communities as compared with those of England.

Taking all these conditions into account, it would seem that their descendants should have advanced and not retrograded if the enlightened ideas of the early settlers were of English origin, for here such ideas had the widest field for their development.[1]

Stagnation, Lord! Looking back! Or standing still! I pray for churches that
seem to have reached some kind of plateau, whereby they do not immediately
or obviously decline, but do not grow, either – in other words, perishing on the
vine! Lord, keep us ploughing, keep us moving, keep us advancing. I pray this for
my own church. I pray this for my own spiritual life.

---

1   From *The Puritan in Holland, England, and America.*

December 12ᵀᴴ

AND THERE WAS TREMBLING IN THE HOST, IN THE FIELD, AND
AMONG ALL THE PEOPLE: THE GARRISON, AND THE SPOILERS, THEY
ALSO TREMBLED, AND THE EARTH QUAKED:
SO IT WAS A VERY GREAT TREMBLING.
(1 Samuel 14:15 *KJV*)

At the shutting in of the evening, there was a very great earthquake, in new England, and the same night another, although something less than the former... they being great and terrible works of God, and are usually ominous to some strokes and visitations of his hand unto places and people where they are; and sometimes the Lord in the very acting of his power in them, hath declared his severity to the children of men, to their great overthrow and confusion... as if man were not always worthy to tread upon so solid a foundation, we see [the earth] oft times quake and shake, and rock and rend itself, as if it showed that he which made it, threatened by this trembling the impiety of the world, and the ruin of those that dwell on the earth.[1]

Almighty God, yours is the power and the glory.

---

1   From *Chronicles of the Pilgrim Fathers.*

[JEHOSHAPHAT SAID], "LORD, THE GOD OF OUR ANCESTORS, ARE
YOU NOT THE GOD WHO IS IN HEAVEN? YOU RULE OVER ALL THE
KINGDOMS OF THE NATIONS. POWER AND MIGHT ARE IN YOUR
HAND, AND NO ONE CAN WITHSTAND YOU."

(2 Chronicles 20:6)

Ought we not then to fear and tremble before… God, who (as one sayeth), by his handmade nature doth so terribly shake the earth, and no land can be sure, no place so strong that can defend us? Nay, the more strong, the more dangerous; for the higher, the greater we fall. Let us therefore say with the wise man, Eccl. iii.14, I know that whatsoever God doth, shall stand forever; nothing can be put to it, nor anything taken from it, and God doth it, that men should fear before him.[1]

You are God indeed. You are my God.

---

1   From *Chronicles of the Pilgrim Fathers*.

SO CHRIST HIMSELF GAVE THE ... TEACHERS ...
(Ephesians 4:11)

It pleased God to put a speedy period to the life of Mr. John Norton,[1] who was a burning and a shining light; and although the church of Boston, in a more special manner, felt the smart of this sudden blow, yet it reflected upon the whole land. He was singularly endowed with the tongue of the learned, enabled to speak a word in due season, not only to the wearied soul, but also a word of counsel to a people in necessity thereof, being not only a wise steward of the things of Jesus Christ, but also a wise statesman; so that the whole land sustained a great loss to him. At his first coming over into New England, he arrived at Plimouth, where he abode the best part of one winter, and preached the gospel of the kingdom unto them; and ever after, to his dying day, retained a good affection unto them. From thence he went to Boston, and from thence to Ipswich, in New England, where he was the chosen teacher of their church.[2]

Lord, speak to me that I may speak
In living echoes of thy tone;
As thou has sought, so let me seek
Thine erring children lost and lone.

O lead me, Lord, that I may lead
The wandering and the wavering feet;
O feed me, Lord, that I may feed
Thy hungering ones with manna sweet.[3]

---

1   1606–63.
2   From *Chronicles of the Pilgrim Fathers.*
3   From Frances Ridley Havergal's hymn.

BUT SELECT CAPABLE MEN FROM ALL THE PEOPLE – MEN WHO
FEAR GOD, TRUSTWORTHY MEN ... AND APPOINT
THEM AS OFFICIALS ...
(Exodus 18:21)

[There] followed the death of that eminent servant of God, Mr. Samuel Stone,[1] who was another star of the first magnitude in the firmament of New England. He was a learned, solid, and judicious divine, equally able for the confirmation of the truth, and confutation of errors. His ministry was with such conviction and demonstration, and when he set himself to application, very powerful. He was teacher to the church of Hartford fourteen years, together with Mr. Hooker,[2] and sixteen years after him, thirty years in all ... He was honourably buried at Hartford.[3]

Thank you, Lord, that you do not leave your church without leaders. You provide the right people, in succession, for every season. We can rely upon your provision and your timing. My prayers today are for churches seeking new leaders and new church officers for one position or other. As you gifted Samuel Stone and Mr Hooker to the New England congregations, I pray you will gift those churches as they seek your will.

---

1   Samuel Stone (1602–63), Puritan minister. Co-founder of Hartford, Connecticut.
2   Thomas Hooker (1586–1647), Puritan leader. Co-founder of the Connecticut colony.
3   From *Chronicles of the Pilgrim Fathers*.

I WILL GIVE YOU HIDDEN TREASURES, RICHES STORED
IN SECRET PLACES ...

(Isaiah 45:3)

The congregation had had its share of minister trouble before it reached the New World. In the beginning William Brewster and his friends had worshipped for a time at Gainsborough[1] under the brilliant but erratic John Smyth,[2] whose later excursions into Se-Baptism[3] and other "hellish errors" so scandalized his one-time brethren and caused all of the English Separatists such pain and embarrassment. After the Gainsborough Group had amicably divided and the Saints along Scrooby Water formed a congregation of their own, they enjoyed great spiritual content for a year or two under the "grave & reverend" Richard Clyfton,[4] who brought many benighted souls to the light by his "paines & dilligens" [sic] ... In their panicky flight to Leyden they lost their pastor, for Clyfton refused to go and abandoned his flock, preferring the company of the "Franciscans".[5] While hurt and upset by this, the congregation quickly dismissed him as a renegade and soon regarded his defection as a blessing in disguise, for it enabled John Robinson to step forward and come into his own as the greatest of the early Separatist leaders. The Saints at Leyden enjoyed his "able ministrie & prudente governmente" [sic] for more than ten years, a period none of them ever forgot, for it was the happiest and most wholly satisfying of their lives. They would never know another like it.[6]

"A blessing in disguise." Loving God, help me to trust in your ways, in your timing, and in your goodness, even when some blessings are disguised.

---

1 See January 4th.
2 Reverend John Smyth (c.1570–c.1612). He was a keen student of logic and metaphysics, and would often frustrate his congregations by applying principles of logical syllogisms to biblical teaching.
3 The doctrine of baptizing oneself.
4 See March 3rd.
5 See https://en.wikipedia.org/wiki/Franciscans
6 From *Saints and Strangers*.

IF THOU FAINT IN THE DAY OF ADVERSITY, THY STRENGTH IS SMALL.
(**Proverbs 24:10 KJV**)

With so many of the Old Standards gone, a younger generation began to rise in the higher councils...

Events in England presented the new regime with several delicate problems. With the restoration of the Stuarts in 1660 the Anglican bishops were again in the saddle and tracking down their enemies. The skies had suddenly darkened, no one knew what to expect, and all the news was bad. "Episcopacy, common prayer, bowing at the name of Jesus, the sign of the cross in baptism, the altar, and organs are in use, and like to be more," a Massachusetts agent reported from London; "the Lord keep and preserve his churches, that there may not be fainting in the day of trial."[1]

When my soul is faint and thirsty,
'Neath the shadow of His wing
There is cool and pleasant shelter,
And a fresh and crystal spring;
And my Saviour rests beside me,
As we hold communion sweet;
If I tried, I could not utter
What He says when thus we meet.[2]

---

1   From *Saints and Strangers.*
2   From Ellen Lakshmi Goreh's hymn "In the Secret of His presence".

... MARK THEM WHICH CAUSE DIVISIONS AND OFFENCES CONTRARY
TO THE DOCTRINE WHICH YE HAVE LEARNED; AND AVOID THEM.
(Romans 16:17 *KJV*)

At a meeting in Plymouth... the council of the United Colonies urged prompt steps
to rid the country of Quakers by driving them into the wilderness. At the same time a
letter was dispatched to Rhode Island to insist that they not be allowed to take refuge
there.[1]

> Lord, this is a painful and distressing reading. Nevertheless, it reflects real life –
> and real church life! There are those times when awkward and difficult matters
> need to be addressed, and dealt with. I pray, therefore, for those who carry such
> responsibilities. Help them as they try to do the right thing. Help, too, those who
> are on the receiving end of decisions and policies such as this one, which might
> have a lasting effect on their wellbeing.

---

1   From *Saints and Strangers.*

ADAM AND HIS WIFE WERE BOTH NAKED...
(Genesis 2:25)

The congregation at Newbury was electrified one Sabbath morning when a comely young woman walked into the meeting house quite nude – "to show the people", she said, "the nakedness of their rulers".[1]

It's difficult to know how to pray in response to this story, Lord, but maybe I can offer a prayer for those who feel as though their protests and complaints are getting them nowhere, fast, and that desperate measures are therefore necessary. I think especially of modern-day activists, whose measured actions have been ignored, and who feel the need for more drastic actions. Help me, I pray, never to be guilty of ignoring the valid feelings of unhappy complainants. Help me never to regard their distress as my inconvenience, lest I inadvertently push them towards behaviour born of desperation. Teach me that responsibility. Teach me to listen carefully for the story behind the complaint.

---

1   From *Saints and Strangers*.

THEY WERE LOOKING INTENTLY UP INTO THE SKY AS HE WAS GOING,
WHEN SUDDENLY TWO MEN DRESSED IN WHITE STOOD BESIDE
THEM. "MEN OF GALILEE," THEY SAID, "WHY DO YOU STAND HERE
LOOKING INTO THE SKY? THIS SAME JESUS, WHO HAS BEEN TAKEN
FROM YOU INTO HEAVEN, WILL COME BACK IN THE SAME WAY YOU
HAVE SEEN HIM GO INTO HEAVEN."

(Acts 1:10–11)

A blazing star, or comet, appeared in New England... concerning which it hath been observed, that such was its motion, that, in all likelihood, it was visible to all the inhabitants of the earth; and that, also, in its motion, the blaze of it did turn to all the quarters of the world; and that by its turning according to the several aspects it had to the sun, it was no fiery meteor caused by exhalation, but that it was sent by God to awake the secure world.[1]

A reminder today, Lord Jesus, that you will return one day! Keep me ready. Lord, I pray for my loved ones and friends who do not (yet) believe in the second coming, and have not (yet) trusted in you for their salvation. Before that great and awesome day, Lord, touch their hearts and minds. Have mercy.

Lo! he comes with clouds descending,
Once for favoured sinners slain;
Thousand thousand saints attending
Swell the triumph of his train:
Alleluya! Alleluya! Alleluya!
God appears, on earth to reign.

Every eye shall now behold him
Robed in dreadful majesty;
Those who set at nought and sold him,
Pierced and nailed him to the tree,
Deeply wailing
Deeply wailing
Deeply wailing
Shall the true Messiah see.[2]

---

1   From *Chronicles of the Pilgrim Fathers*.
2   From a hymn written by John Cennick and Charles Wesley.

WHEN YOUR JUDGMENTS COME UPON THE EARTH, THE PEOPLE OF
THE WORLD LEARN RIGHTEOUSNESS.

(Isaiah 26:9)

It pleased God to go on in a manifestation of his displeasure against New England, in a very remarkable manner, by striking dead, in a moment, three persons in the town of Marshfield, in the jurisdiction of New Plimouth... namely, one named William Shirtliff,[1] and a woman and a youth; which said dispensation of God's hand, being considered, with some circumstances, gave cause to the beholders to be much astonished; the said Shirtliff having his wife by the hand, and sitting by her to cheer her, in respect that the said storm was so fierce, he was slain, and she preserved, though in some measure scorched with the lightning; yea, he had one of his children in his arms, and himself slain, and the child preserved. We have likewise received intelligence of four more, that about that time were slain by thunder and lightning, about Piscataqua, and... more hurt. At the time of this storm of thunder and lightning, in the which those of Marshfield died, there arose likewise a very great whirlwind, that, when it came, it tore up trees by the roots, though through mercy it did little other hurt... If God's judgments have thus been abroad in the earth, how ought the inhabitants of New England to learn righteousness?[2]

How easy it is, Lord, in this modern era, to casually dismiss such natural
phenomena as just that, and to regard any mention of your involvement as
something akin to superstition. Yet, how much wiser to see you in all things, to
acknowledge your mighty power, and to cultivate an appropriate fear of your
awesome nature. Teach me that reverence, I pray.

---

1   Or Shurtleff (b. 1624).
2   From *Chronicles of the Pilgrim Fathers*.

"Be dressed ready for service..."
(Luke 12:35)

Though New England had no public school system worthy of the name for almost two centuries, New Haven took early steps to encourage education, passing its first school law in 1638. Massachusetts followed four years later, "it being one chief project of that old deluder, Satan, to keep men from the knowledge of the Scriptures" by keeping them ignorant, so that the "true sense and meaning of the original might be clouded by false glosses of saint-seeming deceivers". The Pilgrims had announced their intention of providing a common school as early as 1624, excusing their delay by saying that they had been prevented by "want of a fit person or hithertoo means to maintaine one" [*sic*]. Whatever their intentions, nothing was done about the matter for almost half a century. What little instruction youngsters received was obtained at home from their parents, many of whom were illiterate.[1]

A half-century of delay! Lord, it is hard to ignore the whiff of excuses in this statement! Assist me, I pray, not to procrastinate on those matters I know require my attention in the next few hours. Give me that divine prompt I need from time to time.

---

1   From *Saints and Strangers*.

"... LOVE ONE ANOTHER."
(John 13:34)

Education of girls was a vain and idle thing, the Pilgrim Fathers agreed. At best, it was a silly affectation; at worst, a danger to the established order. Women should mind their own business, and that business was cooking, spinning, washing sweeping, and bearing children – often. Consequently, as more than one foreign visitor noted, the women of New England were all "pitifully Toothshaken" [*sic*] and apt to look much older than their years.

"Uxor praegnans est",[1] reads an almost annual entry in Judge Sewall's[2] diary, and in this regard his was not an unusual family...

Along with the high birth-rate went an appalling infant mortality rate – the result of cold and draughty houses, bad diet, want of medical knowledge and surgical care, and congenital weakness born of too frequent parenthood... The rate of maternal mortality ran also high. The old burying grounds of the Saints, as anyone can verify, are filled with stones to young wives who went to their graves prematurely, worn out by childbirth, and often with five or six of their infants buried beside them.[3]

> **Oh, Lord! Forgive us for those social and moral issues that your church has all-too-often handled badly, and has, to make matters worse, attempted to justify with selected verses of Scripture. Forgive us, Lord, for misusing the Bible in order to mistreat others, and for doing so in your name. Teach us how to love you by loving others, I pray.**

---

1   A literal translation, from Latin to English, would read "his wife is pregnant with".
2   Puritan Judge Samuel Sewall (1652–1730). He is reputed to have sent twenty people to their deaths on charges of witchcraft.
3   From *Saints and Strangers*.

THE LORD REWARDS EVERYONE FOR THEIR RIGHTEOUSNESS AND
FAITHFULNESS.
(1 Samuel 26:23)

In spite of… perils and hardships, these settlers prosecuted their undertaking, and never seem to have faltered in it for one moment… Although… as one of them describes it, they "died sometimes two or three a day… and the living were scarce able to bury the dead, and the well not sufficient to tend the sick," and when they felt obliged to level their graves, lest the Indian should find out how their number was reduced, there was no disposition whatever to abandon the enterprise. They felt themselves called of God, as much as His people of old, to lay the foundations of a new church, and a Christian Commonwealth, and they vigorously prosecuted their work, until they saw those foundations well laid, and the walls rapidly rising above them. They made their settlement a permanent one. They led the way for so many other colonists, and for so many others of like principles with themselves, and this did so much to determine the character of [America]. And one of the results has been, the virtual settlement, and such a settlement, of this whole country.[1]

Faithful God, keep me faithful. This is my simple prayer today.

---

1   From *A Memorial of the Pilgrim Fathers.*

… RENDER TO CAESAR THE THINGS THAT ARE CAESAR'S, AND TO
GOD THE THINGS THAT ARE GOD'S.
(Mark 12:17 *KJV*)

The Pilgrims established… Pure and Free Churches. The Reformed Churches of Europe had… come out of the darkness of the Middle Ages and the corruption of the Papal Church… Perhaps it is not strange that they brought with them so many of the errors and superstitions of those times. Even the English Church was only imperfectly reformed. It was the attempt to bring back the medieval faith, and especially those forms of worship and that extent of priestly and church power, which caused the sufferings of the non-conformists, and the flight of so many from England.

Our fathers held that the Bible was a sufficient rule of faith and practice, and that men had a right to read and to interpret it, responsible only to God. Whatever that book taught, they regarded themselves under obligation to receive; whatever they understood it to forbid, they considered it wrong, for wither the Church or the State to require. Upon this ground of religious freedom as one of the rights of men, they refused conscientiously to conform to some of the practices of the State, and rather than do it preferred to submit to all the pains and penalties of non-conformity.[1]

What a thought, Lord – what a reminder – that state and church are both subject to you! This is a great perspective, a useful "filter" through which to view events, policies, and decisions. Help me to keep it in mind.

1   From *A Memorial of the Pilgrim Fathers*.

"Remember the Lord in a distant land..."
(Jeremiah 51:50)

Plymouth [England]... became an important place in the memories of the Pilgrims. It was first of all a place of haven after danger, a place where they were "kindly used and courteously entertained" by people of much the same opinion as themselves – one last place of comfort and familiarity on a voyage to the unknown. Plymouth was also the testing place of many of them. About twenty persons had to turn back, for whom there was no room – the doubters, those whose courage failed them... Plymouth to some must have been a place of heart-searching and disappointment. To others, about whose constancy there was no doubt, a place of strengthening of purpose. Plymouth stayed in their minds, long after the *Mayflower* had sailed... When the Pilgrims reached New England... they settled in a place called Thieves' Harbour – or by the... West Country men who had been fishing that coast, "Plymouth". The "Thieves' Harbour" name disappeared, but the Pilgrims, although none of them were West Country men,[1] instead of taking some nostalgic place-name from their own native north or east, kept to the name of "Plymouth". This kinship with the old Plymouth persisted.[2]

> Home is where the heart is, Lord! Today, I thank you for the gift of precious memories. I thank you for that wonderful human capacity of reminiscing with regard to valued friends and times past. Thank you for those treasured places and people that have served as important "markers" on my life's way. They have been to me as lights along the pathway. Thank you.

---

1   Plymouth is in the south-west of England.
2   From *The Pilgrim Fathers at Plymouth*.

Just as Plymouth, New England, did not forget Plymouth in Devon, so the Devonshire Plymothians remembered their part in the adventure of the Pilgrim Fathers with pride. In 1891... a tablet was erected to mark the spot where the Pilgrim Fathers embarked. Amongst the cobbles paving the Barbican pier is a granite block with the inscription "Mayflower 1620" cut in it, protected by a sheltering canopy. On a house nearby – the sixteenth-century "Island House" – is a board on which the names of the Pilgrims are set out... The Barbican Tablet also commemorates "the visit to Plymouth in July of that year (1891) of a number of the Pilgrims' descendants and relatives".

Although Plymouth has greatly changed – even since 1891 when the Descendants of the Pilgrim Fathers visited the city – the nucleus of the old town the Pilgrim Fathers knew, remains. The clusters of houses... and the Mayflower Steps are still grouped in narrow streets and alleyways as they were in the sixteenth and seventeenth centuries. Although the old "Causey"[1] by which the Pilgrims embarked disappeared in 1626, the Mayflower Stone marks its site as nearly as possible.[2]

"O Thou who changest not, abide with me..."[3]

---

1   Causeway.
2   From *The Pilgrim Fathers at Plymouth*.
3   From Henry Francis Lyte's hymn "Abide with Me".

YOUR BEGINNINGS WILL SEEM HUMBLE, SO PROSPEROUS
WILL YOUR FUTURE BE.
(Job 8:7)

In 1820, on the bicentenary of the historic landing, the celebration at Plymouth [America] first began to assume more than local significance. On that occasion the Pilgrim Society made its bow to the public by organizing a large procession. Escorted by the Standish Guards, "an independent company lately organized", it marched through the streets to Town Square, halting near the fragment of rock still lying there, to hear an address…

"We have come to this Rock to record here our homage to our Pilgrim Fathers, our sympathy in their sufferings, our gratitude for their labours, and our attachment to those principles of civil and religious liberty for which they encountered the dangers of the ocean, the storms of heaven, the violence of the savages, disease, exile, and famine, to enjoy and to establish… We seem even to behold them as they struggle with the elements and with toilsome efforts gain the shore. We listen to their chiefs in council; we see the unexampled exhibition of female fortitude and resignation; we hear the whisperings of youthful impatience, and we see… chilled and shivering childhood, houseless but for a mother's arms, couchless but for a mother's breast, till our own blood almost freezes."[1]

Honouring the past by living well in the present and looking towards the future: thanksgiving, application, and hope. Thank you, Lord, for these things: all that the past still has to say, all that the present has to give, and all the promise of what is yet to be. As this year moves towards its natural conclusion, help me, I pray, to focus on that specific trio of blessings.

1   From *Saints and Strangers*.

"... WE WOULD LIKE TO SEE JESUS."
(John 12:21)

Of Plimouth Plantation,[1] fascinating in its every detail, altogether an extraordinary human document, was given to the world in 1856, when a transcript was published at Boston. For the first time in their posthumous lives the Pilgrims stood out strong and clear, in three dimensions, rather than as thin silhouettes in black and grey. They began to breathe once more – and love, and hate, and fight, as only they could. It became unmistakable that, in spite of their revolt against many aspects of it, they had gone to Holland and had come to the wilderness trailing the glory of Elizabethan England, that age of towering imagination and high bold enterprise. In addition, Bradford's pages filled in many huge gaps in the Pilgrim story, opening up new and unsuspecting scenes, brightly illuminating many incidents that had been tantalizingly obscure before.[2]

Thank you, Lord God, for the Bible, in which these same principles bring you "to life", as it were, so that we may all the better know of you and your love. The gospels speak of Jesus, and illuminate his life in a way that we might not know about otherwise. Thank you for the revelations of Scripture. Show yourself to me as I scan the precious pages of your written word.

---

1   Referred to elsewhere in this book as *History of Plymouth Plantation.*
2   From *Saints and Strangers.*

YOU TRANSPLANTED A VINE FROM EGYPT; YOU DROVE OUT THE
NATIONS AND PLANTED IT. YOU CLEARED THE GROUND FOR IT, AND
IT TOOK ROOT AND FILLED THE LAND.
THE MOUNTAINS WERE COVERED WITH ITS SHADE, THE MIGHTY
CEDARS WITH ITS BRANCHES.
(Psalm 80:8–10)

We… do well to value the principles and maintain the institutions of the Pilgrims.

If these principles are entitled to respect, it is because they are true and just; and if these institutions have any peculiar worth, it is because they are better than others, and can do more for society and the church. And the world has need enough of their influence…

We propose no monument to their memory, but to preserve their institutions and extend their influence. This land [America] is their monument. When the traveller visits St. Paul's Cathedral, and looks around for a monument to its architect, as he gazes up into its magnificent dome, he reads this inscription – *"Si Monumentum requires, circumspise"* (If you seek his monument, look around you.) So the best memorial is the land [the Pilgrims] have settled and blessed. Look around you, and see what a good land they selected for their settlement, and when it shall have been more fully possessed and developed, what a magnificent inheritance it will have become for a people.[1]

> Within this context, Heavenly Father, my prayers today are for the United States of America. I pray for the president, and for all who lead the nation. I pray for its citizens, and all who live, move, and have their being within its borders. I pray your blessing upon America, asking you to guide that land and its people according to your will.

---

1   From *A Memorial of the Pilgrim Fathers.*

December 31ˢᵗ

THE LORD HATH DONE GREAT THINGS FOR US; WHEREOF
WE ARE GLAD.
(Psalm 126:3 *KJV*)

With firm faith in… God, and with the full conviction that they were under his guidance… and with a sincere desire to extend their Redeemer's Kingdom among men [the Pilgrim Fathers] bravely confronted the difficulties before them, and set about accomplishing their mission.

There lies the *Mayflower*; a name so sacred to our hearts as the ark in which our faith, and ecclesiastical government, and substantially the gem of [American] civil institutions, were preserved; a vessel of only 180 tons; less than the average size of the fishing-smacks that now sail from that harbour… but with her… emigrants on board, containing within her poor accommodations, we must think, more of sincere faith, and religious motive, and Christian enterprise, and more of truth, and freedom, and benevolence, than were ever gathered in one ship before since the Saviour sailed the sea of Galilee. They are imperfect men, and have been trained in a rough school, but they have as much of charity and gentleness as most, and more of conscientiousness, and courage, and faith, and hope, than any. They owe supreme allegiance to Christ, and identify themselves with his kingdom, and to be loyal to this king, and promote his cause in the earth, is alike their purpose, and their inspiration.[1]

Thank you, God, for the Pilgrim Fathers!

---

1   From *A Memorial of the Pilgrim Fathers.*

NOTES

NOTES

THROUGH THE YEAR WITH THE PILGRIM FATHERS

THROUGH THE YEAR WITH

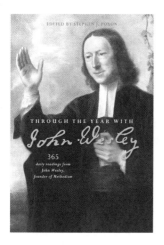

365 DAILY READINGS FROM JOHN WESLEY, THE "FATHER OF METHODISM"

"John Wesley was an explosive force in his own lifetime and beyond. The generosity of spirit of John Wesley, "the friend of all and the enemy of none" is here displayed again and again. As is the simplicity of his life, the depth of his faith, his determination to go on declaring the good news of the gospel until his last breath. This is a little gem of a book... day after day for an entire year, will lift the spirits of twenty-first century men and women and equip them to face the challenges of today's world."

– Lord Leslie Griffiths

Through the Year with John Wesley refreshes and presents key passages from the theological and reflective writings of the Reverend John Wesley, the renowned "father of Methodism".

A deeply spiritual man of high integrity and indomitable character, Wesley strove to present great Christian truths to the non-churchgoing masses of England throughout the 1700s, making a powerful impact upon the nation; the like of which has rarely been felt since.

Each day the reader is presented with passage that has been selected from Reverend John Wesley's thoughtful, passionate, and prolific writings. These passages have then been carefully married by Stephen Poxon to appropriate verses of Scripture and a daily prayer to bring to life Wesley's words.

Hardback ISBN 978 0 8572 1823 0 | Paperback ISBN 978 0 85721 888 9
eISBN 978 0 8572 1824 7

THROUGH THE YEAR WITH

William Booth

365 DAILY READINGS FROM WILLIAM BOOTH,

FOUNDER OF THE SALVATION ARMY

"Some talk of changing the world. Others actually do it. If there is a voice for our day and our time, bringing social reform and spiritual passion together, it's William Booth."

– Major Danielle Strickland

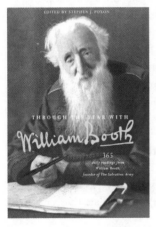

William Booth – pawnbroker's assistant, firebrand preacher, advocate of women's rights, friend of the poor, confidant of statesmen, politicians and royalty, father of eight children, champion of the marginalised, and founder and first General of The Salvation Army. General Booth's courage, oratory, and passion changed Victorian Britain. He resolutely ignored his critics – including those who decried him as the Anti-Christ – and reached out to those who considered themselves well outside the concern of Almighty God. Prayer and practicality were his hallmarks: he ridiculed the idea of preaching to a beggar while that beggar was cold and hungry. William Booth worked tirelessly, campaigning, researching, negotiating, adapting music-hall songs – and writing. This book introduces us to his heart and convictions. Here we find the urgency, thought, and humanity which drove him on.

"A glorious treasure trove of daily readings from the pen of William Booth... a superb anthology of devotional gems."
– Jonathan Aitken

"William Booth was first of all a preacher and a student of the Bible. Stephen Poxon has quite brilliantly linked William's words to Scripture."
– Colonel Bramwell Booth

978-0-85721-614-4 | £12.99 | $19.99